Anonymous

Two Hundredth Anniversary of the First Reformed Protestant Dutch Church of Schenectady, N.Y.

Anonymous

**Two Hundredth Anniversary of the First Reformed Protestant Dutch Church of Schenectady, N.Y.**

ISBN/EAN: 9783337296148

Printed in Europe, USA, Canada, Australia, Japan

Cover: Foto ©Lupo / pixelio.de

More available books at **www.hansebooks.com**

# 1680.

*Nisi Dominus Frustra.*

# Two Hundredth Anniversary

### —OF THE—

## First Reformed Protestant

## DUTCH CHURCH,

### OF SCHENECTADY, N. Y.,

## JUNE 20th and 21st.

*Een dracht maakt macht.*

# 1880.

## Committee on Publication.

WILLIAM VAN VRANKEN.   BARENT A. MYNDERSE.
JACOB W. CLUTE.        OLIN S. LUFFMAN.

Daily and Weekly Union
Steam Printing House, Schenectady.
1880.

# Contents:

I. THE PROCEEDINGS, *June 20th and 21st.*

II. THE SERMON, *By the Rev. Wm. Elliot Griffis, Pastor of the Church.*

III. HISTORY OF THE CHURCH, *By Professor Jonathan Pearson, of Union College.*

# Present Officers of the Church.

### Pastor,
WILLIAM ELLIOT GRIFFIS.

## The Consistory.

### Elders.

| | |
|---|---|
| JACOB V. VROOMAN, | WILLIAM VAN VRANKEN, |
| CORNELIUS LANSING, | JOHN WESTINGHOUSE. |

### Deacons.

| | |
|---|---|
| WILLIAM VAN DERMOOR, | WELTON STANFORD, |
| JACOB W. CLUTE, | JONAS HALLENBECK. |

*Clerk* — WELTON STANFORD.
*Treasurer* — JAMES H. BARHYTE.

### Advisory Committee.

| | |
|---|---|
| JUDSON S. LANDON, | BARENT A. MYNDERSE, |
| OLIN S. LUFFMAN, | HENRY ROSA. |

*Organist* — CHARLES E. KINGSBURY.
*Sexton* — JOHN B. STEVENS.

# The Great Consistory.

JOHN G. VAN VOAST,
DUNCAN McDONALD,
CASPER F. HOAG,
WILLIAM VAN VRANKEN,
NICHOLAS YATES,
FRANCIS J. VAN DE BOGERT,
GEORGE S. HARDIN,
ABRAHAM VROOMAN,
DANIEL VEDDER,
CHARLES N. YATES,
WILLIAM B. SCHERMERHORN,
JACOB N. CLUTE,
AARON BARRINGER,
THOMAS H. REEVES,
JOSEPH Y. VAN DE BOGERT,
JACOB V. VROOMAN,
MARTIN DeFOREST,
JAMES H. BARHYTE,
BENJAMIN L. CONDE,
ANDREW T. VEEDER,
JOHN W. VEEDER,
DUNCAN ROBISON,
JOHN WESTINGHOUSE,
WILLIAM VAN DERMOOR,
E. NOTT SCHERMERHORN,
JAMES MILMINE,
JONAS H. CLUTE,
RICHARD MARCELLUS,
HARMON CONSAUL,
ALBERT VAN VOAST,
ALEXANDER THOMPSON,
CHARLES E. KINGSBURY,
JOHN VAN DERMOOR,
ALBERT VAN VOAST, Jr.
CORNELIUS LANSING,
WELTON STANFORD,
JONAS HALLENBECK,
JACOB W. CLUTE.

# Resolution of the Consistory.

———:o:———

At a meeting of the Consistory held April 30th, 1880, the Pastor suggested, Elder Van Vranken moved, and Elder Lansing seconded the motion, that,

On June 20th and 21st, the Two Hundredth Anniversary of the church should be appropriately celebrated.

Proposed and carried unanimously.

The following Committees were then appointed by the President of the consistory:

| COMMITTEES. | CHAIRMEN. |
|---|---|
| Memorial Exhibition | William Van Vranken. |
| Invitation and Programme | Jacob Vrooman. |
| Entertainment of Friends | Jacob W. Clute. |
| Ushers | Jonas Hallenbeck. |
| Decoration | Jay Westinghouse. |
| Services in Holland Language | Cornelius Lansing. |
| Press | Welton Stanford. |

# THE PROCEEDINGS.

Sabbath Morning, June 20th 1880.

Between the years 1670 and 1680, the First Reformed Protestant Dutch Church of Schenectady, was founded in the wilderness of "the far West," on the south side of the Mohawk River, within the palisaded fort and settlement, founded in 1662, by Arendt Van Curler and his fifteen pioneers and their families. The first church was a log structure a few feet square, with scarcely enough panes of glass to make more than one large modern window sash.

On the 20th of June, 1880, the people of the same church celebrated their bi-centennial, in that gothic stone edifice, built in the pointed style, with "storied windows richly dight" with the heraldry of the Dutch Church, which is the pride of Schenectady city, and which for architectural beauty, has no superior in the denomination. It is the fifth edifice, the first being burned by the Indians in 1690, the second and third in succession being outgrown, the fourth being burned by fire. The present, springing from the ashes of its predecessor, was dedicated August 6th, 1862. Of its beauty, and fitness, Dr. T. S. Doolittle has written in that encyclopaedia of the Reformed Church—Corwin's "Manual."

To celebrate the bi-centennial properly, the pastor had come with his sermon, the sculptor with his chisel, the musicians with song, the ladies with floral device and festal evergreen, and the artist with his banner, motto and symbol. Over the "Forefathers' Door" was cut and gilded the prayer from 1 Kings 8: 57, in classic Dutch, "The Lord our God be with us, as He was with our fathers." On the "Bride's Door," over its orange blossoms were cut and laid in gold, "His banner over me was Love." These completed the series of five Scripture passages, chiseled over the four doors of the church, the main entrance having two.

Inside, evergreens draped every pillar, and hung pendant from the lofty peak of the roof to the corbels of the columns. On the eastern walls, over the arched windows, were the historic mottoes :

> THE CHURCH UNDER THE CROSS.

> NISI DOMINUS FRUSTRA.

and

> EEN-DRACHT MAAKT MACHT.

On the walls next to the tower vista, were on one banner:

> LEYDEN,
> UTRECHT,
> DORDRECHT,
> ANTWERP,

surmounted by two satin flags of Holland. On the opposite hollow, was an immense shield eight feet square, painted with the heraldic devices of a tortoise, on green ; a pelican feeding her young with her own blood, on orange ; a lion, on red ; an eagle, on white. These symbolized the four nationalities, which in succession held the soil—the aboriginal Mohawk ; the Dutch settler ; the English conqueror ; and the American possessor.

The polished marbles of the pulpit, were covered for the day, with solid banks of roses and other flowers, the figures :

> 200

being conspicuous in buttercups. On the left of the pulpit was a baptismal bowl made of white rose-buds, and dedicated to the memory of the 12,000 children baptised in the church, and whose names are on the records. To the right, was an hour-glass in daisies, emblematic of ancient pulpit horology, and the flight of the hours during two centuries, and in memory of the the 18 pastors, and 3,500 members of the church. Over the preacher's head in white roses, was the shape of the bell, four feet high, which from 1732 to 1848, or 116 years, had summoned the people to church, and which told of the 3,000 marriages solemnized during two hundred years.

On immense pennants, fifteen feet long and eight wide, flanking the pulpit, were the names of the eighteen pastors of the church from 1684 to 1880.

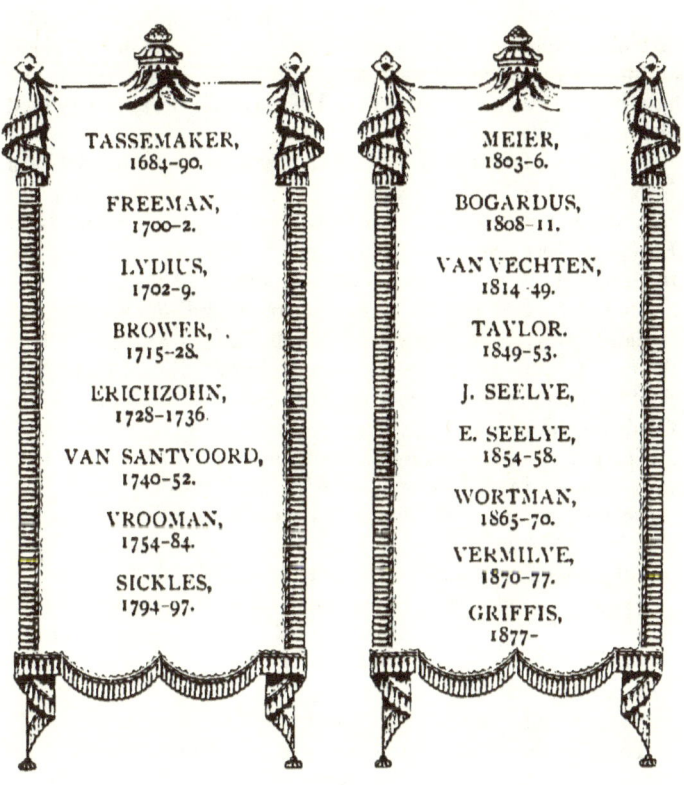

TASSEMAKER, 1684–90.
FREEMAN, 1700–2.
LYDIUS, 1702–9.
BROWER, 1715–28.
ERICHZOHN, 1728–1736.
VAN SANTVOORD, 1740–52.
VROOMAN, 1754–84.
SICKLES, 1794–97.

MEIER, 1803–6.
BOGARDUS, 1808–11.
VAN VECHTEN, 1814–49.
TAYLOR, 1849–53.
J. SEELYE,
E. SEELYE, 1854–58.
WORTMAN, 1865–70.
VERMILYE, 1870–77.
GRIFFIS, 1877–

1784.
ROMEYN.
1804.

Of these, one was killed and burned by the Indians, and six died at their post with the harness on. Seven, or probably nine churches went out from this, the mother church, and one college was born of her. In the centre of the choir, over the pulpit was the honored name of (Dirck) Romeyn, 1784–1804, who was the seventh pastor of the church, and, with his people, the founder of Union College. Born a British subject, a Hollander by blood and tongue, an American citizen while pastor of the church, the flags of Holland, England and the United States were fitly twined about his name.

On that perfect day of June 20th, 1880, radiant with Sabbath beauty, twelve hundred eager people, nearly all of Dutch descent and name, filled the church. The College President, Rev. Eliphalet Nott Potter; a former pastor, Rev. W. J. R. Taylor; the ministers of two of the youngest children of the church (the Second Reformed church of Schenectady, and the Second Rotterdam), Rev. E. C. Lawrence, and Rev. Ira Van Allen; the oldest minister of the Reformed church, Rev. Staats Van Santvoord, and the church's present pastor, Rev. W. E. Griffis, filled the pulpit.

The pews to the right and left of the pulpit were reserved for the members of the Great Consistory and visiting clergymen. After a chant by the choir, and the usual invocation and salutation by the pastor, the hymn, beginning with "Before Jehovah's awful throne," was sung to the tune of Old Hundred.

The eighth chapter of Deuteronomy was read by Rev. Eliphalet Nott Potter, D. D., President of Union College. Prayer was offered by the Rev. W. J. R. Taylor, D. D., pastor of the Clinton Avenue Reformed church, of Newark, N. J., and former minister of this church from 1849 to 1853.

The Rev. E. C. Lawrence then read the following commemorative hymn written for the occasion, by the Rev. Charles S. Vedder, D. D., pastor of the Church of the Hugenots, Charleston, S. C., and a former member of the church and consistory. Three stanzas were sung by the congregation standing, to the tune of "Auld Lang Syne."

## COMMEMORATIVE HYMN.

#### BY A SON OF THE CHURCH.

Our eyes, O Lord, behold the light our fathers longed to see,
When, undisturbed by foes or fear, their hearts might worship Thee :
They found the pleasant land we tread a rude and forest waste,
They planted here the sacred seed whose precious fruit we taste.

They came from homes as dear as ours beyond the swelling tide,
And thought to make as dear homes here by this fair river side.
They bought, with native, honest faith, the fertile soil we own,
And wrought no deed of wrong for which their children must atone.

Thou calledst them then, O Lord, to stand, from friend and help afar
The lonely, feeble frontier-post of home and foreign war.
Each house became a fortress strong, each house inured to strife,
And every hand was taught to shield its dearest ones with life.

Near where we bow, an humble shrine arose in love to Thee,
Where honest hearts kept firm the faith they saved beyond the sea,
But even its sacred walls were pierced, that through each opened seam
Bright weapons thrust, might flash reply to savage shot and scream.

Around the spot where now in peace our christian altars rise,
And happy homes look up and smile beneath these tranquil skies,
The war-whoop rang, one winter night, two centuries ago,
And lurid flame and deadly blade flashed in a stream of woe.

Thy sun, O Lord that fatal eye, unwarningly went down,
It rose to light a blackened waste, where stood a living town,
It shone on slaughter's ruthless stroke, in midnight darkness sent,
On pastor, people, church and homes in one red burial blent.

\* \* \* \* \* \* \* \* \*

But they, O Lord, whom thou didst save to plant thy standard here,
Their faith to try, and steadfastness ; their love and holy fear,
No other fear could daunt nor chill — no other love betray,
They built again the church and homes whose heirs we are to-day.

And still again, as needs increase, and one in flame ascends,
Fair structures rise, till now the fifth our father's faith defends,
Where faithful men, a lengthening line, have heralded Thy love,
And countless trustful, happy hearts have tasted joys above.

Our father's God, be thine the praise their grateful children bring,
Be ours the strong and living faith whose victories we sing ;
And when two hundred years again have passed their solemn way,
May worthier lips sing worthier praise than ours can sing to day.

A thank-offering was then presented by the people, in aid of Foreign Missions; those who preferred contributing towards the erection of a memorial tablet, to be set in the niche of the eastern wall of the church edifice.

The choir then sang the stirring anthem from Haydn's Oratorio of the Messiah :

"Now elevate the sign of Judah."

The Historical discourse by the pastor, from 1 Kings, 8:57, the same text as that carved over the Forefathers' Door, lasted one hour and a half. The close and eager attention of the audience, proved that it was not one minute too long.

Prayer was then offered by the Rev. Cornelius Van Santvoord, D.D., of Kingston, N. Y., a lineal descendant of the fifth minister of the church, Rev. Cornelius Van Santvoord, whose pastorate in Schenectady was from 1740 to 1752.

Recognizing with warm affection the Scotch element within the blood and membership of the Dutch church, past and present, the 914th hymn—a paraphrase of the 90th Psalm, was sung to the tune of Dundee.

The Rev. Ira Van Allen, pastor of the Second Reformed Church of Rotterdam, pronounced the benediction.

The audience slowly, and with apparent reluctance, gradually dispersed. Friends, visitors and citizens joyfully lingered for congratulation, for grateful memories sake, and for the enjoyment of the imperishable historical associations of the edifice and occasion.

## THE AFTERNOON SERVICES.

According to the programme issued, Divine services in the Low Dutch language, commemorative of, and similar to those used in the first edifice of the Dutch church, in the village of Schenectady, A. D. 1680, were held in the church at four o'clock. The threatening rain did not fall, and the main auditorium of the church, including aisles, and gallery, with the consistory room, were filled with an audience estimated at fifteen hundred persons.

According to the old custom, the ministers, attired in gowns, walked from the pastor's house to the church, ascending the pulpit after silent prayer. The Voor-lezer, (fore-reader) occupied the reading desk in front of the pulpit, and the Voor-zanger (precentor) and his Koor-helpers, (choir-singers) occupied front seats. The Magistrates of the city. (Mayor, Common Council, Supervisors etc..) filled the reserved seats near the pulpit. The Great Consistory had the pews to the right and left of the minister reserved for them. Of the audience, the males sat on the right, or eastern half of the church, and the females, on the left, or western half. According to ancient local custom, all bonnets, as well as hats were removed. The services, as measured by the hour-glass, were exactly one hour long. The programme printed in Dutch was as follows:

## Zondag des Namiddags,
### Vier uur.
# Godsdienstoefening
in de
## Nederlandsche Taal,

ter herinnering van en gelyk aan die in gebruik in het eerste Kerkgebouw

van de

### Neder Duitsche Gereformeerde Gemeente,

van het dorp

### Schenectada, 1680, A. D.

1. Voorgebed en Zegewensch.. .. .. ..............
2. Lezen der Tien Geboden door den Voorlezer................ .... ...Ouderling Daniel Vedder
3. Gezang — „Gemeenschap der heiligen." (Gezongen door den Vorzanger en Koor-helpers......... .. .................
4. Gebed..... .. ........... ......Domine Vanderwart
5. Lezen der Twaalf Artikelen des ge-loofs................. ...Ouderling Cornelius Lansing
6. Dank offer ter hulpe van Hope Seminaire, Holland, Michigan.
7. Lezen der heilige Schrift, 90. Psalm..... Domine J. Lansing
8. Predikatie.. Text Jer 6:16............Domine Vanderwart
„Soo seyt de Heere; Staet op de wegen ende siet toe, ende vraget na de oude paden, waer doch de goede weg zij, ende wandelt daer in, soo sult gy ruste finden voor uwe ziele."
9. Gebed........................ ........Domine Vanderwart
10. Zegespraak............. ...Domine S. Van Santvoord

The actual order of exercises, was the following:

Invocation, and Salutation, by the Rev. Herman Vanderwart, pastor of the Reformed church of Scotia N. Y.

The Voorlezer, Elder Daniel Vedder, of the Great Consistory, then read the Ten Commandments.

A hymn, "The Communion of Saints," was then sung by the Voorzanger, and his assistants, a choir of five male voices. The singers were, Henry Ramsey, Daniel Vedder, Cornelius Lansing, Christian Tate and Charles W. Parks.

The "Twelve Articles of the Christian Faith," as they are called in the Holland tongue, (The Apostles' Creed) were then read by Elder Cornelius Lansing.

After a statement in English, concerning the origin of the settlement, and college at Holland, Michigan, a thank-offering in aid of Hope College, was made by the people.

The Ninetieth Psalm was read by the Rev. A. G. Lansing, of New Salem, N. Y.

The sermon was preached by the Rev. Herman Vanderwart. The text was from Jeremiah, 6:16. "Thus saith the Lord, stand ye in the way and see, and ask for the old paths, where is the good way, and walk therein, and ye shall find rest for your souls."

So clearly enunciated, so impressively delivered, and so manifestly eloquent was this sermon, that the whole vast assemblage seemed one earnest listener. There were probably as many as one hundred in the audience, mostly elderly people, who understood most of the once familiar language of the church and city.

The preacher offered prayer in his native Holland speech.

The pastor, the Rev. W. E. Griffis, made an address in English, recalling the circumstances attending the first settlement of the city of Schenectady in 1662, by Arendt Van Curler and his fifteen fellow-pioneers with their families. He showed how they bought their lands and lived at peace with the Indians. After stating that the bones of the first two generations of the settlers, including those of the victims of the massacre of February 8th, 1690, lay unmarked and almost unknown under the cobble stones of the pavement, at the end of Church on State street, formerly called the "Street of the Martyrs," he pleaded that a monumental stone, or other memorial should be erected by the citizens of Schenectady to mark the spot and keep alive the memory of the virtues of the founders of the city.

The benediction was then pronounced by the Rev. Staats Van Santvoord, the oldest minister of the reformed church, and after our honored and venerable citizen, Gen. William K. Fuller, of Schenectady, the oldest living graduate of Union College.

### Evening Session.

The Baccalaureate Sermon before the graduating class of Union College was delivered by the Rev. W. J. R. Taylor D.D., after an historical address by President Potter, in which he gave a graceful and forcible account of the connection between Union College and the Reformed Dutch church of Schenectady. It was highly appropriate that the Baccalaureate and Commencement exercises of the college should blend with those of the bi-centennial anniversary of the church, as Union College was her child.

Union College grew out of the "Schenectady Academy," which was organized and built by the people of the Dutch church in Schenectady in 1784, at the corner of Union and Ferry streets. After ten years of prosperous life, and almost wholly through the influence of Dr. Romeyn and the people of the Dutch church in Schenectady, the academy secured a collegiate charter. The church then gave in trust to the Trustees of Union College, the building and endowments amounting to over thirty thousand dollars. The first commencement in 1797, the Jubilee Services of 1845, and the 85th commencement exercises in 1880, were held in the Dutch church. For many years in the early history of the college the students attended the Dutch church services in a body. Union College has educated about one hundred and thirty ministers of the Reformed church in America.

The sermon by Dr. Taylor, a descendent of Dr. Direk Romeyn, and a former pastor of the church, preached from the text 1 Chronicles, 12:32.

"And of the children of Issachar *which were men* that had understanding of the times, to know what Israel ought to do; the heads of them *were* two hundred; and all their brethren *were* at their commandment."

Of this able, pertinent and scholarly discourse, the editor of the Schenectady *Evening Star* remarks:

"It showed what the times required in the young men about to go forth from the institution to adapt them to wield and influence the world. What hostile forces are at work to undermine the foundations of society. What weapons are needed to repel and counteract them; and how young men may be fully furnished to meet the demands of their age, and come off victorious in the contests surely to be waged with stern antagonists of whatever type. The discourse was ingenious in its conduct, sage in its counsels, philosophical in its discriminations and reasonings, and pervaded by a lofty, ethical and religious tone; all conveyed with great earnestness and force of utterance, which could hardly fail of leaving salutary impressions upon those in whose special behalf the address was given."

A hymn, and the benediction by Rev. Staats Van Santvoord, D. D., closed the interesting services.

### Monday, June 21st.

According to the programmes distributed some days before, and sent out to friends, who visited the city for the purpose of celebrating with the people of the church their bi-centennial, there was held a

### MEMORIAL EXHIBITION,
Of Historic, Devotional, Literary, Ecclesiastical and Religious Relics of the Past,

*From Monday, June 21st, at 12 p. m., to Wednesday, 6 p. m.*

FREE TO ALL!

Friends, Citizens and Strangers Cordially Invited.

The rare and rich collection of antiquities, such as few American homes can show, was arranged in five sections, in which the articles were grouped around the pictures of the five church edifices, with their respective dates, 1683–1701; 1702–1734; 1734–1814; 1814–1861; 1862–1880. Below is only the barest sketch of what well deserves a volume by itself. In the angle between the Banker screen and the tower room door was an oil painting of the Burning of Schenectady and the Massacre of February 8th, 1690, by Mr. S. H. Sexton, now owned by Hon. A. A. Yates. The baleful scene represented is Church street, during the height of the bloody carnival. The house defended by Adam Vrooman, the parsonage of Domine Tassemaker, and the little church at the end of the street, near the palisades, are shown in the spirited painting. In this section were gathered pieces cut, sawed, or made into walking canes from the old palisades; a brick from one of the first dwellings with "1666" indented upon it; Indian snow-shoes, such as those on which the French and their allies travelled from Canada to the massacre; a Mohawk spear with the totem, or crest, of a tortoise embroidered on its pennant; wood from the parsonage built in 1691; a deed of Van Slyke island in the river opposite Schenectady, signed by Governor Petrus Stuyvesant; skull of one of the victims of 1690, cloven by a tomahawk; various Indian relics; and church documents dated prior to 1690, and many antiquities from Holland.

In the second section was a picture wrought in silk embroidery, and supposed to represent the second edifice of the church, which, like the first, stood on Martyr's (State) street, at the end of Church, showing the adjoining burying ground, and the streamlet long since filled up, which ran through the original settlement. Among the attractions of this group was a woodcut portrait of Domine Bernardus Freeman, second pastor of the church; numerous Dutch Bibles dated from 1637 to 1741, substantially bound in leather and brass for family use, or faced with silver chains for women to carry to church; household linen and goods woven and spun by the Dutch ladies of nigh two centuries ago; New Year's cake-moulds, silver tankards, spoons and cups of the time of King William III; the church records of Marriage and Baptism from 1691 to 1734, and various Indian relics.

Section third, comprising the period between 1734 and 1814, was the richest and most interesting of all. There was a painting by Giles F. Yates, of the old stone edifice built in 1734, with its clock-tower and belfry; the great royal charter granted by King George II, of England, with its huge wax seal resembling a buckwheat cake; an oil painting of Domine Reinhart Erichzon, then pastor; the church door and key, the latter without a barrel, and forged on a blacksmith's anvil; numerous portraits and paintings of the period, and a large case of silver, revolutionary flags, documents and relics, loaned by the Sanders family of Scotia; the tablet stone of the Schenectady Academy; many church books and papers of great interest, and a piece of the old church bell cast in Holland; and a remarkably varied and curious array of table silver, warming-pans, hour-glasses, door-knockers, porcelain, faience, old blue ware, china, carding forms, Continental money, church script, watches, jewelry, and numerous articles of household and personal adornment, most of them belonging to former ministers and people of the church.

In section fourth was a painting of the fourth church edifice, built of brick, and surrounded by fine trees; portraits of the pastors who officiated therein, and of the Rev. Andrew Yates, Rev. Abram J. Swits, and Tayler Lewis; the old pulpit seat saved from the fire of 1861 by John McNee, the faithful sexton; the architect's designs; candle-sticks and lamps from the old consistory room, and many other curious and eloquent tokens of the past.

In section fifth everything was so new that in the presence of such grand and ancient witnesses of the past in other parts of the room, no description need be given.

During the four days of the exhibition there were thousands of gratified and instructed visitors, some of whom came again and again expressing delight and wonder at the richness of the antiquities thus set forth in worthy array to the public for the first time.

### Monday Afternoon.

At 4 p. m., agreeably to the invitation given from the pulpit the day before, a party of about one hundred gathered informally, with the pastor of the church acting as guide, to study the artistic beauties of the church edifice, the masterpiece of the architect, Edward Tuckerman Potter.

The symbolism of the following portions of the edifice was pointed out and explained. A fuller account of them is given in Prof. Pearson's History of the Church, chapter xii.

1. The capitals of the Banker screen, the cycle of the twelve months of the year, and the love, courtship, union and paternal cares of the birds expressing the relations of mother and son—the screen having been given by Mr. Gershom Banker, in honor of his mother.

2. The situation of the organ, and the carvings of Jubal's organ and pipe of Pan, wreathed in ivy, on the corbels at the base of the supports.

3. The pulpit, made of marbles cased in walnut, with the three orders of stone; the foundation, resembling the yellow earth; the building stone, "polished after the similitude of a palace;" the gem, or crowning stone. The colors of these polished marbles are respectively variegated yellow, veined green, and mottled dark red. They were imported from France and were cut from the Jura Alps.

4. The monograms, inscriptions and carving on the pulpit shaftlets, scripture foliage, the olive and palm, with the text in raised letters, "We preach Christ crucified."

5. The four triplet windows, and the stained glass dight with the wheat and grapes—the "corn and wine" of the promised land.

The north rose window dight with the Faith, Hope and Charity; the south rose window dight with the coat of arms of the House of Orange; the two windows of the consistory room dight with the arms of the Clute and Cuyler families, and the four tower windows containing views of four of the edifices, were noticed in detail.

6. The carved corbels from which spring the arched ribs of the roof, containing on their south faces forms of foliage, such as the rose, oak, ivy, clover, paas-flower (hepatica), pfingster, and ideal forms. On the north faces of the corbels are carved the initials of the builders and finishers of the church enifice, viz.: architect, master stone-cutter, master mason, master carpenter and master painter.

7. The symbolism of the temporary mottoes, designs and floral decorations used in celebrating the bi-centennial aniversary.

8. The inscriptions and carving over the four doors of the edifice: Forefathers' Door, facing the east toward Holland, contains a text in gold, from the Dutch Bible, of which the English is,

"The Lord our God be with us, as He was with our fathers." The Door of the Congregation, or main entrance, having four arches, bears the welcome, "Enter into His courts with thanksgiving, and into his gates with praise." The capitals of the porch wrought from Nova Scotia sandstone, resting on columns of polished red granite, are carved with the products of the Mohawk valley, hops and Indian corn; wheat, rye, oats, and barley; broom corn; acorns and cone-bearing branches of the oak and pine.

In the peak above the doorway are carved in monogram the letters I. R. D. C., and on opposite sides A. D. 1862, wreathed in folliage.

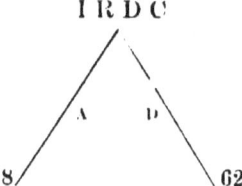

Over the Bride's Door, facing the west, is cut and gilded the text "His banner over me was love," while two white shaftlets of Carrara marble uphold capitals wreathed with sprays of orange blossoms and leaves. The workmanship of the arch of this door is probably unique in America.

Under the western gate, through which the Bride's Door is approached, is a stone, the history of which is chiseled deep upon it:

| DOOR SILL OF 3d CHURCH EDIFICE, 1734–1814. |
| --- |

The old threshold still in a place of honor, connects the past with the present, and like a scarred veteran still holds the honorable mark of service—the bolt hole.

The doorway of the Consistory Room, which is used also for devotional meetings, has this text cut on the imposts of its arch, "To show forth thy loving kindness in the morning, and Thy faithfulness every night."

Set into a niche in the rear wall of the church is the tablet stone of the fourth edifice, built in 1812 and burned down in 1861. It is of white marble, and appropriately inscribed.

After looking at the remains of the foundation wall of the old Consistory Room of 1814-1861, and at the barn upon the Benjamin property in which the bodies of the victims of the Benkendal massacre, July 18, 1748, were laid for identification, the party dismissed. They had obeyed the spirit of the 48th Psalm: "Walk about Zion, and go round about her; tell the towers thereof. Mark ye well her bulwarks, consider her palaces, that ye may tell it to the generation following."

The promise, amid the inspiration of the hour came with new force and beauty:

"For this God *is* our God for ever and ever: He will be our guide *even* unto death."

MONDAY EVENING.

The seventh page of the Programme of the bi-centennial exercises read as follows:

## MONDAY EVENING.

June 21st, 1880,

7 O'CLOCK.

## RE-UNION

### OF FORMER PASTORS AND MINISTERS

who have held membership in the church, with members of the church and congregation.

1. MUSIC—Anthems and Hymns.
2. ADDRESSES BY THE PASTORS.
3. Reading of letters of congratulation from absent members, friends, and ministers, who have gone out from the church.

The living ex-pastors of this church are the Rev. Julius Seelye, D. D. (1845-1858), now President of Amherst College; the Rev. W. J. R. Taylor, D. D., (1849-1853), now pastor of the Clinton Avenue Reformed Church, Newark, N. J., the Rev. Denis Wortman, D. D., (1865-1870), Pastor of the Reformed Church of Fort Plain, N. Y.; and the Rev. Ashbel G. Vermilye, D. D., now in Europe.

In response to the above, the church was comfortably filled with adults, most of whom were children when Dr. Taylor was their pastor. The pulpit was occupied by Dr. Taylor, Dr. Wortman, the pastor, and the Rev. Horace Stanton, pastor of the Clinton Square Presbyterian church, Albany, N. Y., who represented the "alumni" ministers of the church.

After brief devotional exercises, Dr. Wortman was introduced, and read a neat, witty, lively, and at times pathetic series of reminiscences that caused every one to listen with delighted attention. He reviewed the time of his own pastorate and the changes since, congratulated the church and pastor on the present and future, described his predecessors, showing that this church during the present century had been served mainly by young men, the average age of the pastors being that of 36 years. He very wittily, and at the same time pointedly, advised the church to secure a fire-proof safe or repository for the valuable papers and records, and advised the election of a permanent curator. He then graphically reviewed the course of the world's history during the life of the church, and after a vivid description of the local life of two centuries ago, closed with the old Dutch New Year's salute, which in English is:

"I Wish you a Happy New Year—
Long may you live,
Much may you give,
Happy may you die,
And inherit the kingdom of Heaven by and bye!"

Dr. Wortman's address was afterwards reprinted in the Schenectady *Daily Union*, of July 10.

After a spirited anthem by the choir, Dr. Taylor followed in a congratulatory address, in which the floral emblems, the bell, baptismal bowl, hour-glass and chanticleer, the mottoes and symbols were all touchingly alluded to in suggestive phrase.

He dwelt upon the lessons of the occasion, and exhorted the people to improve the rich legacy of the past, and consecrate themselves more earnestly to the work of the future.

Three stanzas of the commemoration hymn were sung, and then followed the reading of letters of love and congratulation from the Rev. Julius E. Seelye, D. D., President of Amherst College, Rev. Ashbel G. Vermilye, D. D., former pastors; Rev.

Charles S. Vedder, D. D., of Charleston, S. C.; Rev. T. W. Chambers, D. D., one of the pastors of the Collegiate church of New York city; Rev. Prof. R. B. Welch, D. D., of Auburn Theological Seminary; Rev. T. Hamlin, of Troy, and Rev. A. W. Raymond, of Paterson, N. J. The letters of the ex-pastors are given below.

AMHERST COLLEGE, AMHERST, MASS., June 10, 1889.
REV. W. E. GRIFFIS:—

*Dear Brother,* I have delayed my reply to your very attractive invitation, in the hope that I might see some way open to accept it. I greatly regret to find this impossible. The anniversary to which you invite me occurs the week before our commencement, and my college duties will compel my presence here at that time. But I shall be with you in heart, and my thanksgivings and prayers shall join with yours in grateful recognition of the past, and in earnest supplications for the future.

All my memories of that dear old church are tender and precious. Though I was the first of her Dominies who was not born a Dutchman, and though some people wondered how such a *novus homo*, as I was called, could find a fit home in so venerable a household as the First Reformed Protestant Dutch church of Schenectady, no one of her children could have had a more cordial welcome than I, and if the Dutch blood had flowed in my veins for the two hundred years in which I once heard our most worthy and excellent Judge Sanders, of Scotia, declare, on the floor of General Synod, it had flowed through his, I do not see how it could have given me any more intimate relations with the elders, deacons and members of that church, than it was my high privilege to enjoy. It was in the first year of my ministry there that the General Synod referred to the Classes, who referred to the Consistories the question whether the word Dutch should be omitted from the name and title of the church, and though I was only ecclesiastically a Dutchman, I confess it gave me a pleasure when our Consistory voted with only one dissenting voice to retain the historical name, and had I been a member of the church when, fifteen years later, the same proposition was renewed and carried, I am not sure but that I should still have preferred the old name to the new.

As I think of the house in which I preached—lacking, indeed, the grace and beauty of the present edifice, but with a solid unobtrusiveness and dignity worthy of the people who built and worshipped in it—as I think of those people, loving, trusting and devout, earnest and firm in their convictions, not easily moved but deeply moved when moved at all—as I think of the children—where shall I find their like?—who so often ran to meet me in the street, now no longer children, but greeting me as I return, with children of their own. As I look over the list of one hundred and forty one, who were added to the church during the five and a quarter years of my ministry there, and of the thirty-eight members of the church who, during that time, left the ministrations of the earthly sanctuary for the worship of the temple not made with hands; as I think of those who since have gone, and of those who have come until now, I should find almost a congregation of strangers, where twenty-two years ago every face was so familiar,—many words both sad and joyous come to my lips which I would like to utter to the congregation which will gather on the 21st inst., to rehearse these and other memories of the past.

I congratulate the church on its long history, and on its prospects for the future—brighter, I verily believe, at the present time than ever before. May the Lord of all grace give to the present pastor, His choicest benediction, and ever lead His people there from grace to grace, till He brings us all into glory!

Very truly yours,
JULIUS H. SEELYE.

LONDON, May 24th, 1880.

*My Dear Brother Griffis:*—On reaching London, day before yesterday, I found there your very kind letter of May 3, inviting me to the 200th anniversary of the old Dutch church, at Schenectady. But in accordance with plans proposed before I left home, having accomplished the work for which I went to Antwerp, I have now just commenced, with my family, a more extended tour through Europe, to last (Providence permitting), during another year. Of course, the venerable occasion with its reunions and reminiscences, must go by without me. I can only send my most cordial wishes for the success of the anniversary itself, of your own ministry as my successor in the pastorate, and a hearty "*God save and keep you*" for the church and its people—among whom, whatever changes death and time may have worked, I still hold many esteemed friends. Men die, institutions live. A congregation is not the same for any ten years together. There are changes going on, and which ought to go on, continually; and no two pastors do precisely the same work, have the same difficulties to meet, or find and leave a church each just where his predecessor did. Your present 200th anniversary will be a record of immense changes. Nevertheless the institution lives; these changes are themselves a part of its life; and if it subserve the purposes for which it was intended, there is no nobler institution on earth, nor one so worthy to live and continue as a church. I have been living during the past year among churches old, splendid in architecture, but devoted to bigotry, and which do not subserve the moral improvement of men. Whilst the old church at Schenectady has age, can celebrate an unusual age, and has for its worship a building of choice architecture, may it always have in view the true purpose of a church, and enter upon a new life continually, constantly improving the past. May this celebration be to you and yours, pastor and people, only a happy mile-stone in the march of your unity, and progress, and prosperity. Grace, mercy and peace be abundantly multiplied unto you all.

Truly and fraternally yours,

A. G. VERMILYE.

The Rev. Horace C. Stanton, one of the many members of the church who have entered the ministry, made an address, depicting in lively phrase his personal experiences of the fire of August 6, 1861, which destroyed alike his father's home and the church; and in well chosen words portraying the past, improving the lessons of the hour, he pointed out the auguries of the future.

The pastor of the church then called on the city ministers for their blessing upon the church and people. In response, the Rev. Horace G. Day, the oldest city pastor, spoke eloquently in unison with the spirit of the hour, and with fervent, christian charity, scanned the lessons of the past, and on behalf of the Baptists exhorted the church to hold firmly the common faith of Christians.

The Rev. T. G. Darling, D. D., of the Presbyterian church, spoke gratefully of the help rendered the people of his church during the straits of their early history, and expressed the hope, after eloquently surveying the past, that the two churches might ever be one in faith and mutual love.

The Rev. E. C. Lawrence, pastor of the Second Reformed church of Schenectady, which was organized under the ministry of Dr. W. J. R. Taylor, in 1841, then ascended the pulpit. After a cordial greeting and a few earnest words, Mr. Lawrence read the following letter:

To the First Reformed Protestant Dutch Church of Schenectady, New York.

The second church of Schenectady presents her warmest greetings to her venerable mother on this glad and festal occasion, congratulates her upon the success and prosperity which have marked her progress during the last two centuries and glories in her noble history, the long line of her able, eloquent and devoted pastors, in her stalwart defenders of the true faith once delivered to the saints, and in the large-hearted and laudable munificence which reared this beautiful building.

Long may our beloved mother live, and every year renew her youth and beauty! Long may her spiritual field, like this rich old Mohawk valley, be fat, and fertile, and flourishing, and well cultivated! Let it indeed be the very garden of the Lord! Let joy and gladness be found therein, thanksgiving and the voice of melody! Most honored and happy mother, thy loyal and loving daughter invokes upon thee the choicest of Heaven's blessings and the continual favor of Almighty God who crowneth thee with loving kindness and tender mercies. With proud and grateful heart thy daughter salutes thee by the hand of

Her pastor.

June 21, 1880.   E. C. LAWRENCE.

The pastors of the Episcopal, Methodist and Congregational churches not being present on account of other engagements, could not or did not respond. The happy exercises were brought to a close by singing the hymn,

"Lord, at this closing hour,
Establish every heart,"

to the appropriate tune of Denis, the benediction being pronounced by Dr. Taylor. The audience and speakers then adjourned to the Consistory Room, where in informal reunion, and the interchange of greetings and memories, the time was spent until 10:30 p. m. The precious collection was then left for the night in charge of two young men.

"Except the Lord keep the city, the watchmen waketh but in vain."

On Wednesday, June 23d, the 85th commencement exercises of Union College, "the child of the Dutch church in Schenectady," were held in the church, the first being celebrated in the old 3rd edifice in 1797. In the addresses of President Potter, Bishop Doane, and Hon. Chauncey M. Depew, of the Board of Regents of the State of New York, frequent and emphatic reference was made to the connection of the church and college. In addition to the other decorations, there was placed in front of the rear gallery a conspicuous welcome to the Hon. John Welsh, who delivered the Chancellor's oration, and with his party of fellow visitors represented the city of Brotherly Love.

| Schenectady | WELCOME | Philadelphia |
| 1662 | | 1880 |

The names to the two cities stood significantly together. Their founders, Arendt Van Curler and William Penn, both bought their lands from the Indians, lived at peace with them, and for the foundations of the Empire and Keystone states professed and practiced principles that have made these the leading States of the American Union.

On Thursday evening, June 25th, the 63d anniversary of the Sunday School was celebrated in the church. It 1817 the first Sunday School in Schenectady was organized by the Dutch and Presbyterian people in union. Previous to this members of the Dutch church had engaged in mission work in the eastern part of the city among the inhabitants of Albany hill.

The exercises consisted of singing by the school, "the class of 1817" being arrayed in antique dress of the pupils of the early part of this century, and the presentation of flowers, with recitation of scripture verses and mottoes. The floral offerings were formed into the date

| 1680 |

After an address by the pastor, distribution was made of the abundant baskets, wreaths and boquets of flowers to some of those who had taken part in the preparations for the exercises of the week. As an expression of the gratitude and happiness felt by all the people, we here append the names of some of the committees and workers, who contributed toward making the enterprise with all its exercises a unity of success.

## COMMITTEE ON INVITATION, PROGRAMME AND ARRANGEMENTS.

Jacob V. Vrooman,    Jacob W. Clute,    W. E. Griffis.

### COMMITTEE ON DECORATION.

Chauncey Yates,
Lyman W. Clute,
Olin S. Luffman,
William Van Epps,
Fred. C. Jacobs,
William Schermerhorn,
Byron E. Near,
Wm. Van Dermoor,
Louis G. Verbeck,
Harvey Van Voast,
John E. Myers,

Mrs. Stephen Vedder,
Mrs. Jay Westinghouse,
Miss Mary Van Vranken,
Mrs. Andrew T. Veeder,
Mrs. Olin Luffman,
Mrs. Charles N. Yates,
Mrs. Welton Stanford,
Mrs. William Schermerhorn,
Mrs. Henry J. Clute,
Mrs. John E. Myers,

### COMMITTEE ON FLORAL EMBLEMS.

Miss Mary Cleary,
Mrs. Maxwell Ellis,
Miss Anna McNee,
Miss Libbie Thompson,

Mrs. Clay Whitely,
Mrs. William Johnson,
Miss Cornelia Bond,
Mrs. E. T. Lawsing.

### COMMITTEE ON MOTTOES, SYMBOLS AND BANNERS.

Jay Westinghouse,
Harvey Lyon,

Charles N. Yates,
Henry Swere.

### COMMITTEE ON MEMORIAL EXHIBITION.

William Van Vranken,
Andrew J. Barhydt,
Daniel Vedder,
W. T. L. Sanders,
Austin A. Yates,
G. Lansing Oothout,
Benj. L. Conde,
Jonathan Pearson,
J. Vanderveer,
Cornelius Lansing,
Casper F. Hoag,
John E. Myers,
Jacob F. Clute,
Edward Rosa,

Mrs. Austin A. Yates,
Miss Cornelia Boardman,
Mrs. E. Brinton,
Mrs. B. A. Mynderse,
Mrs. C. P. Sanders,
Miss C. Veeder,
Mrs. Edward Rosa,
Mrs. Maxwell Ellis,
Mrs. C. Van Slyck,
Mrs. Levi Clute,
Mrs. Levi Young,
Miss Annie Gleason,
Miss Elizabeth Yates.

#### COMMITTEE ON ENTERTAINMENT OF FRIENDS.

Jacob W. Clute,  
Judson S. Landon,  
Henry Rosa,  
B. A. Mynderse,

Mrs. J. W. Clute,  
Mrs. J. S. Landon,  
Mrs. Henry Rosa,  
Mrs. J. H. Barhyte.

#### USHERS.

Jonas Hallenbeck,  
James Van Voast,  
Harvey Van Voast,  
William Vrooman,  
John Juno,  
Byron E. Near,  
Fred. C. Jacobs,  
William Van Epps,

William Van Deusen,  
William Van Dermoor,  
Welton Stanford,  
Jacob W. Clute,  
Gulian V. P. Lansing,  
Louis G. Verbeck,  
John E. Myers,  
Wm. Schermerhorn.

#### COMMITTEE ON DUTCH SERVICE.

Danniel Vedder.

Cornelius Lansing.

#### COMMITTEE ON PUBLICATION OF HISTORY AND SERMON.

Jacob W. Clute,  
William Van Vranken,

B. A. Mynderse,  
Olin S. Luffman.

#### COMMITTEE ON SUNDAY SCHOOL ANNIVERSARY.

C. E. Kingsbury,  
Levi Young,

Mrs. William Johnson,  
Mrs. H. J. Clute,  
Miss Lou Rosa.

#### COMMITTEE IN CHARGE OF MEMORIAL EXHIBITION AT NIGHT.

Fred. C. Jacobs,  
William Van Epps,  
P. T. Brinton,

William H. Young,  
James Butler,  
Edward S. Vrooman.

#### ORGANIST AND CHOIR.

C. E. Kingsbury,  
James B. W. Lansing,  
J. W. McClellan,

Miss Abbie Bauder,  
Miss Vandenburg.

SCHENECTADY, June 21, 1880.

*Dear Pastor:* — We most heartily thank you for the very interesting and instructive discourse delivered by you on Sabbath morning, June 20th inst., upon the occasion of the celebration of the two hundredth anniversary of the founding of our church.

Its publication in connection with an account of the other exercises of the occasion, and with the history of the church, prepared by Prof. Jonathan Pearson, will furnish a memorial of the past history and present position of the church, most honorable in itself, and one which we venture to hope will be carefully preserved by those who shall come after us, even after the lapse of other centuries.

Permit us to add that we congratulate ourselves that the long line of our learned and honored pastors rests as the church enters upon its third century with one who so thoroughly understands and so faithfully portrays the spirit and devotion of his predecessors,

Rev. WM. E. GRIFFIS, Pastor First Reformed Church, Schenectady.

Very truly yours,

MARTIN DeFOREST,
DANIEL VEDDER,
J. V. VROOMAN,
T. H. REEVES,
WM. VAN VRANKEN,
EDWARD ROSA,
JAS. H. BARHYTE,
J. S. LANDON,
J. A. BARHYDT,
STEWART MYERS,
CHARLES N. YATES,
WM. CHRISLER,
B. A. MYNDERSE,
CORNELIUS LANSING,
JOHN WESTINGHOUSE,
WM. VAN DERMOOR,
C. E. KINGSBURY,
HENRY ROSA,
A. A. YATES,
A. FRAME,
E. T. LAWSING,
G. L. OOTHOUT,
JAMES H. CLUTE,
P. FENWICK,
JACOB W. CLUTE,
RICHARD MARCELLUS,
ANDREW T. VEEDER,
C. VAN SLYCK,
CORNELIUS THOMSON,
CHAUNCEY O. YATES,
GEORGE SHAIBLE,
CASPER F. HOAG.

# HISTORICAL DISCOURSE.

→∞0↔

1 KINGS, 8 : 57.
"The Lord our God be with us, as he was with our fathers."

It is with no trivial thought or shallow emotion, that we engrave these words in enduring stone over that portal of this edifice which is consecrated to the memory of the fathers, and which looks toward the land whence they came; that we choose them for the text of our memorial discourse; that we breathe them to-day as our heartfelt prayer; that with them on our lips and in our hearts, we survey the past; and that holding them as a lamp to our feet we step into the unknown path of the future, and begin a third century.

The past is to us an open book, all inscribed by the finger of Providence. On the white page of the present the characters are being traced. The future is to us a book closed. In trembling hope before that shut volume, we pray "The Lord our God be with us," with earnestness equal to the exultant gratitude with which we utter the fact, "as he was with our fathers."

Cast with me your retrospect over two centuries, and contrast the present with the past; and if to-day we have reason for thanksgiving that to us the lines have fallen in pleasant places, and a goodly heritage is ours, let us honor the fathers, who in simple virtue, laid the foundations of this city, and in the faith once delivered to the saints, consecrated to Almighty God their sabbaths, their sanctuaries, themselves and their children.

Who were the fathers? Whence and why came they to this continent, and into this valley — not then a teeming highway of empire, rosaried with threads of iron and water, beaded with cities, and glistening with unnumbered harvest fields and happy homes, but lonely, untilled and desolate, save as the Iriquois broke its solitude? Whence and why came our fathers? Historian, poet and artist tell us with pride, that the first settlers of

New England and the carolinas were exiles seeking "freedom to worship God," and martyrs driven before the persecuting sword "to found a faith's pure shrine." Nor do we deny it. As citizens of a great republic, we with their descendants honor their memory, and will with them "call it holy ground, the spot where first they trod," though with more of truth than they, we can say of ours, "They have left unstained what there they found, reedom to worship God." Yet frankly we confess it, without shame we tell it, that our fathers left Holland, and founded this Empire State in pursuit of commercial enterprise alone. The first settlers of Schenectady entered this fair valley to find what they had already left behind them in Holland.

Why were not the Hollanders political exiles or religious refugees? Simply because they had no need to be. They were under no ban, no persecution. They could not flee from despotism or persecution, for Holland was already free. Her protestant faith, her toleration were already gained. Her Reformers, Gansevoort and Agricola had begun the Reformation fifty years before Martin Luther. Guido de Bres had formed the Confession of faith which is still ours, in 1563. The first martyrs, Esch and Voes, who were burned at the stake at Antwerp in 1523, lighted by their own bodies the first candles of liberty that made the Dutch republic under William the Silent a beacon of liberty that lighted the world. The poor people of Holland called themselves "The Churches of the Netherlands under the Cross," and when come to national freedom, unity and power were not only among the first churches of Protestant Europe in the Reformation, but were the first to accord liberty of conscience and toleration of faith. Under the banners of the Princes of Orange, inscribed with the emblem of a pelican feeding her young with blood from her own breast, the Hollanders not only won liberty, but they granted it to others. Even the Pilgrim fathers found a home in Leyden, and there learned some of their best lessons of liberty before they came to America. That Holland was the asylum for exiles of every land, one need only examine and analyze the oldest names of our own congregation to see in them the tell-tale evidence that the liberty of brave little Holland was shared by many nationalities. Our fathers could not fly for liberty or conscience sake from the home-land, for these they had already possessed for nigh a century, and these — religion and liberty, they brought with them here.

So then, by virtue of historic truth, we claim for our fathers equal renown with the Pilgrims or the Hugenots, and a yet more ancient heritage of freedom. With pride we confess it to-day that our fathers kindled not the beacon of liberty first in this wilderness, but already lighted and burning brightly, they brought hither the torch from the home hearth-fire.

On the shores of Manhattan and Long Islands, on the Hudson at Albany and Kingston, on the Delaware at New Amstel, the Hollanders had already settled with their churches, pastors and schoolmasters, when this valley was still owned by the Six Nations of Indians, whose totem or coat of arms was a tortoise. The Mohawks were considered as dwelling in the head, as the Senecas were in the tail, and the other tribes in the several feet. Schenectady, or the place "beyond the pine-plains," was the frequent site of the council-fire of the tribes, and the eastern capital of the confederacy. The founder of our city, Arendt Van Curler, bought, twenty-one years before William Penn, from the Mohawk sachems, in 1661, the Great Flat of this valley, and the next year led a band of fifteen hardy pioneers with their families from Renssylaerwyck, now Albany. Their motive in leaving this settlement and striking into the western wilderness was to escape local annoyances, and enjoy a freedom more exactly like that of Holland. They entered the wilderness, pathless then save an Indian trail of pine and sand, which still stretches in ancient barrenness before the eye of the railroad tourist from Albany, their goal being the fertile lands near us. Reaching Norman's Kill — that stream as historic as Penn's elm tree — at which the Dutch and the Mohawks in 1618 entered into eternal friendship, the pioneers after a march eastward in which they had followed the line of trees "blazed" by the Indians, turned to the north, until they halted on the south side of the Mohawk river, where we now live. The aboriginal name of the site chosen was retained in justice to the hospitable savages. Would that this policy of embalming in our speech the ancient birthright names of the great natural features of our country had been more generally followed.

Quickly the lands were allotted, the forest trees cut down, the rude houses built, and the seeds cast into the soil. A stockade of tree trunks, with bastions at each corner, marked the parallelogram, whose sides are now Washington avenue, Front, Ferry and State streets, while Church and Union crossing each other at right angles cut the settlement into four squares, which again were subdivided into sixteen. Two gates were built, one on Front street, near the river, and one at State, opening toward Fort Orange, or Albany. Thus, before the hostile savages of Canada could swoop upon them, a village had sprung up in the pine woods. The festal garlands that decorate our church to-day were gathered from trees miles away. Two centuries ago, the entire site of the city was embowered by them. Church and Union streets of the future were for years dotted with stumps, and to the echoing and rustling forest, then full of all the wild voices of nature, the people listened as they sat on their sills or rude "stoeps" at eventide, and every breeze floated to them freighted with the resinous aroma of the encircling woods. So sudden was the building of the village that the bear, the wolf, the deer and the wild turkey, and even the buffalo, surprised on their way down from the highlands back of the river, now called College, Prospect, and Paige hills, to drink in the Binne-kill, were sometimes shot within the limits of the palisades. The river then, as often now, was swollen with the melting of the Adirondack snows, and the magnificent sight of the flats and islands covered with a sheet of turbid water, and receiving their top-dressing of enriching silk, gave first augury of that wondrous fertility which for two centuries has made the soil of the Mohawk valley productive to a proverb.

With the same peaceful disposition as that much lauded in Penn and his Quaker founders of the city of Brotherly Love, the settlers lived side by side with the dusky Mohawks. Their admiration for the simple, manly character of Van Curler, the founder, led them for many years to address the governors of the Province, both Dutch and English, as "Corlaer." By the name of the founder, also, was the village known to the French and Canada Indians from whom there was ever the threatening terror of massacre and pillage. More than one description of the fort and hamlet was sent to the court beauties and favorites of Louis XIV, at Versailles, (in the archives of which place they have been found), by the French officers and gallants at Montreal and Quebec. For the sake of winning courtly favor at Versailles, was Schenectady finally destroyed and our ancestors massacred by the Frenchmen in Canada.

For eight or ten years, the villagers had no church, but met occasionally for worship in private houses, or were content with family prayer and the home reading of the scriptures and confession of faith, or the reading of a homily by the "voorlezer." Occasionally one of the domines from Albany came up to preach and administer the sacrament, baptize the children, or bury the dead. Or, the people here would make a journey to Albany to enjoy the ministrations of religion, which kept them Christians, even amid the toils of a rough frontier life. For nearly a century Schenectady was the outpost of colonial civilization. Whether under the red white and blue flag of Holland, or the red cross and lion of England, they were equally unprotected from the merciless savages both red and white.

When was this church first organized? Dr. E. T. Corwin, the biographer of the Reformed church says in his Manual about 1670. Professor Jonathan Pearson, in his history of our church thinks it certain that the church had an existence in 1674. As all the papers and books of the church kept by the first pastor, Tassemaker, were burned with his own body in the massacre of 1690, perhaps the exact date will never be known. Yet of this we are certain, that as early as 1680 the church had a consistory and stated services were held by the ministers from Albany. Our list of elders and deacons begins with the year 1680. Therefore we call this year of grace 1880, our bi-centennial, although we might claim greater age. The Rev. Gideon Schaets, of Albany, organized the church, and visited it at various times from the first year of the settlement, until 1694. Both our first pastor, Tassemaker (or Thesschenmacher), and Domine Schaets were pupils or adherents of the famous Voetius, who was Professor of theology at the University of Utrecht, and a belligerant opponent of the now extinct sect of Labadists, a species of Quaker Communists (of a good kind). Two of these people who afterwards located colonies on the Hudson river visited both Albany and Schenectady, and revenged themselves on the two Dutch domines by writing a pamphlet in which they mercilessly criticized the style, manner and doctrine of the two Voetians Schaets and Tassemaker.

Our first church edifice stood within, and near the southern line of the stockade, at the end of Church street, on State. The parsonage and pasture lot — for the early Dutch always built a house for the domine, as soon as they built a church — was within the bounds of the present church lot at the corner of Church and Union streets, and was occupied for this purpose for 130 years. Dutch ministers were very scarce after the English conquest in 1664. Only one came from Holland during the years from 1662 to 1676. Petrus Tassemaker (or Thesschenmacher), our first pastor, was a graduate of Utrecht University, and an enthusiastic pupil of Prof. Voetius, whose orthodoxy was not considered to possess the exact tint of true blue, by the only four Dutch ministers then in America. They, however, organized a Classis, and ordained him, so that our infant church secured the fruits of the first Classis that ever met, and of the first Dutch ordination that ever took place in America.

All that is known of our first pastor in his relation to our church is that he was a good student, a man of culture and travel, that he especially disliked the Labadists, and that he labored in the gospel both for the Dutch and the Indians here during six years. Within a few feet of this pulpit stood the little parsonage, at the door of which the silent savages and Frenchmen sent by Frontenac stood, hatchet in hand, on the midnight of February 8th, 1690, until the war-whoop was raised. Then a blow, the scalp torn off, the house fired, his body cast into the blazing timbers, was burned to the shoulder blades. His head was barbarously carried away on a pike, but his ashes were scattered no man knows whither. The settlement was annihilated. The mighty King of France, Louis XIV, and his Consort, Madame de Maintenon, at Versailles, were told the full story of the masacre of the heretics by Monseignat, and Schenectady became the theme of grave debate in Paris and London. We propose to remember their sorrows upon the walls of this edifice—the church of the fathers and of their children. To the memory of our first pastor and his flock, the martyrs of 1690, we shall soon erect a marble tablet inscribed in letters of gold. The minister left no descendants to mourn for him, but many of the children in the sixth and seventh generation of the murdered fathers still live as worshippers in our church to-day.

The first pastor of our church, like all the others until Dr. Romeyn, or after the Revolution, were educated in Holland; for the fathers then and the children now, alike demand that their ministers be liberally educated. With the names of Leyden and Utrecht, their Alma Matres, as also with the fir tree and pine and box together, we to-day beautify the place of God's sanctuary in which they ministered. Nor do we forget Dortrecht in which the national synod was held in 1819, and the national faith confirmed; nor Antwerp, in which the first confessors and martyrs of the Dutch church, the old church under the cross, lived, and suffered, and died; nor the ancestral motto in the mother-tongue, "Eendracht maakt macht;" with the scripture word alike of warning and cheer, "Nisi Dominus frustra."

It was more than sullen obstinacy and defiant hatred of their enemies that led the survivors of the massacre—a pitiful remnant—to come back to the ashes of their former homes and resolve to build anew. It was true courage, as brave, as sublime, as the martyr's heroism or the warrior's rage. Into this wilderness they came to begin anew their toils, and to light again the altar.fires of devotion. Until the peace of Ryswick, in 1697, there was no safety in this valley except behind fortifications, with the loaded rifle always at hand. From 1694 to 1699 the Rev. Godfrey Dellius, the assistant of Domine Schaets in Albany ministered once a month in the "Dorp," and labored to christianize the Indians. After the declaration of peace, they were again strong enough in 1700, to call a minister, and build a new church. Our second pastor was the Rev. Bernardus Freeman, a scholarly, christian gentleman, able to preach in English as well as Dutch, and later in the Indian tongue. With his courteous manners, abilities and character he won the hearts of Hollander and Mohawk alike. He translated several books of the scriptures, the creeds, and a portion of the English liturgy into the English language. A volume of sermons, and one of miscellaneous writings, and some of his translations—proofs of a studious life—are still in existence, preserved at New Brunswick, N. J. To one of these books is prefixed his portrait showing the author in the gown, bands and luxurious wig or curled hair of the period. After five years of service at Schenectady Dr. Freeman was called to Flatbush, L. I., where a house erected by him is still standing.

This earnest endeavor of our Dutch fathers to civilize and christianize the Indians deserves more than a passing notice. There have been Washington Irvings to caricature, almost to indecency; there have been writings to malign and bigots to lampoon and belittle the Dutchmen, but the historian or essayist of genius who will portray in stately and winning diction their true characteristics and show their virtues, is yet to arise. All the world has heard of John Eliot, of Massachusetts, preaching to the red man. Pen, painting, poem and eulogy have embalmed his fame; yet the Dutch domines of Albany began preaching to the Indians three years before Eliot held his first service. Hundreds of names of genuine Indian proselytes are still on the roll of our church and that at Albany. Our own fathers looked upon the Mohawks as something more than brutes, or creatures merely from whom money and beaver skins could be obtained. Three of our own pastors were missionaries to the Indians. Our own church records show that hundreds of the sons of the forest were influenced for good. Many were truly converted and sat in worship with our fathers in the old churches on the Street of the Martyrs. There they partook of the same communion together. There the Indian pappooses were held in the arms of their dusky mothers, who stood in beads and blankets, before the same baptismal font, (whose ancient shape we reproduce in the white rosebuds of yesterday,) at which waited the white lady and her infant in christening-quilt of silk and embroidery. There, too, the Indian lover stood with his Indian bride, and in the name of the Father, and of the Son, and of the Holy Ghost, in the words of the Christian ritual, vowed to love and cherish one wife in his wigwam; and, when our fathers came annually to pay their pew rent or subscriptions in beaver skins, the Christian Indians came also with like gifts for the sanctuary. When the domine died, the Mohawks out of sympathy presented peltries and strings of wampum as tokens of condolence. We erect on our walls on this festal day the heraldic insignia, not only of Holland, of Britain, and of America, the pelican, the lion and the eagle, but also the tortoise, in remembrance of our Indian Christians and church members. Our extant records shows a portion of the good work done among these Indians, viz.: 39 marriages, 101 baptisms, and 14 communicants received into the church, from 1702 to 1717, and indicate much good accomplished in these fifteen years; the records of the work of previous years being unfortunately lost to us.

We wonder how many intelligent Americans who confound the geographically Low Dutch with the morally low "Dutchmen," the Hans Breitman type of people, who never came from Holland, or who form their ideas of the Hollanders from the caricatures of Irving, are acquainted with facts like these?

And when the Mohawks dwindled away, and the Oneidas and Tuscaroras lingered on their reservations in western New York, this church assisted liberally, for many years, until 1830, to maintain missionaries among them, under the auspices of a society that was organized mainly by her pastor, Dr. Romeyn, and of which he was president.

To accommodate the increasing number of white worshipers and Christian Indians, a subscription paper was circulated, and a second church was built in 1703, on the site of the first edifice, at the south end of Church street, on State, then called the "Street of the Martyrs." Its dimensions were 55 by 46 feet. It was probably built of stone. The burying ground to the west of it, was 15 feet wide and 56 feet long. The first three edifices were erected in the middle of the street and were loopholed for musketry, since attack from the Canada French and Indians was a possible event until the close of the French and Indian war, in 1763. Many a husband, father or brother, while out on a trading expedition, canoeing the rivers, or tilling the soil, fell before the hidden foe. A puff of smoke, a whistling bullet, a fallen victim, a yell, a scalp, covert regained, and all was over. A mutilated body brought home to a mourning household, a funeral in the little church, a procession on foot to God's acre on Green street beyond the fort, or news of some fresh captive carried off to Canada, were common events until the Revolution.

It was a sad day for the church and village when Dr. Freeman left them, and for eight years, except for the visit of an Albany minister about three times a year, there were no religious services. From 1709 to 1715 the Rev. Thomas Barclay, a missionary of the London Society for the propagation of the Gospel, and military chaplain of the fort at Albany, preached once a month, and read the English liturgy in the church, and hoped to bring the villagers into the English church; but the Dutchmen clung to their ancestral faith and ritual, and in 1715 secured a pastor from Holland, the Rev. Thomas Brouwer. Little is known of his life, except that he must have made good proof of his ministry, since he received 108 persons into the church, baptized 505 children, and married 53 couples during the thirteen years of his service here. He was buried under the pulpit of the church in which he served, and his dust removed to a similar place when the third church of 1734 was built, and his bones now lie in Vale Cemetery. In this respect his remains are honored above those of his flock, who still sleep in their unmarked graves beneath the cobble stones of the street pavement, over which the wheels rattle, and the feet of the unthinking passer-by tread. Were I a son of Schenectady and a rich man, I should ask from the city, or purchase a few square feet of ground at the end of Church street on State, where stood the first two church edifices, and beneath which still lie the bones of the ancestors, and I should erect in enduring granite a monument to the historic past, and to the memory of the founders of this city whose dust lies beneath. And could I dispose of the city funds, I should prefer to spend one hundred dollars in this method of permanent adornment, than to allow five hundred dollars to fizzle away in smoke after the Chinese fashion. Better yet than powder or marble, perhaps would it be for some public-spirited citizen to erect as a memorial to the fathers, a free public library. Certainly I should rejoice if some one of Dutch blood, if not of Dutch name should thus worthily honor the past, and benefit the present generation.

The fourth pastor of the church was the Rev. Reinhardt Erich zon, a native of North Holland, who, like Dr. Romeyn, was called from Hackensack, N. J. A man of more than ordinary ability, he was first president of the Coetus, the General Synod of that day, and which made the Declaration of Independence of the Dutch church in America from that of Holland. During the eight years of his pastorate here, (1728–1736,) the royal charter of the Church was procured from King George II of England, and the new stone church on Union and Church streets was built. He was probably the first of the pastors who was already married when he first came to Schenectady. Several of his descendants are still living in our congregation. He was called to Freehold, N, J., in which place we have been able to secure a portrait of him which may be seen to-morrow. Two hundred and six persons were received into the church during his ministry here.

A subscription for a new church with a clock and bell having been circulated, and sufficient wheat and guilders having been subscribed, building began in 1732, and the church was dedicated January 13, 1734. This third edifice, 80x56 feet, built of graywacke or blue sandstone, with a space of ten feet around it for the funeral cortege to pass around the church, is remembered by a few of the older members of the church, whose number diminishes yearly. The belfry was surmounted by the orthodox vane on which a cock of St. Nicholas, as became a Dutch church, greeted the dayspring, and gave the direction of the wind.

Within, the pulpit stood on the west side, on a narrow pedestal, with a conical sounding board beyond. An hour-glass could always be seen on a bracket in front of the minister, who, after he had consumed one hour in the service, reversed the glass for the sands to run afresh. Behold it on my left, transfigured in flowers ! In front of the pulpit was the chancel (Dophuisje) surrounded by a railing, within which the minister stood while handing the bread and wine to the communicants, or administering baptism. In the service the men and women sat apart, the men on raised seats along the wall, and the women in slips or bancken, in the body of the house. Hats or bonnets did not trouble the head of the women until after the Revolution, but wearing hoods in winter, and their own braided hair in summer, with kerchief over their shoulders, they sat with heads uncovered during services.

In 1800 family or square pews were first set apart. No such thing as a flue or chimney was visible in the church architecture, and stoves were unknown until 1792. From early times the men warmed their hands by casing them in their stout coat pockets. The women brought small foot stoves in their sleighs to church in winter, or had their husbands, slaves or servants carry them, often a distance of two or three miles. Occasionally some one fainted on account of the fumes of the charcoal, but in general gas and cold alike were borne without complaint, for linsey woolsey and stout lungs were the fashion then. The first stoves erected were mounted on platforms nearly as high as the gallery but were finally lowered to the floor, as the philosophers of the time, who had charge of the stoves, discovered that heat rises.

The old bell that for 116 years called with its silvery notes the people to worship, was cast in Holland, by the renowned Johann Albert de Grave, in 1732. Tradition says that several pounds of silver in coin and plate were contributed by the citizens of Amsterdam, as a missionary offering to this church in the far off American wilderness, and were melted into the bell.

Though weighing only 600 pounds, it gave out, when rung, such perfect vibrations, that its marvellously clear and sweet tones were often heard ten miles up the valley. Two inscriptions girdled the bell near the top, which was decorated with a row of grapes and leaves. The Dutch legend read as follows: "The bell of the Low Dutch congregation of Schenectady, at their own request, 1732;" the Latin, "De Grave and N. Muller of Amsterdam made me." In 1848, after 116 years of service, the beautiful bell was hopelessly cracked. Being removed, much of its metal was recast into a heavier bell, which, however, was unsatisfactory. A new one having none of the old metal in it was finally put up in the belfry, and after 13 years of service was encircled by the great fire of August 6th, 1861. It gave one sad final note as it fell, was melted in the intense heat, and ran in molten streams on the ground. Enough of the old bell of 1732 was saved to make thereof a few clock and tea bells, which still exist in the congregation. With sweet and perfumed memories of the old bell, the skillful fingers of the ladies have reproduced this morning before our eyes, its form in a transfiguration of beauty. Does it not seem to you on whose ears fell the music of the old church bell, that out of the grave of bygone days, it has arisen this Sabbath day, in the bright resurrection of flowers?

The clock and clock-tower must have been taken down sometime during the last century, as few living persons remember them. Yet on the old church seal used to stamp documents, there was a distinct representation of it, and our records show that it was not only built, but a man was employed to keep it in order for some years.

It is interesting to know that the church still possesses among her papers, the original subscription lists for building each one of her five edifices, except the first, and for purchasing the bell and clock. It has been with a thrill of imagination, that I have composed this discourse, not from vague tradition, but from a study of the actual documents, now time-stained and crumbling, which were touched by the hands of the fathers of one or two centuries ago.

Our fifth pastor, after an interval of several years, was the Rev. Cornelius Van Santvoord, a graduate of Leyden, a brilliant scholar and writer, whose works are still extant, one of which has been translated by my friend, Rev. M. G. Hansen, of Coxsackie, N. Y. He preached fluently in English, French and Dutch. He was called from Staten Island, and ministered in Schenectady twelve years, dying January 6th, 1752, at the age of 55 years. He was buried under the pulpit of the old 3rd church, and his remains now sleep in Vale Cemetery. During his ministry 151 persons were received into the church, 645 children baptised, and 174 couples married. One terrible event during his pastorate must be noticed briefly.

Scarcely had the generation, who witnessed the first massacre, passed away, when this church and village were plunged into mourning by another appalling calamity. On a summer's day, July 18, 1748, a party of about forty townsmen went out to Benkendal, three miles from this church, to assist in raising a barn still standing. Hearing the sound, as they believed, of the wild turkey, and seized with the hunter's joy, they were led into the dreadful ambuscade, and became the helpless targets for a hundred French and Indian rifles. Several were carried captive to Canada, and toward sunset of that dreadful day, on the floor of the old barn visible from our north windows, only a few feet distant, two rows of the ghastly slain were laid for recognition by their wives or children. It was a sad day for this church and the village. It was in the midst of alarms like these, that our fathers lived. They loopholed their church walls, posted the sentinels at the gates, and those who lived beyond the palisades came to church with their rifles on their backs and powder-horn at their side.

For three years after the death of their pastor the church was shepherdless. It is a tax on the imagination for us at the present time to realize how difficult it was in those days to procure a minister. Our fathers insisted that he must have a University education, in Holland. None but one trained up in the Dortrecht theology would do, and the expense and trouble of settling a minister were very great. The expense of his passage across the ocean, and freight and carriage of himself and his goods must be paid to his place of destination. If a church called away a minister before a certain number of years had elapsed they must pay to the consistory half the money it cost them at first. Besides this a parsonage must be built, and so it happened, that to call and settle the next minister, it cost this church for passage and freight only, $563. In addition to this, they tore down the old parsonage erected about 1691, and built another one a story and a half high with many gables like steps. This stood inside our present lot until 1814, when it made way for the fourth church edifice.

The Rev. Barent Vrooman, the sixth pastor was born in Schenectady, and was a descendant of one of our former elders, grand Adam Vrooman, who defended his home at the corner of Front and Church streets so bravely during the massacre. Barent Vrooman after preaching a few months in the region of New Paltz, where he laid the corner stone of a church still standing, came to Schenectady when 29 years of age, and served the church during thirty years, amid all the distractions of the French and Indian wars, and the Revolution. He was six feet four inches high, of commanding figure, very kind to the poor, benevolent and sociable, fluent in delivery, and active in the church at large. His people were very devoted to him, and he gave his best years to them, until he dropped dead with palsy. There is not much sentiment in ledgers and cash books, nor pathos in receipt books, but I confess to have been deeply moved in comparing the bold, strong signature of the young Barent Vrooman of 30, and the same sign-manual in trembling, crooked lines of Barent Vrooman in his old age. During his long pastorate he baptized 3,521 children, married 383 couples, and received 453 members into the church.

For 113 years after the founding of the village, there was no other church except the Dutch in this place, though several English families lived here as early as 1710. In 1735 the Episcopal church was organized, but it was not until 1762 that a small stone edifice was erected, in which the Scotch and English worshipped alternately. Like a good Dutch church, it bears on its weathervane the cock of St. Nicholas. Nor were any of the Reformed churches in this county or Classis organized until near the close of the last century, except that of Niskayuna, at which services were held as early as 1749, the first pastor being a Mohican Indian. It will be thus understood why the ministers of this church were kept so busy in marrying couples and baptizing children. All the Dutch families in the county were adherents to this one church, and other nationalities availed themselves of the services of the domines here. Our record of baptisms and marriages, except during the ten years of the revolutionary period, are quite complete, from the year 1691, those before the massacre having been burned in the first parsonage. These records are extremely valuable, and should be placed beyond all danger of loss by fire. From them Prof. Pearson compiled his valuable genealogical work on "The First Settlers of Schenectady and their descendants," and also the History of this, our church, soon to be published; and what is more, never received one penny for his labor of love. Scarcely a week passes but that the church records are consulted to establish personal identity, legal questions, pensions and other financial claims, and historical facts. Inquirers come or write from Canada, Texas, California, and along the Mohawk and Hudson vallies. The citizens and the church alike are interested in seeing these memorials preserved. A fire-proof safe is greatly needed.

The church that to-day celebrates her 200th anniversary is the mother of nine Reformed churches and of Union College. Every one of the Reformed churches in the Classis of Schenectady owes more or less of their first beginning to this church. They are her children, stepchildren or grandchildren, and the two churches of Glenville, the two of Rotterdam, Princetown, and the 2nd Church of this city sprang directly from us, and in several instances were liberally aided. Union College now in her 85th year, is the child of this church. To the Rev. Direk Romeyn, our seventh pastor this city owes grateful memory, for having given it the first impulse to systematic public education. Of all the names of men to whom Schenectady is indebted, I know none more worthy of honor than that of Direk Romeyn. A prince and a leader in the Reformed church, an exemplar of christianity, a public-spirited citizen of large ideas, the companion of statesmen and men great in knowledge, action and character, his reputation was national as well as local. He took the lead in this state in the support and patronage of classical learning, in securing the freedom of the Dutch church in America from that of Holland, with the aid of Livingston, in writing her constitution, and establishing her Theological Seminary—the oldest in America—and in organizing the foreign missionary work, for all christians. His experience during the Revolution— the time that tried men's souls—broadened his whole nature.

He was born a British citizen, was by language and lineage a Dutchman, but when with us an American, and died under the stars and stripes. And these three national colors we fitly entwine around his name. He looked to the future, not to the past. He gently but earnestly won the people from dead issues, and bade them step on. He taught them that they were Dutchmen no more, but Americans, and that the language so dear to the lessening number of greyheaded fathers, must be abandoned for the future speech of this nation and continent. Yet in all rounds of his busy life he was an humble christain, and a faithful preacher of Christ's gospel. His tomb we to-day garland with flowers, and his name we write in letters of gold, and place it in the centre of the illustrious dead because we believe him to have been the best and ablest of all our pastors. After serving this church for twenty years, he fell asleep in Christ, April 16th, 1804. His sepulchre and that of his honored consort are with us in Vale Cemetery. During his ministry the church having expanded to its largest size, and having 484 members on it roll and a congregation of 2,500, employed an assistant, the Rev. Jacob Sickles, from 1794 to 1797, and the Rev. J. H. Meier, 1803–1806. Both of these young men were graduates of the Theological Seminary, in which Dr. Romeyn was professor. The first, while here, accepted a call to Coxsackie ; then, after three years, he went to Kinderhook, where, after laboring 34 years, he died, in 1845. Mr. Meier, after three years of promising life and service here died of consumption, and was buried at Albany. During the pastorate of Dr. Romeyn, in addition to all his other labors he married 945 couples, (nearly one a week), baptized 3,541 children, (nearly 177 a year, over 3 a week), and received 248 persons into the church. To him also we owe the careful revision and preservation of the church records. He was the last of the line of preachers in Dutch. He himself often preached in English, settled the battle of the tongues, and persuaded the people to realize that they were no longer Dutch, Scotch or English, but for all times Americans ; and that as such they could honor the fathers and the traditions of the past, yet be none the less American christians. As head of the educational institutions of this city, Union College unites with us in honoring the memory of one who was the embodiment of Christian unity, and as the leader of the church, the founder of the college. And here charge us not with vain boasting, if we publish a fact which is so far forgotten in this town, as to be fresh news to many, yet which the records of the church and college, in paper and chiseled stone prove, and of which at the semi-centennial of the college in 1845, copious mention was gratefully made. At Dr. Romeyn's instance, under his influence and chairmanship, a meeting of the citizens was called in 1784, to build an Academy which was to become a College. Twenty-seven out of the thirty-one citizens who signed the agreement and subscribed handsomely were elders, deacons, members or worshippers in this church. Our church built the Academy that stood on the north-west corner of Ferry and Union streets. After ten years of prosperity, and through the prominent influence of Dr. Romeyn, aided greatly by the late Governor Yates, the charter of Union College was obtained. There may even be some still living who remember the evening of February, 1795, when the brick Academy building on Ferry street was illuminated with candles which were lighted all at once by signal, while the bell on the roof kept pealing merrily, and the rooms were full of happy boys, and the streets were crowded with sympathizing people, as, with the charter received from the Legislature, the academy was merged into the college. And how then did our people act? In true Christian liberality of spirit and heart they gave over to the Trustees of Union College, the building and endowments worth at least thirty thousand dollars. Although people of Dutch decent, loyal to the faith of their fathers, they did not make it a Reformed Dutch College. This they had already at New Brunswick. But they gave this city a Union College, and with their money, and prayers, and anxious thought they nourished it during its infant years. There has been more than one fling at the Dutchmen of this town, but the epithets "stingy," "ignorant," "bigoted," cannot fairly belong to them, nor ought the city or the college ever forget what this church has ever done for them. As one who is proud to be a successor of Dirck Romeyn, and to minister to the children of the founders of Union College, I can only say to the President and officers of the College, "Keep alive in belief and practice the principles of the founders."

As we enter into a summary of this, the nineteenth century, and dwell upon facts within the memory of some still living, I must be brief almost to injustice. The tenth pastor of this church was the Rev. Cornelius Bogardus a pupil of Dr. Romeyn, and a graduate of our Theological Seminary ; for since the Revolution the churches no longer sent to Holland for their pastors, and the English language was everywhere in use in the pulpits. Mr. Bogardus, though a promising young man, lived but four years in the ministry at Schenectady, dying like his predecessor, Meier, of consumption, December 15, 1812, at the age of 32. Yet during these four years, he received into the church 157 members, baptized 444 children, and joined in marriage 117 couples. He was the last minister who preached even occasionally in Dutch, and the last who officiated in the old stone church ; for already in 1805, the plan of building a new edifice was agitated, but not till Dec. 3rd, 1812, were the contracts signed for a new brick building. There being no more French or Indians to fear, the edifice was built back from the street. The old parsonage was demolished to make room, the old church torn down, and a handsome and fashionable looking edifice of brick stared at the old folks with suspicious newness, and rejoiced the young ones with its smart modern look. Other innovations must have made some of the old heads shake, for the sexes were not separated as of old, and family pews were introduced. Indeed, it nearly broke the hearts of the aged folks to have them leave the building, and instead of demolishing it at once, it was taken down piecemeal. Need I describe the old fourth church ? You remember it far better than I, who from documentary and hearsay evidence only can describe it. The memories of childhood and of dear ones gone, and of glorious privileges, and grand singing and precious seasons of revival and grace sanctify that old church to many of you. Those who never saw it, may be told that it seated about 800 people, had three aisles, and galleries on three sides, 24 square pews along the walls, and 72 in the middle blocks. Its organ and chandeliers were the gift of Nicholas Vander Volgen, and were beautiful, tasteful and serviceable. On the 20th of November, 1814, the last services were held in the old stone church, which for eighty years had re-echoed the voices of Erichzon, Van Santvoord, Vrooman, Romeyn, Sickles, Meier and Bogardus, in which many a historic personage of the Revolution worshipped, in which the first commencement of Union College was held, and the students in their gowns, in seats along the wall, were regular worshippers. Tears for the old, smiles for the new church mingled together. The Rev. Andrew Yates preached morning and afternoon. On the following Sabbath, the new church was dedicated, and the Rev. Eliphalet Nott preached twice. For 47 years this edifice stood, until the fire of August 6th, 1861, when by "the act of God," this people were called again for the fifth time to erect a new edifice to his glory.

With that fourth church building is associated inseparably the memory of the Rev. Jacob Van Vechten, who held the longest pastorate in the history of this church, who under God was the instrument of reaping the richest spiritual harvest, who introduced needed reforms, and brought back the qualifications for baptism and membership to the Bible standard. Our eleventh pastor, Van Vechten, was a graduate of Union College, and for many years one of its active trustees. He began his pastorate here January 8th, 1815, serving faithfully and laboriously until March 6, 1849, during which time 910 members were received into the church. Of retired and studious habits, suffering under infirmity for many years, he aimed to purify the church, and to promote spiritual and experimental rather than formal religion. It had been the custom before him to baptize all children whether of godly or ungodly parentage, legitimate or illegitimate. Dr. Van Vechten required the scripture test of faith and experience. Instead of receiving at the communion table all who could recite the Heidleberg Catechism, he taught that only those who had experienced the renewing power of repentance and grace should be members of Christ's church. Honor to this faithful man's name. Perhaps better than in his latter life he himself would have believed, he illustrated the truth, that progress is possible, even in so conservative a thing as religion, and in such an institution as the Dutch church.

The next bishop of the church at Schenectady, the twelfth in true apostolical succession, was the Rev. W. J. R. Taylor, who has a D. D. at the end of his name that means something. He shall have short notice here, for he shall speak for himself as baccalaureate preacher this evening. Our twelfth pastor will, we hope recall some of the memories of his life here to-morow night. He has held more than one honored post in the church and Christian world since he left us, and he comes now fresh from General Synod with the laurels of a Christian Statesman upon his brow. We, as a church and people agree with him that no test of church-membership save that which Christ imposed should bind the conscience of a Christian man. Do not our own consistory records show, that be he opposed to all secret societies, or be he a free-mason, or be he odd fellow, or be he what he will, so that he is a servant of Christ, he shall sit with us at the communion table and be our brother in the Lord; while we at the same time hold Christ and his church supreme over all human claims or institutions. My elder brother, be your life long, your faith strong, and your good works many!

Nor can I speak at length of our next pastor, thirteenth on the roll, whom we almost fear will be made President of the United States, and who has been made willy-willy a member of Congress at the expense of a postage stamp. The President of Amherst College remembers with happy emotions that you were his only people and this church his only pastoral lore. He preached first here May 22nd, 1853, and according to a way you have since repeated, you gave him a unanimous call nine days afterward. Like four or five of your pastors, he obtained a good wife in Albany. Though a Yankee born, you, sons of Dutchmen, loved him as your own blood. After five years of faithful labor, in which among other good things, he taught you to double your contributions to benevolence and be all the happier for it, he left you to become the Professor and College President he was born to be. Whether before a congregation, a college class of students, a conclave of Japanese statesmen, of Hindoo pandits, or United States Congressman, he incarnates the best principles of Christianity, liberal scholarship, and American institutions. Long life and God's blessing to Julius Seelye.

Our fourteenth pastor, Edward Eli Seelye, was a graduate of Union College, and received two calls to this church, the latter of which he accepted. He was installed Nov. 1st, 1858, and after serving three years in the old brick church, saw its destruction, and then applied himself with the consistory and people to a delicate and arduous task, that of erecting this splendid edifice.

He lived to see the glorious dream of that poet-architect, Edward Tuckerman Potter, actualized in stone and wood. Nor must we ever forget that this splendid cathedral, in which 18 bishops of the New Testament sort have had their seats, was honestly and generously brought to its perfection under the superintendence of Casper F. Hoag and Martin DeForest, with the other members of the Building Committee. The only fault I find in the details, is that a meaningless arrow was put upon the spire, instead of that emblem which historically befits a Dutch church as it does none other, the cock of St. Nicholas, the symbol of life and resurrection, of the soul greeting the dawn light of heaven after the night and darkness of death. After preaching the dedication sermon, and enjoying for one year the inspiring beauty of this church, he was stricken down with the only sickness of his life, and died in August, 1864. A mighty soldier of God in the pulpit, powerful with pen and presence, he was the man for the crisis through which this church was called to pass. He made sinners tremble and saints rejoice. His memory is honored among you, nor will the remembrance of his rugged strength alike of intellect and physical frame, and of his kindly heart, soon fade from among you. Like seven other pastors of this church, Tassemaker, Brouwer, Van Santvoord, Vrooman, Romeyn, Meier and Bogardus, he died at his post with the harness on. He loved God, and never feared the face of man.

Of our fifteenth minister, Denis Wortman, need I speak to you, who love him so? Of his gentle life, his pure example, his loving heart and sympathetic nature? No, I have no need. His memory is yet fresh in your minds, and he himself will be with us in the flesh and spirit also to-morrow evening. God bless the gentle and the genial christian Denis Wortman.

Nor does the spirit of this hour, dedicated as it is to the past, allow me to speak at length of another living pastor of the church, the Rev. Ashbel G. Vermilye. All the other pastors of this church, except Julius Seelye, were of Holland birth or descent. Our sixteenth pastor represented "The Huguenot Element in the Reformed Church," who under the protection of our fathers sought refuge and freedom in America with them. Like Vrooman and Romeyn, his tall and commanding form was seen as that of a leader and counsellor in Classis or Synod. He was always willing and ready to do routine legislative work, from which most pastors shrink. After five years in Schenectady he resigned, and accepted the charge of the American chapel at Antwerp, in which field he has been eminently successful. He has sent us a letter of love and congratulation which we shall read to-morrow night. The next pastor whom you called is perhaps the only one of the eighteen ever installed within the church edifice.

"And what shall I more say?" Is it necessary, it this inspiring hour, to enter into details concerning that which hath been accomplished in the centuries flown? Of the 12,000 children baptized by our pastors here, since the first child born in the fortified village was presented at the baptismal font? The rosebuds that transfigure before us the silver bowl are not so numerous as the invited children of the Saviour, who have lived and died within our pale, Shall I recount the 3,000 couples who hand in hand, before God and their pastors, have plighted their love to each other, and their faith in God? Let this bell to-day with its bloom and fragrance vibrate afresh the sweet memories of our own past lives, who have received the nuptial benediction, and let it awake to our imagination the throng of happy lives and homes lighted by connubial love, which glow like living pictures, in the past.

Need I speak in detail of the 3,500 members who made their vows and consecration, and have sat with joyful hearts at the sacramental table? Shall I tell of the rapture of communion enjoyed in Christ's banqueting-house, by those who have dwelt under his banner of love? Let this hour-glass, fashioned as it is out of daisies, tell us alike of the daisies that have bloomed on the graves of those who sleep in Christ, and of the golden hours of love and gladness spent by them in the house of God. Already we have called up from the past the five edifices, and the eighteen pastors who have served this church. Shall I narrate how seven colonies went out from this church to become the Classis of Schenectady; or, again, how Union College was born of and nourished by her? Shall I conjecture that her wealth spent for congregational purposes probably amounts to $600,000, and that her benevolent contributions equal perhaps $100,000? Shall I remind you, to show you that the church still lives in strength, of her two Mission Schools on Prospect hill and Water Street? Or, of her four hundred members, her well attended devotional meetings, and her active Sabbath schools.?

It is not on these we dwell to-day, nor of these do we make boast. Not unto us be the glory! If we have aught of joys to-day, this is our chief; that, supreme above all, we have for two centuries preached and believed in "Jesus, the saviour of men." Withal of human infirmity, shortcoming and loss, we yet believe that to our fathers from Holland, there was given of God as large a measure of truth, as was ever vouchsafed to any church or body of people called Christians. Fully assured of this, yet ever ready to receive truth, whether new or old, we enter upon our third century holding their faith as ours, and praying as they prayed:

> "The Lord our God be with us,
> As he was with our Fathers."
>
> Amen!

# HISTORY OF THE CHURCH.

SOME FACTS

FOR THE

HISTORY OF THE

## Reformed Protestant Dutch Church

— OF —

SCHENECTADY.

Compiled by
JONATHAN PEARSON,
UNION COLLEGE.

# PREFACE.

[Professor Pearson's manuscript is reprinted without alteration or suppression of any part. The editor's notes are in brackets, and signed with his initials. W. E. G.]

The following compilation is mainly original matter, never before published,—the result of several years research by the author among all sources of information within his knowledge. It contains the frame work of the history of the REFORMED PROTESTANT DUTCH CHURCH OF SCHENECTADY, based mainly upon cotemporaneous documents and void alike of tradition and sentiment. The above written name for this church though not the earliest, nor that by which the General Synod is now known, is used here, as being that given in the charter of 1734, and preventing all ambiguity.

In 1715 this congregation was called the "Reformed Nether Dutch Church,"—in 1727 the "Nether Dutch Reformed Church," or "*Nederduytse gereformeerde gemynte*, and more simply the "Dutch Church."

The authorities consulted in the preparation of this work were mainly the papers preserved in the "Deacon's chest," and the other church records. The *Doop* and *Trouw* books begin in 1694; the earlier registers were doubtless destroyed in 1690, in Domine Thesschenmaecker's house.

The treasurer's accounts go back a few years earlier, but are imperfect.

The consistorial minutes were not regularly kept until 1784, when Doctor D. Romeyn became minister of the church. They were written in the Doctor's fair hand, in the Dutch language, until nearly 1800, afterwards in English. The great mass of the older papers consist mainly of land leases, long since cancelled; nothing like a historical sketch exists, and no recognition of the hundreth anniversary of the organization of the church is to be found. The earliest recorded effort to write a historical narrative of the church was made in consistory, Jan. 1, 1806, when Messrs. Cornelius Van Santvoord and Joseph C. Yates were appointed a committee to prepare for the use of the "Classis an accurate account of the organization, original and present members, remarkable events and everything important respecting this church." This late attempt was probably never carried out.

At a later date, Jan. 12, 1813, the consistory directed Abraham Oothout, Maus Van Vranken and the Secretary, (Isaac De-Graaf,) "to examine the papers contained in the old box belonging to this board, and to destroy all such papers as they may deem useless!" What possible use could be made of those old papers written in the illegible chirography of the seventeenth century and in a tongue then almost dead?

Who can tell how much of the early history of this church perished in this examination? Strange as it may seem the name of the donor of one of the best estates early and longest held by this church, to wit, the "Poor Pasture," is entirely unknown to this generation.* Governor Lovelace's patent for the same once known to be in the "old box," with other "useless papers," has perished. The book of records kept by Ludovicus Cobes, notary and secretary of the village in 1677, in which were written the deeds, wills, marriages contracts, etc., of that date was among the church papers until near the close of the last century, but is no longer to be found.

Whether it was destroyed, with other unreadable and therefore useless papers, by the committee appointed for that purpose in 1813 no one can tell. Suffice it to say that few and scanty are the trustworthy records of the past. Old wives' fables and traditions, often false and lying, the author has rejected, unless corroborated by contemporary written documents.

The established church of New Netherland was that of Holland, founded upon the principles propounded by the Synod of Dort, in 1618 and 1619. For some years the intrusion of other sects was tolerated, but during Stuyvesant's administration an attempt was made to suppress dissent and several persons were imprisoned and banished the Province for their contumacy. The matter went so far that the Directors in Amsterdam were compelled to interfere, and a dispatch dated April 16th, 1663, administered the following rebuke: "In the youth of your existence you ought rather to encourage than check the population of the colony. The consciences of men ought to be free and unshackeled so long as they continue moderate, peaceable, inoffensive and not hostile to the Government. Such have been the maxims of prudence and toleration by which the magistrates of this city have been governed; and the consequences have been that the oppressed and persecuted from every country have found among us an asylum from distress. Follow in the same steps and you will be blessed."

Persecution afterwards ceased, but the wrongs already committed were not easily forgotten.

---

*This was written before the bi-centennial anniversary. See the tablet in the church.

# HISTORY OF THE CHURCH.

## CHAPTER I.

SETTLEMENT OF THE VILLAGE AND ORGANIZATION OF THE CHURCH

In the spring of 1662 Arent Van Curler, late superintendent of Rensselaerswyck, with a little band of colonists, started from Beverwyck (now Albany) to take up the "Great Flatt" and found the present town of Schenectady. The wide plain lying between these two towns was then an unbroken forest without a road. They traveled first westward until the Norman's Kill was reached, then struck northward, following the Indian trail of " blazed " trees. After a circuit of more than twenty miles they reached the seat of their future labors. The year preceding, their leader had obtained from the Mohawks, title for a village site and the fine arable land lying west and north of it. This little company consisted of the following fifteen persons:

Arent Van Curler, Sander Leendertse Gleen,
Philip Hendricks Brouwer, Tennis Cornelise Swart.
Marten Cornelise Van Esselstyn, William Teller,
Catalyntje De Vas, widow of Pieter Jacobse Borsboone, *de* Arent Andriese Bratt, *Steenbackker,*
Pieter Danielse Van Olinda, Jan Barentse Wemp,
Jacques Cornelise Van Slyck, Gerrit Baucker,
Symon Volkerts Veeder, *de* Pieter Adriaense, alias, Soege-*Bakker,* makelyk,
Harmen Albertse Vedder.

The greater portion of the flats and islands lying immediately west and north of Schenectady was allotted to these fifteen individuals, excepting P. D. Van Olinda, who had farming lands in Niskayuna and elsewhere. For greater security against floods and Indians their home lots were laid out together, upon that portion of the present city lying west of Ferry street, and the whole plot was surrounded with palisades.

Within a few years after the settlement was begun material changes had been made in the ownership of these lots; some of the first settlers died, others removed and new ones took their places; of whom the most prominent were the following:

Claas Frederickse Van Petten,
Cornelis Cornelise Viele,
Hendrick Meese Vrooman,
Claas Lourense Van der Volgen,
Isaac Cornelise Swits,
Elias Van Guysling,
Ryer Jacobse Schermerhorn,
Sweer Teunise Van Velsen,
Jacobus Peeck,
Jellis Van Norst,
Jan Van Epps,
Ludovicus Cobes,
Bastiaen De Winter,
Philip Philipse DeMore,
Johannes Pieterse Quackenbos,
De. Petrus Thesschenmaecker,
De. Barnhardus Freerman,
Jonatan Stevens,
William Hall,
Frederick Clute,
Gerrit Ryckse Van Vranken,
Ahasuerus Marselis,
Johannes Myndertse,
Manasseh Sixberry,
Christiaan Chtistiaanse,
Hans Janse Eenkluys
Jan Pieters Mebie,
Daniel Janse Van Antwerpen,
Carel Honse Toll,
Claas Andriese DeGraaf, 
Robert Yates,
Isaac Du Trieux (Truax),
Joris Aertse Vander Boast,
Reynier Schaets,
Douw Aukes De Vrees,
Jellis Fonda,
Symon Groot,
Jan Janse Jancker, alias,
   Van Rotterdam,
Frans Harmense VanderBogart,
Dr. Jacobus Van Dyck,
Caleb Beck,
Barent Janse Van Ditmars,
Daniel Kettelhuyn,
Johannes Kleyn,
David Marinus,
Pieter Onderkirk,
Johannes Pootman,
Gysbert Van Brakelen.

Most of these are familiar names in Schenectady to this day; nearly all have been perpetuated in their descendants. They are chiefly of Holland origin; indeed down to the middle of the last century Schenectady was almost purely Dutch. Being a border settlement its growth was necessarily slow. To the ordinary hardships of a frontier life were added the almost constant alarms created by the long French and Indian wars and the oppressive trade regulations, by which all traffic in furs with the natives was prohibited to the inhabitants of Schenectady and appropriated by those of Albany. With such discouragement, it is a wonder that Schenectady gained in population at all; and that the spot was not abandoned altogether, especially after that sad destruction of life and property on the 8th and 9th of February, 1690.

Few or no accessions were made to the miserable remnant who survived that fatal night, until after the peace of Ryswick, in 1697, and it is probable that at no time previous to 1700, did the population exceed two hundred and fifty souls.

The first settlers of Schenectady were chiefly citizens of Albany; in transferring their residence to the former town many still retained their houses in the latter. Indeed, Schenectady was but a distant suburb of Albany, settled by her own children, and closely connected with her by ties of family and intermarriage. Not only was Albany the headquarters for trade in this part of the Province, but she was also the seat of the higher judicial court and of the mother church.

At the first settlement of Schenectady in 1662 there were but five Dutch churches and ministers in the Province, viz: those of

New Amsterdam, whose ministers were......... { Johannes Megapolensis.
{ Samuel Drisius.
Beverwyck (Albany),..................................Gideon Schaets.
Breuckelyn (Brooklyn),..............................Henricus Selyns.
Esopus (Kingston),...................................Hermanus Bloom.
Midwout and Amersfort (Flatbush, L. I.),.........Johannes T. Polhemus.

Of these the church at Beverwyck, founded twenty years before, was the oldest in the Colony except that of New Amsterdam.** Her first Domine (1642 to 1647), was Johannes Megapolensis who now ministered in New Amsterdam; the second, Gideon Schaets (1652-1690). The latter probably assisted at the organization of the church at Schenectady, to which he occasionally ministered until his labors ceased in his own church in 1690.

The date and circumstances of this organization are involved in much obscurity, the early records of both churches being lost. But from occasional mention made in cotemporaneous papers and records it is safe to say that the church of Schenectady was in existence between the years 1670 and 1680 and probably earlier. Thus on the occasion of the death of Hans Janse Eenkhuys,

---

** [The Reformed Church in America was first organized by the Rev. Jonas Michaelius, inside the fort, at the lower end of what is now New York city, in 1628. It was called the church of Saint Nicholas. W. E. G.]

in 1683, the deacons petition the court at Albany for letters of administration on his effects and say * * * *dat eenen* Hans Janssen *op den 7 meert 167 4-5 heeft overgedraegen aende aermen van* Schaenhechtade *zeecke syne plantage,* &c. &c., in other words that Hans Janse, in 1675, made over to the poor of Schenectady his plantation, on condition he should be maintained in his old age and weakness, which they say they have done, and paid the expenses of his burial. Now this *plantage* was simply the "Poor Pasture," and was the property of the church from Eenkluy's time down to 1862, when it was sold.

These facts seem to point to the existence of the church as early at 1674, for it is a well known fact that the Dutch churches were the guardians of the poor, the orphans, and the aged, who were without natural protectors; and received and dispensed large alms and property for this purpose.

The next incidental mention of this church is found in the records of the city of Albany. In February, 1679, "the court and *consistory* of Schenectady request that *Domine* Schaets may be sent four Sundays in one year to administer the Lord's supper to said place and community, which request is granted in so far that *Domine* Schaets is allowed to go four times in one year to administer the Holy Sacrament, but not on a Sunday, whereas it would be unjust to let the community [of Albany] be without preaching." *

Thirdly, The prosperous condition of the poor fund of the church from 1680 to 1690 shows pretty clearly that it had been organized some years previous to the former date. At the close of the year 1689 *Domine* Thesschenmaecker audited the Deacons' accounts and found that the unexpended alms contributed for the poor amounted to about 4,000 guilders, of which about 3,000 guilders had been loaned to individuals on bonds dating back in one case to 1681. Though the Dutch were a liberal people in matters appertaining to their church, it is not probable that such an accumulation of alms was made entirely within the ten years above mentioned, especially when their numbers are considered, and that in this time the parsonage house was constructed and their first *Domine* was called and maintained. It

---

* Annals of Albany, I, 103.

is fair therefore to conclude that the Dutch church of Schenectady was certainly an organized body in 1674, probably much earlier.

The first twenty years of the village was a struggle with the hardships of frontier life; its energies were spent in removing the forest and subduing the soil. For religious privileges it was dependent upon Albany; until in 1683-4, when the little hamlet having grown sufficiently strong in numbers and wealth, called its first minister. The earliest mention of *Domine* Thesschenmaecker in the church records is found in a book of miscellaneous writings, the first leaves of which unfortunately are wanting. The following is a copy and translation of the first page in its present mutilated condition:

| Uytgyeve. | [1683?] | (Translation). Expenditures. [Paid.] | [1683?] |
|---|---|---|---|
| aen Myndert Wemp, | F. 48 | To Myndert Wemp, guilders, | 48 |
| aen een kan, | 8 | To [paid for] a pot, | 8 |
| aen Jan Roelofsen voor * * | 24 | To Jan Roelofsen, for * * | 24 |
| 5 Witte broden, | 1 | To 5 white loaves, | 1 |
| aen domine Tassemaker * * | 24 | To domine Tassemaker * * | 24 |
| aen emanual Consaul, | 6 | To Emanual Consaul, | 6 |
| aen Lubbert gysbertse voor 2 dagen Wereke, | 6 | To Lubbertse Gysbertse for two days work, | 6 |
| aea spyckers van Albanie, | 6 | To nails from Albany, | 6 |
| aen den ½ dusent harde steen, | 18 | To half thousand hard bricks, | 18 |
| aen 2 bevers aed Laseysers tot set huys tepingelen, | 48 | To two beavers to Laseysers shingling the house, | *48 |
| aen 12 gulden aen * * voor stacken en * * ver verbruyck aen de heyminge, | 12 | To 12 guilders * * for stakes * * for use of the fence, | 12 |
| 27 april voor wyn tot het naght mael aen domine tasschenmaker betalt. | 20 | 27 April, For wine for the Lord's supper paid to Domine tasschenmaker, | 20 |
| 27 May domine Schats Vereert, | 36 | 27 May, presented to Domine Schaets, | 36 |
| Schoonmaken van der Kerche, | 13 | cleaning the church, | 13 |
| * * * * | *1.10 | * * * * | *1.10 |
| * * * * | *5. | * * * * | *5. |
| * * * * | *2.10 | * * * * | *2.10 |
| Voor wyn van hat naght mael, | 20. 0 | For wine for the Lord's supper, | 20. 0 |

*Parsonage house.

| | | | | |
|---|---|---|---|---|
| aen Adam Vroom, | | 24. | To Adam Vrooman, | 24. |
| nogh aen domine tasschemaker voort maken vande hayninge aen het erf, | | 45. | Also to Domine tasschemaker for making the fence to the lot, | 45. † |
| nogh voor 7 meal witte broot tot het avent mael C. F. 1.10 a meal, | | 10.10 | Also for white bread 7 times for the Lord's supper C. F. 1.10 a time | 10.10 |
| Claas permurent aen dagen ryden, | | 18 | Claas Purmerent [Van der Volgen] one day carting, | 18. |
| 2¾ dagen aen de heyninge, | | 22 | 2¾ days on the fence, | 22. |
| Voorts singelen van 't huys, | | 12 | for shingling the house ‡ | 12 |
| aen 2 Vragsten postengasacht, | | 6 | To two loads of posts sawed | 6 |
| 2 glass Ramen. | | 10 | 2 glass windows, | 10 |
| Somma, | F. 516-13* | | Total, | florins 516-13 |

From these accounts we learn the following facts:

1. That *Domine* Thesschenmaecker came to Schenectady before the death of *Domine* Schaets (1690).

2. That the first house of worship was then built.

3. That the consistory this year (1683 ?), was building a parsonage house and fencing the lot. For although it is not stated that *'t huys* was for the Domine's use, we can hardly conceive of his being engaged in building, and the church in paying for, a dwelling for any other person.

Of the five houses of worship built by this church, the one above-mentioned was the first. We know little about it except that it was small and inconvenient—too small indeed for the few worshippers in 1701, ‖ and that it stood at the junction of Church, State and Water streets. After the massacre of 1690

---

† Parsonage lot.

‡ Parsonage house on the present church lot.

* The money of accounts of the Dutch was the guilder or florin and stuyver, 20 of the latter to one of the former. There were the guilder sewant and the guilder beaver ;—the latter of the value of about 40 cts., or three times that of the former. The guilder of accounts was commonly valued at one shilling N. Y. currency.

‖ In a petition to Governor Nanfan, in 1701, for aid in erecting a new house of public worship they say:—"the place where itt is now Exercised in nott bein Large Enough to containe the whole assemply oft ye Inhabitants & Indian Proselytes," &c.

it was also used as a block-house * and like the dwellings of the village was probably built of wood. It has usually been assumed that this church was burned by the French and Indians, but of the truth of this tradition there is no proof.

The parsonage lot, now the church site (excepting 56 feet added to the east side at later dates), was used as such 150 years down to 1813. The original dimensions were 100 by 200 feet, Amsterdam measure,† and it has been in possession of the church from the time of its organization. The house erected upon it for Domine Thesschenmaecker, who was an unmarried man, must have been of humble dimensions judging from the number and cost of the *"glass Ramen"* purchased for it in the above account. It became the funeral pile of its first occupant when the village was burned in 1690.

## CHAPTER II.

### 1684–1690.   DOMINE PETRUS THESSCHENMAECKER.

Domine Thesschenmaecker ‡ is best known for his tragical end. He came to this country from Guiana whither he had gone from Utrecht, a young theological student,‖ and is first mentioned in the following petition of date 1676.

> To the Rt. Honorable Sr. Edmond Andros Kt. of Sauemares: under his Royall Highness Duke of Yorke and Albany and dependances: The humble petition of Seuerall of the Inhabittanse of Esopus humbly shewith unto yor Honor,
>
> Whereas this place is destitute of a minister for the Instruction of the people: It is our Ernest desiar and humble request with all Submission that yor Honor will be pleased to be aiding and assisting in the procuring one for us that can preache both Inglish and Duche, weich will be most fitting for this place, it being in its minority and having great charges is not very able to maintaine two ministares;

---

\* In an ancient deed dated 1692 it is called "'*t blokhuys (te weten de kerche)*."
† The Amsterdam foot consisted of about 11 in. English.
‡ The abbreviated form of his name, Tassemaker, we have used in the historical discourse, and on the tablet erected in the church.   [W. E. G.]
‖ Hist. Mag. IX, 323.

nether to be at the charge of sending for one out of England or Holland; and we are Informed Mr. Peettar Tasetmakr is at liberty, who is a person well knowne to yo$^r$ Hon$^r$ and officiated in this [place] for sum time; And if to bee procured, is very well approved and much desired by moste, hee being a man of Sober life and conversacon having Deportted himselfe to sattisfaction of ye Inhabitance,—

Wherefor wee Humbly pray that your honor will bee pleaseb to bee Instrumentall in the same and yo$^r$ Hono$^{rs}$ humble Petticeners shall ever pray, &c.*

This appears to be a sufficient certificate of his fitness for the sacred office, but whether he returned to Esopus on this flattering call is not known. It appears that at this time he had not been ordained, for in 1679 on application from New-Castle, on the Delaware, the Governor in the following warrant directed Domine Newenhuysen to examine and induct him into the ministry of the Protestant Reformed Church. Probably he was then a resident of Staten Island.

To the Constable of Staten Island.

*Sr Edmond Andros Kt. &c.:*

Upon application from New-Castle in Delaware, That (being destitute) Mr. Peter Teschenmaecker may bee admitted to bee their Minister. By Vertue of his maj$^{ties}$ Letters patents and Authoritie derived unto me, I doe hereby desire and Authorise you, to examine the said Mr. Teschenmaecker and if you shall find fittly Qualifyed that then you ordaine him into the ministry of the Protestant Reformed Church to preach God's word and Administer his Holy sacraments and give him Testimonialls thereof as is usuall.

Given under my hand and seale of the Province in New Yorke the thirteenth day of September in the 31st yeare of his Ma$^{ties}$ Raigne Annoq Domini 1679.

To Mr. Gulielmus Newenhuysen ministr or pastor of this Citie or any three or more of the minis-t$^{rs}$ or Pastors within this Government. } E. A.

Prepared and examined by mee,
MATTHIAS NICOLLS, Sec$^r$.

---

* Doc. Hist. III, 583.

In two respects this was an unusual proceeding. First in that the Provincial Governor, though empowered by royal letters patent to license and collate ministers of the gospel, should exercise this right, especially in the Dutch churches; and, secondly, that a minister of this church should be ordained in this country. Almost to the middle of the last century it was thought indispensable that a theological education and licensure should be obtained abroad. This together with the subjection to the authority of the Classis of Amsterdam, formed the subject matter of the great controversy which agitated the church for more than thirty years until united in 1771 through the efforts of Dr. John H. Livingston.

In accordance with Governor Andros' order of warrant, above cited, "Domine Schaets, of Albany, Domine Van Zuuren, of Long Island, and Domine Van Gaasbeeck, of Esopus, met with Domine Van Nieuwenhuysen, at New York, and formed themselves into a Classis, composed of all the Dutch ministers within the Province with members of their consistories."

"The following is a translation of the original record of the *first Dutch Classis ever held in North America:*

"*Copy of the acts done in our meeting at New York the* 9th *of October,* 1679, *in the matter of Domine Petrus Tesschenmaecker.*

"On this day, the 9th of October, 1679, was handed in a call of a minister for the congregation of the South [Delaware] River, which calling has fallen on the person of Domine Petrus Tesschenmaecker, a candidate for the sacred ministry.

"But considering that this matter is without example in this Government, the Low Dutch ministers who are here, on the request of the Honorable Knight, Governor Edmund Andros, and on the exhibition of the *testimonia examinis preparatorii* of the aforesaid Domine Petrus Tesschenmaecker (written by the Dutch and English consistories at tne Hague), having been content (considering likewise the distress of the above named respective congregation), to confirm and consecrate this candidate to the office of the ministry there.

"And because before all, it is necessary that an Overseer (*apziendar*) should be proved, so the Reverend Assembly, consisting of the Low Dutch clergyman of this Government, together with other Ecclesiastical persons, approved as good the aforesaid attestation *examiyis preparatorii* without special opposition; and it was resolved to proceed to the *promotie* itself."

"Thereupon Domine Tesschenmaecker being summoned within was acquainted with this approbation of the Reverend assembly, and was further asked, whether he accepted this calling, to serve in the same according to the ecclesiastical orders of the Reformed Synod of Dordrecht and other special instructions, and would also promise conformity to the said orders. The answer was "yes," undertaking and binding himself to observe the same."

"This being done, Domine Tesschenmaecker was first heard in his *propositie* upon the text Matt. 5: 20., the treatment of which gave the Reverend Assembly sufficient satisfaction."

"Thereupon the Reverend Assembly addressed itself to the examination, having appointed as examinator Domine Wilhelmus Van Nieuwenhuysen, minister of the Holy Gospel in the Metropolis of the Government of New York."

"The examination being sustained the Reverend Assembly was likewise contented with the answers of Domine Tesschenmaecker, so that finally, the confirmation accorded to our church order and formulary followed hereupon, in the name of the Lord." Signed,

"*Casparus Van Zureren,*
minister in Long Island,
*Conventus pro tempore Scriba.*"

"These interesting documents were sent to the Classis of Amsterdam in a joint letter signed by the four Dutch clergymen in New York. In that letter they rely on Governor Andros' authorization as the justification of their action, which they declared was "in all respects conformable to praiseworthy usuage and order of the church in the Fatherland (to the upholding of which we have also obliged him by promises and the giving of hands as wee ourselves were obliged thereto by your Reverences), there having yet further come to us excellent testimonials of the deportment and preaching of Domine Teschenmaecker, signed by the Consistories of the Low Dutch and English congregations in the Hague; and he himself (*examinandus candidatus*) exhibiting very good and proper gifts as in his *propositis* so in his answers, to the complete satisfaction of all the members of our Assembly."

"The Classis of Amsterdam afterwards approved this action and of the settlement of Domine Tesschenmaecker at the Delaware, where, however, he remained but a short time. In the winter of 1682, he preached on Staten Island, and in 1684 he was called to the church in Schenectady." *

After his ordination Domine Thesschenmaecker departed immediately for his new field of labors; for November 20th, following, he received a patent † for a lot of land at New Castle, 300 by 480 feet, respecting which the Colonial Secretary received a letter ‡ dated January 17th, 1679-80, promising his fee of 40 shillings in wheat.

Here he remained three years until 1682, "when in consequence of some disagreement with his congregation he left and accepted a call from Schenectady." ||

In the latter place he labored six years with reasonable success; and in spite of the distant mutterings of war between Britain and France the little community grew in numbers and wealth. The virgin soil of the neighboring *Flats* and islands yielded abundantly, and the population, gaining confidence, ventured beyond the palisades of the village and gradually crept up the Mohawk river, occupying the fertile lands on either bank.

It was while resting in fancied security that the place was surprised, on the 8th day of February, 1690, and totally destroyed. Approaching the place at midnight the French and Indians found the gates open, the guards withdrawn, and the village in profound slumber. The work of destruction commenced under such favorable circumstances was soon completed;—day dawned upon a ghastly scene,—the labors of thirty years in ashes,—sixty of the inhabitants slain,—twenty-eight captives selected for the long winter march to Canada,—and the miserable remnant, wounded and frost-bitten, painfully seeking relief in flight towards Albany. The French commander had ordered his men

---

* Hist. Mag., IX: 325-6.
† Patents IV. 90?
‡ "De. Tesschenmaecker hath promised to make satisfactory in ye Spring for ye pattent and ye other wrytings, 40 shiilings in wheat, as by yorself demanded, wh I think is soe reasonable as can be considering ye trouble wh to my knowledge yrself had in gt buisnesse." Eph. Herman to Matthias NicolL —Alb. Records, Jan. 17, 1679-80.
|| Anthology of New Netherlands, p. 100-1.

to spare the life of the clergyman, but his savage allies knew no difference between minister and people;—he was slain and burned in his house. *

Domine Thesschenmaecker left no heirs. A farm of "eighty acres and a proportional quantity of meadow ground" granted to him 3 Nov. 1685, on the south side of Staten island,† was claimed by the inhabitants of Richmond county as a poor fund. ‡

For seven years from this sad event, till the peace of Ryswick in 1697, there was no safety North and West of Albany outside of the fortifications. Many forsook their plantations and sought places of greater security, and it is a matter of surprise that the hardy pioneers of Schenectady clung to the soil in the midst of such discouragements. It argues well for their pluck and endurance.

Until 1700 the church was without a pastor, and indeed it does not appear that the people had any religious privileges, except such as might be had by a visit to Albany, until 1694, when Domine Dellius began to minister to them occasionally. His first recorded visits this year were on the 11th of April and 9th of October, on which occasions new members were added to the church and children baptized. In 1695 he came four times, viz: on the 2d Jan., 27th Mar., 26th June and 9th October. In 1696 five times—Jan. 8th, Ap. 15. July 1. Sept. 19th and Dec. 30th. In 1697 three times—Ap. 6th. June 30th, and Nov. 10, and in 1698 four times—27th Ap. 20 July, 19th Oct., and 28th Dec. In all eighteen visits in five years.

In 1699 Domine Dellius returned to the Fatherland and Domine Johannes Petrus Nucella succeeding to his place as minis-

---

* "Dom. Petrus Tesschenmaker the minister at Schenectady has met with misfortune. He and most of his congregatoin were surprised at night and massacred by the French and Indians in their interest. His head was cloven open and his body burned to the shoulder-blades." Domine Selyns to the Classis of Amsterdam. Anthology of New Netherland, p. 116.

† Patents, IV, 902.

‡ 1692, 2 Nov. Upon reading Anoy$^r$ Peticon of the s$^d$ Representatives [of the county of Richmond] setting forth that Mr. Tuschenaker having some reall and personall Estate in Staten Island was killed by the French and Indians at Schenectady and in his lifetime had promised the s$^d$ Estate to the Poor haveing noe heirs, praying an order for the some.

The s$^d$ Peticon is likewise referred to the Attorney Generall who is to report what may be proper therein to be done.   Leg. Council, 4, 28.

ter of Albany, visited Schenectady once—on the 31st of August. The following year he came twice, viz: on the 9th January and 25th May.

The number of members added to the church by these two ministers was twenty-five; the number of children baptized seventy-six, seven of whom were Indians.

Taking into consideration, therefore, the fact that at this time all children were christened, some idea may be formed of the number and increase of the population when only sixty-nine were baptized in six years.

During the same period five couples were maried by Domine Dellius and seven by Johannes Glen, "*Justis Van de peace.*"

But no sooner was peace proclaimed in 1697 than both village and church began a new career of prosperity. Within five years a second minister was called, and a new and larger house of worship was erected.

## CHAPTER III.

1700-5. DOMINE BARNARDUS FREEMAN,* SECOND MINISTER OF THE CHURCH AND MISSIONARY TO THE MOHAWKS.

When Domine Dellius returned to Holland in 1693, his church gave him leave of adsence for ten months, but subsequently commissioned William Bancker and others of Amsterdam to procure another minister in case he remained beyond that time.

This commission was in the following words:

[TRANSLATION].

*Gentlemen :*

By Capt. Band on the 8th June was our previous [letter sent] to you with the accompanying instructions concerning the return of Mr. Dellius, and hope it was [received] by you; not doubting that you took careful thought that at the limited time then expressed it may be accomplished in a proper manner. Our fellow brother, Evert Bancker, has showns us certain writings of his brother [Willem] Bancker of Amsterdam to have a care

---

* He sometimes wrote his name Freeman, but oftener Freerman.

that the commission which should advance the call of a preacher may not limit him to the Reverend Classis of Amsterdam alone; —and now we understand from Messrs. Peter Van Benghn and Myndert Schuyler by another account how that last voyage a certain proper person was proposed by you for a preacher at New York, but afterwards the aforementioned Classis would not hear to it, and this gave you great dissatisfaction. If Domine Dellius does not give perfect assurance to you of his return here, well understanding that he must take ship from England in good time; that is, within ten months after his departure from here, we desire whenever you can not come to an understanding with the aforementioned Classis, to serve yourself with such a Classis as you shall find convenient, hoping that you with De. Dellius, or in his absence by your own Godly and good conduct, may effect the accomplishment of our desire;—that is a very proper person, rather a young man than a married, be he a Bachelor of Divinlty, who is to be made a preacher, or one who is already a preacher, with needful gifts, just as it shall appear best; and next summer may he come to us in love and unity to salvation, that God's churches may no longer remain waste without a teacher.

Albany, 1699, Nov. 15.

       Messrs.

         Yours to serve:
the elders and deacons of the Church of Christ of Albany.

       ALBERT RYKEMAN,
       P. SCHUYLER,
       JACOB LOKERMANS,
       ANTHONY BRIES,
       JOHN CUYLER,
       EVERT BANCKER.*

*Messieurs:*

 *Met Capt. Band op de 8 Juny oure voorgaende om Ul; me doe by gaende Instruction wegens het verbreck van de heer dellius & verhope Ul; syne tyd is ge worden nist twivelende dan Ul; neempt soryvuldige agthinge dat tot de be paelse tyd doen maels geer presseert in geen derly manierss mag tae gedaen werde. Onse mede Broder Evert Bancker heef ons Vertoond Seker anschrivens van syn Brod; Bancker van Amsterdam;—om sorg to hebben dat de gecommittend (?) die het Bersopvan aen predicant sonden Vorderen niet mogte bepaelt syn alleen an de E. Classis van Amsterdam; dochquam na oure verhael ho dat laeste Reis seker bequaem persoon doer Ul; was Voergestel*

In the execution of the above commission, William Bancker, being then in Amsterdam, selected Do Barnhardus Freeman, and on the 5th of March, 1700 gave him the following call:

In accordance with the commission of the Consistory of Albany, of date the 15th November, 1699, to me given, to select for the church a proper person, either a preacher or a student of theology, and after a proper qualification to send him over:— So it is that I, the subscriber, having observed the good and edifying conduct of Do Barent Freeman, Bachelor of Theology, to the same in the fear of God the aforewritten call have offered, to the end that his Reverence the church of Jesus Christ in Albany with the Holy Ministry may serve and upbuild, with the preaching of God's word upon the Lord's day, as also during the week, so far as it may be convenient; also the Holy Sacraments to administer, the church discipline to exercise to edification, and in prayers to visit the sick to consolation, diligently to Catechise, and also four times a year, at the request of the Reverend Consistory aforesaid, to preach at a village named Schenectady and administer the sacraments; and to conduct himself in all other respects as God of his faithful servants requires as an example to the Church of Jesus Christ. All for a salary therein agreed upon. And seeing that the aforesaid Do Freeman this

Voor predicant tot N. Yorke, Waer no de ge melde Classis niet wilde horen; & dat suek Ul; groot ouvergenoegs gap. Indien De. dellius niet geep Volkome nytslog aen Ul; Wederkomste hier, Medt Verloop Van Voors; tvdt uyt England weer scheep moet gaum; dat is nae syn vertreck van hier binner tier maenden; Versooke wy wanneer Ul; salgoed Vinden; Verhopende Ul; met de meer gemelde Classis niet konde over aen housen Ul; salgoed Vinden; —Verhopende Ul; met Dellius ofin syn absentie gyl; doer Godvrughtige yver en goed beleidt magh beschikke de overkomste van ouse Begere; dat is een pray bequaem persoon, liver een jong man als getrowt hetsy proponent die daer predikant werd gemaekt of selfs een peedikant, met nodige gowen soo als het beste sall voorsalle; en naest komende somer tyd by ons magh come in liefee en enigheit tot salighat, op dat de K. K. giles niet langer sonder beroer magh verwoestan soo bliven.

Albany 1699 Nov. 15.  Messieurs.  Ul; Dienst willige.
oud; en diaconen der kerke Jesu Christe van Albany.

ALBERT RYKEMAN,
P. SCHUYLER,
JACOB LOKERMANS,
ANTONY BRIES,
JOHOUNES CUYLER,
EVERT BANCKER.

above written call has also in the fear of the Lord accepted, and it is now needful for the carrying out of the same that his Reverence should be further and immediately examined, and after the examination be ordained to Holy ministry with the laying on of hands. So we have requested the Reverend Brethren of the Reverend Classis of Lingen that they would execute this Holy design, not doubting that such would redown to the glory of God's Holy name, and the upbuilding of Jesus' church there.

Done in Amsterdam the 5th of March in the year 1700.

WILLIAM BANKER. *

De. Freeman, the subject of the above call, was a man of mature age, a native of Gilhuis in the county (Graafschap) of Bentheim. In 1698 he was a member of the church of Amsterdam, and on the 9th of March of that year was licensed to preach by the Classes of Worden and Overrhynland. Immediately after the above call from the church of Albany, he was ordained by the Classis of Lingen (16th March, 1700), and departed for his

---

* Volgens de commissie Van de kerckenraedt van Albany van datum den 5 Nouember Anno 1699 aan my verleent our een bequaem persoon tsy predikant of proponent voor de kercke uyt te kiesen en na bahoorlyge qualificatie derwaerts over te senden. So its dat sch ondergeschevener Gelet hebbende op de Goede en stigtelyke gaven en bequaemheden als mede op het vroom en en Seer stigtelyk gedragh van De. Barent Freerman Proponent in de H. theologie den selven in de Vreezegods de voorschreven Beraepinge geoffersert hebbe, ten einde eyn Eerwaerde de Kerke Jesu Christi in Albany, met den H. Predica-dienst en opbouwen met het predicken van Gon's woord op den dag des heren als ook in de week, soo als daes in gebruick is, ook de H. Sackramenten te Bedienen de Kercklyke discipline to t stigtinge te offenen en in de gebeden den Cranken te Besooken tot troost Catagesatic wel waer te nemen en ook viermael hoers op het versook van de Eerwaerde Kerckenraad voorz : of een dorp genaempt Schoneghtade te predicken en de Sackeraments te bedienen in alles Verder dat God van syne trouwe dienaers eyscht sich te gedragen als een voorbeelt der gemeente Jesu Christi alles op een tractament daer taestande en de wyle de vaer naemde de. Freeman dese voor-schrevens Berapinge ook in de vrese des heren heeft aengenomen, en nu nodig is dat tot uytooninge van deselve synd Eerwaerde verder perempoeir Geeramineert worde en na gedane examen in den H. dienst met oplegginge der handen worde Beverstight, soo versoeken wy de E. Bryderen van de E. classis van Lingen datoe liver dit H. Voornemen te achterolgen niet tweifelende ofoulks sal dienen tot groot mokinge van God's H. naem en opbouw van Jesu Kercke aldaer.

Actum in Amsterdam
den 5 Maart Anno 1700.                             WILLIAM BANKER.

distant charge accompanied by Do. Johannes Lydius. On the 20th of July they arrived in Albany where the latter remained, while the former passed on to Schenectady, and on the 18th commenced his labors as pastor of the church and missionary to the Mohawks. His appointment to the latter office, brought about doubtless after his arrival in New York, furnishes a reason for the change in his destination.

Domine Dellius had filled the same office many years, and both for political as well as religious reasons it was considered important to continue so powerful an agency among the native tribes.

In regard to this matter the Earl of Bellomont, Governor of the Provinces, said to the assembled Sachems of the Five Nations on the 26th of August, 1700. * * * "I have sent to England for ministers to instruct you in the true Christian religion. I expect some very soon; for the present I shall settle Mr. Vreeman, an able good minister, at Schanectade, who I intend shall be one of those that shall be appointed to instruct you in the true faith. He will be near the Mohacks, and in your way as you came from [the] several castles to this town, [Albany,]. and will take pains to teach you. He has promised me to apply himself with all diligence to learn your language, and doubts not to be able to preach to you therein in a year's time." *

In a communication to the Board of Trade the Governor says: "I send your Lordships a copy of Mr. Freeman's Letter. He is the Dutch minister at Schenectady and a very good sort of a man." † * * * *.

The following is a copy of the letter referred to:

Schenegtade the 6th Jan. 1700–1.

May it please your Excellency.

I have received your Excell$^{cis}$ letter of the 15th Nov$^r$ 1700, whereby I understand that your Excell$^{cy}$ was satisfied with what I had done to promote the Gospel among the Indians, I shall also use my utmost to intreat them to be firm in the allegiance to His Maj$^{ty}$ and for as much as appears to me they are good subjects to His Maj$^{ty}$ whereof they desire me to give your Excell$^{cy}$ an account.

* Col. Doc. IV. 727.
† Col. Doc. IV. 833.

Your Excell<sup>cy</sup> may remember that there are not above one hundred Maquasse in number, thirty-six whereof have embraced the Christian faith, ten whereof through the grace of God are brought over through my means, for I found but twenty six.

I shall do my utmost with the rest. So wishing your Excell<sup>cy</sup> a happy new year and continuation of you health, recommending myself to your favour.

I remain, your<br>Excell<sup>cies</sup> most obedient Servant,"<br>B. FREERMAN. *

As Albany was the headquarters of Indian trade as well as of the yearly Council held with the Five Nations, De. Lydius was also appointed to instruct the natives in the Christian faith, and "ye bettar to enable him to serve them in ye work of the Gospell ye Interpretesse [Hillitie] † was appointed to be his assistant in that affair as formerly." ‡ * * *

In the five years spent at Schenectady De. Freeman became well versed in the Indian tongue so as not only to preach, but to write in it. In this he was assisted by the Provincial interpreter, Lawrens Claese (Van der Volgen), a member of his church. And so attached were the natives to him that five years after he left Schenectady they petitioned Governor Hunter for his reappointment, "and that he live [with us] at our Castle and not at Schinnectady nor Albany." ‖

The condition of the Indian mission in 1710 is set forth in a letter by the Rev. Thomas Barclay to the Secretary of the Society for the Propagation of the Gospel in Foreign Parts:

ALBANY, Sept. 26, 1710.

"Since the death of Mr. Lydias the Indians have no ministers; there are about thirty communicants and of the Dutch church, but so ignorant and scandalous that they can scarce be computed Christians. The Sachems of the Five Nations, viz: of the Masque, Oneydas, Onnondagas, Coyougas and Senekas, at a meeting with our Governor, Col. Hunter, at Albany the 10th of August last, when his Excellency in his speech to them, asked

---

\* Col. Doc. IV. 835.

† Hillite was a half-breed,—sister of Jacques Cornelise Van Slyck. She married Pieter Danielse Van Olinda.

‡ Lord Cornbury to the Five Nations, 1702. Col. Doc. IV. 983.

‖ Col. Doc., V, 227.

them if they were of the same mind with those four Indians that had been over with Col. Schuyler, in desiring missionaries to be sent, and they answered they were, and desired to have forts built among them and a church, and that Mr. Freeman, present minister of the Dutch congregation at Flatbush, near New York, be one of those missionaries which the Queen promised to send them. This Mr. Freeman five years ago was minister of Schenectady, and converted several of the Indians; he has acquired more skill in their language than any Dutch minister that has been in this country, and Mr. Dellius is not so well skilled in that tongue; a great part of our Liturgy he has translated into the Indian tongue; in particular morning and evening prayers, the litany, the Creed of St. Athanasius, &c., besides several places of the old and new Testament. He told me when he read to them the litany they were mightily affected by it. He is a gentleman of good temper, and will affected to our church, and if there was a Bishop in this part of the world, would be persuaded to take Episcopal ordination. I often entreat him to go over to England, but he is afraid of the danger of the voyage, and his wife will not consent to live among the Indians. He has promised to give me his manuscript, and what he has done into the Indian tongue."\* \* \*

Probably this was the first attempt made to translate the church service, or portions of the Holy Scriptures into the language of the Mohawks. In addition to the morning and evening prayers, De. Freeman translated "the whole of the Gospel of St. Matthew, the three first chapters of Genesis, several chapters of Exodus, a few of the Psalms, many portions of the Scriptures relating to the birth, passion, resurrection and ascension of our Lord, and several chapters of the first Epistle of the Corinthians, particularly the fifteenth chapter, proving the resurrection of the dead. But his work was not printed." †

A copy having been presented to the "Society for the Propagation of the Gospel in Foreign parts," was given to their missionary, Rev. William Andrews, who was sent out in 1712, and by him printed in New York two years afterwards.

---

\* Doc. Hist. III, 540.
† Col. Doc. VIII, 815.

The salary of the early ministers of this church was one hundred pounds New York currency ($250), house and garden rent free, pasturage for two cows and a horse, and sixty cords of wood delivered at the parsonage. The salary commenced from the day the Domine sailed from Holland and the expenses of the voyage until he arrived in Schenectady were paid by the church. The following is De. Freeman's first bill, rendered August 25, 1700:

"16 mar. 1700 to 25 aug. the Consistory is indebted to Domine Freeman;

For current salary from the 16 march to the 25th of august,—is five months and nine days and amounts to a sum of fifty pounds and something more,—is in sewant,   gl. 2.000 *

Also expenses incurred on the voyage, in fresh provisions, wine, brandy, vegetables and hens, besides about three weeks expenses upon the Isle of Wight,—is the sum of   gl. 374

gl. 2.374

Schenectady,
BARNHARDUS FREERMAN. †

The above bill shows that the expenses of the voyage were 374 gl. ($46.75), and that the whole amount of salary and expenses was 2374 gl., or $296.75. ‡

Trifling as this amount may seem, the little community were unable to raise it, and on the 3d of September, 1700, applied to the Common Council of Albany for permission to solicit contributions in Albany. In reply the Commonality advise "that

---

* Ano 1700 den 16 martius tot 25 Augustus is de kerkenraat Debet an De. freeman

Voor de rerlespon tractement vanden 16 maert tot 25 august is 5 maenden en 9 dagen en bedraegt een somme van fyftig pont en wat meer is an sewant.—   2,000

† Noch ankostinge op Reise gehad so an Versche waren, wyn, Brandewyn, Creuderye en hoenden neffens omtrent dry weeke expences op het Eylant wigt is een som tot   374

gl. 2.374

Schonegtade
BARNHARDUS FREERMAN.
[See Church Papers.]

‡ This sum is exclusive of 800 gl, paid by the Albany church as part of the expenses of De. Freerman's passage.—Munsell's Collections, I, 53, 54.

they first goe and Visite there own Congregation, and if they do not obtaine said Sallary by them, then to make their application to the Commonality at ye next Court day."

On the 21st of September the application was renewed, " Whereupon ye Commonalty have concluded and doe allow and admitt two or more of said Church wardens of Shinnechtady to goe once Round for contribution to use as aforesaid from ye inhabitants of this Citty and no more, in ye time of the Sessions, which will be first and second of October next ensuing." *

When Do. Freeman was appointed missionary to the Indians by Governor Bellomont, he was promised a salary of £60; for expenses £15, and for the interpreter, Laurens Claese Van der Volgen, who was his assistant £25.

The Governor expected to obtain this salary from the Corporation for the propagation of the Gospel at Boston, but in case he failed there, promised to secure it for him out of the revenue of the province.†

It is presumed that said corporation declined to assume this burden, and as a consequence the General Assembly passed an Act in his favor. In a petition which Do. Freeman addressed to Governor Cornbury, in 1703, he affirms that " he has taken great pains in going to their [Mohawks] Castles and translating Divine things into their language for ye easier bringing ym over, and as he hopes with very good success; for wh reason a continuance of ye said salary was promised him by ye late Lieften't-Governour, Capt. Nanfan, and confirmed to yr Petitioner by an act of Generall Assembly of this Province, wh said sallaries (tho' tis now two years since they were first settled) are unpaid, and no Warrants have yet past for any part thereof." ‡

On the death of Do. Lupardus of Kings county, in 1702, the consistory of the Churches there applied to Governor Cornbury for permission to call Do. Freeman, ‖ who at the same time gave encouragement of his acceptance. The Governor answered:

---

* Albany City Records.
† Mr. Freerman yck veresoeck dat gyu de voor aen went om de heydens tot het Kristen geloof over te brengen en tot gerhoorsaemheyt van be konning gy sult geensins on beetaslt blyve. yck sal nu boston schryve die dispositse hebben van het corperasi gelt en yck Verspreeck ne 60 pous int yaer en so die van boston het wygeren yck Versekere ne het yt de revenue van dese province. etc.—Gov. Bellomonts Letter, Col. Mss. XLIV.
‡ Col. Mss. XLIV, XLV, 134, 179 LIII 7, 70.
‖ Doc. Hist. III 89.

"I have duly Considered the Within petition and having been well Informed that Mr. Bar. Ffreeman has misbehaved himself, by promoting and Encouraging the unhappy divisions among the people of this province, do not think it consistent with her Majesties Service that the s$^d$ Ffreeman should be admitted to be called as is prayed by s$^d$ petition. And the petitioners are hereby required not to call or receive the s$^d$ Ffreeman."*

Fearing their minister might be enticed away from them, the Consistory of the church in Schenectady the next year presented to Lord Cornbury the following petition:

"The humble Petition of the Church Wardins of the Nether Dutch Church of the Town of Schoneghtede, sheweth:

That the four severall towns to witt: Midwout or Flatbush, the Bay, New Utreght and Brockland, by their Certain writing doth Indeavour to Draw Mr. Barnardus Freeman, Present Minister of Schoneghtende, from his Congregation, who are not able of themselves Without your Excellecy's assistance to gett another, and since we, your petitioners, have been att a great Charge and trouble with assistant thereunto from this County for Defraying the Considerable Charge of Mr. Barnardus Freeman's Passage and other Charges that doth amount to the Valiable summe of near upon Eighty Pounds, so that if the sd Mr. Barnardus Freeman should be Drawn from us, as they Indeavor to Doe, we could not Preted that such a small Congregation as we are can be able to Send for another, and they Who are of a greater Congregation could had another before this If they had not Endeavoured to Deprive us their neighbors; therefore we, your Lordship's and Councill's Petitioners, humbly Pray that yr Lordship and Councill be Pleased to take this our Great Case In Your Great Wisdom and Serious Consideration to give Such Incouragements to the Instructing of the Indians, that we may be more Enabeled to the Paying of his Salary and your Petitioners as In Duty Bound Shall ever Pray.

Schoneghtende the 29th of May, 1703.

Claes Wirbessen [Lawrense.   Johannes Glenn, deacon.
Vander Volgen] Elder.   Isack Swits, elder.
Daniel Jansen [Van.   Jan Vrooman, elder.
Antwerpen] deacon.   Claes Van Patten, deacon.

Read in Council 24th June, 1703, and rejected. †

---

* Doc. Hist. III, 89.
† Council Minutes. Doc. Hist. III. 93.

Notwithstanding the above remonstrance and the fact that many persons in the congregations in Kings county were disaffected towards him, he visited the Island and on the second of August 1703 accepted the call under certain conditions.* It was not, however, until the summer of 1705 that he finally left Schenectady for Flatbush. The license thus to change his pastoral relations was granted by Governor Cornbury on the 26th of December of the same year.

About this time Do. Vincentius Antonides, who had been called by the disaffected portion of the churches arrived from Holland, and the congregations were at once divided into two rival factions, who resisted all attempts at compromise for nine years.

Finally, in 1714, peace was declared, and the two ministers henceforward acted together harmoniously as colleagues.

Mr. Freeman was married on the 25th of April, 1705, to Margarita, daughter of Capt. Goosen Gerritse Van Schaick, of Albany. They had but one child—Anna Margarita, who married her cousin, David Clarkson, son of Secretary Matthew Clarkson. He died in 1743, aged 83 years. †

De. Freeman was a learned divine. He wrote and published several works, among which were:

---

* The Consistory of Flatbush addressed a letter to that of Schenectady stating that most of the congregation are in favor of sending to Holland for a minister and that only some "stiff heads" had enjoined them to make a call upon Do. Freeman.—Strong's Hist. of Flatbush, p. 88, and Joseph Hegeman's letter to Reyer Schermerhorn, 21 Dec. 1702.

May 18, 1704, Do. Freeman made complaint to the Consistory of the church in Albany, that they of Boston had called him a heterodox and Anabaptistical teacher; and desired a certificate of his good character and preaching, which was accordingly granted.

31 Oct., 1705, Do. Freeman appeared before the Consistory of Albany with Barent Wemp and complained that the Consistory of Schenectady refused to give him a certificate of conduct, hoping thereby to keep him at Schenectady.—Albany Church Records.

† A letter was written by Do. Freeman Ap. 23, 1741, translated by Rev. Dr. DeWitt, with a preface, and published years ago in the Christian Intelligencer. Dr. DeWitt says, " he died at his residence in Flatbush at the good old age of 83 in 1743." Freeman says in this letter "I do not think that I in my advanced old age, reaching my 80th year, shall see the erection of a Coetus," &c. In a letter of Theodore J. Frelinghuysen, of date Jan. 12, 1743, he says, "so long as father Freeman lived," &c. If therefore, he died in 1743, it must have been between Jan. 1st and 12th.

1. A volumne of thirty sermons entitled, "Trials of Grace or the Balance," printed at Amsterdam, 1721, with a portrait, and dedicated to "the members of the church of Schenectady being my first congregation in this region."

2. *De Spiegel der self-kennis.* 12º.

3. A defense against charges made in a pamphlet entitled, "The Complaints of the Nether Dutch Church in New Jersey of the acts of Theodore J. Frelinghuysen," 1726. 16º. *

During his pastorate of five years in Schenectady he married forty one couples, of whom twenty were Indians.

Two hundred and thirty-seven persons were baptized, among whom were one hundred and one natives; and eighty-six white persons and fourteen adult Indian proselytes were added to the church on a profession of faith. As a prerequisite to baptism the adult Indians were required to accept and profess the twelve articles of faith, to forsake impiety and to love Godliness and promise to abide therein. †

## CHAPTER IV.

1703 – 24.   BUILDING OF THE SECOND CHURCH.   DOMINE THOMAS BROWER THE THIRD MINISTER.

Soon after De. Freeman came to Schenectady, the house of worship then used was found to be too small for the accommodation of the inhabitants and Indian proselytes, but as the little community had not yet fully recovered from the effects of the late incursion of the French and their savage allies, the funds necessary for a new house could not be raised without aid from

---

\* Strong's Hist. of Flatbush, p. 88, and Henry Onderdonk, Esq.

† Na dat sy de dwalf artikelen des geloofs hebben beleden an angenomen, den duyvelrye en godloosheden Versaekt, de godsaligheit bem int, en daer op belooft Volstauding te bliven en wee to beleven, dit gadaen vynde, so syn gedoopt in de kerk ogniondage, &c.
First Church book, p. 134.

abroad. A petition therefore was presented to Governor Nanfan, in 1701, asking permission to circulate a subscription throughout the Province for this purpose.*

This petition being favorably received by the Governor and Council, on the 27th of October, 1701, he issued the following license to the inhabitants of Schenectady to receive cortributions from the people of the Province for the space of six months from that date, and directed all justices of the peace, schouts and other officers of his majesty as well as ministers of the Gospel to use their utmost endeavors to aid this laudible object.

† " By the Honorable John Nanfan, Esq., Governor and Commander in Chief over the Province of New York and territories dependent thereon in America, &c:

---

* To the Hon$^{ble}$ John Nanfan Esq$^r$ Lt. Gouv$^r$ and Command$^r$ in Chief oft y$^e$ Province oft New York in America and y$^e$ Hon$^{ble}$ Councell oft y$^e$ same.

 The humble Petician oft Barnardus Freerman minister oft y$^e$ Gospel att Schanegtade & Ryer Schermerhoorn Esq$^r$ in y$^e$ behalf oft the Inhabitants of said Town,

Sheweth

That whereas the Town oft Schonegtade hath been wholy destroyed by y$^e$ French in y$^e$ late Warr & sins the resattling oft y$^e$ same The Inhabitants oft y$^e$ same being verry low and oft mean Estates have not bein able to Erect a Place convenient for y$^e$ Publick Worchip oft God, the Place where itt is now Exercised in nott being Large Enough to containe [the] whole Assembly of y$^e$ Inhab$^{i}$tants & Indian Proselytes,

 They Therefore humbly pray yo$^r$ houn$^{rs}$ Lycense for the collecting a free will offering oft y$^e$ Inhabitants oft this Province for y$^e$ buylding a convenient Place for y$^e$ Public Worship oft God in y$^e$ town aforesaid and yo$^r$ Petic$^{rs}$ shall ever Pray &c.

B. FREERMAN, Ecll. Skagnagt.      RYER SCHERMERHOOREN.

—Col. Mss. XLV.

† By den Honorable John Nanfan, Esq., Governour an Commandeur in Cheeffe over d Proventie van New Yorke & Territories daeraen dependeren in America, &c. :

Also 't Dorp van Schinnechtady, in d County Van Albany, heeft geheelyk gedistroyert geweest doer d Inloopinge Van d Franse in de gewesene oorlogh en nae d herbowen daervan, de Inwoondeeren hebben geweest en nogh syn in een arm & leegh conditie, dat sy niet maghtigh hebben geweest om een behoorlyk plaets op te Rechten voor de gemeene Godts Dients ; En also niets Strecklyker can syn voor d Vrede en Welvaert desen provintie dan dat de gemeene dienst tot God Almighty sy Punctueelyk ge observeert en geviert in alle parten & Plastsen en besonderlyk aen de frontiers, in een gemeene en bekent plaets daertoe geappointeert, dat de Inwoondeeren en bewoonders deser provintie mogen door haer goede Example van godtvrughtigheyt en Relige-

Whereas the Village of Schenectady, in the County of Albany, has been wholly destroyed through the incursion of the French in the late war, and after the rebuilding thereof the inhabitants have been and still are in a poor and low condition, so that they have not been able to erect a proper place for the public worship of God;—and whereas nothing conduces more to the peace and well-being of this province than that the public worship of Almighty God be punctually observed and celebrated in all parts and places and especially on the frontiers, in a public and acknowledged place thereto dedicated, that the inhabitants and sojourners of this province may through their good example of piety and religious reverence be brought over and persuaded there to dwell to the great strengthening of said frontier, which thereby become a defence for the other parts of this province, if a war should again occur between his most Sacred Majesty and the King of France;

Therefore I, by and with the advice of His Majesty's council for this province and in His Majesty's name, hereby give and grant full and free liberty and license to the inhabitants of said village of Schenectady, in said county of Albany, or to such person or persons as by them or the majority of them shall be employed to gather, collect and receive the free and voluntary offerings and contributions of all and every of His Majesty's faithful subjects,—inhabitants of this Province, at any time after this date and during the time of six months; the said contributions to be employed solely for the erection and building a necessary and becoming place for the public worship of God by the Inhabitants of said Village. And I hereby, in His Majesty's name require all His Majesty's justices, schouts, and all other His Majesty's officers within this Province, together with all

---

ouse Eerbiedinge sy overgebraght en ge parswadeert daer te woonen tot d groote versterking Van d gemezde Frontiers die daer door sullen geworden d Bescherminge voor d andere parten van dese provintie in dien een oorlogh uytvalt tuschen zyn most Sacred Majesteyt en de Franse Coningh. Ick daerom by en met advice van syn Majesteyts councill voor dese provintie en in syn majesteyts naem hierby geve en vergunn voll en Vry Libertheit en Lycence aen d Inwoonderen des gemelde dorp Schinnechtady in de gemelde County van Albany oft aen sodanigh Personen oft Personen als by haer sullen geimplooyeert syn oft by het meeste part van haer to vergaderen en t Verderen en outfangen d vry en gewilllge offeringe en contribusies van alle & een yder syn majestyts getrow onderdanen Inwoonders van dese provintie tot Enige tydt vandata deser gedurende dan tydt en wyle van ses maenden Van dien,

Protestant ministers in their sundry and respective counties, cities, colonies, churches, districts and jurisdictions to use their utmost endeavors and diligence to arouse the liberality of the inhabitants on this occasion, which conduces to the honor and service of Almighty God, the welfare of this province in general and for the peace and security of all the inhabitants thereof.

Given under my hand and seal in Fort William Henry, in New York, this seven and twentieth day of October, A° 1701, in the 13th year of the reign of our Sovereign Lord, William the third, by the grace of God of England, Scotland, France and Ireland, King, Defender of the Faith, &c.

Was signed.

JOHN NANFAN.

pr order of the Council. }
B. Cozens, Sec. Coun. }

This appeal to the liberality of their neighbors was successful, and the church was probably finished in the year 1703.* The site was that of the first house of worship, at the junction of Church, Water and State streets, and the dimensions, fifty-

---

en de gemelde Contribusies alleenlyk geimployeert to werde voor en tot het opreghten en bouwen van een noodigh en behoorlyk plaets voort gemeene Godts Dienst by Inwoonders der gemelde dorp van Schinnechtady, in d County van Albany. En hierby ick versoek in syn majesteyt naem alle syn majesteyts Justicen der vrede, Schouten en alle andere syn majesteyts officieren binnen dese provintie, als mede alle prostestant Ministers in haer Vershyde & Respective Counties, steden, colonyen, Kercken, Districts & Jurii, dicties te gebruycken & doen gebruycken haer en Eyder van haer Uytterste deavour en neerstigheyt voor en tot opwercken de Inwoonderen haer mildadigheit op dese Occasie, welcke dient tot d Eeer en Dienst van Gott Almightigh, het goet Welfair van dese provintie int generall en tot d Vrede en securiteyt van een yder Inwoonder daerin.

Gegeven onder my hant en segel in fort William henry, in New Yorke, dese seven en Twentigheste dagh van Octobr, A° 1701, en int 13d jaer der Regeringe van onsen Souverainen heer William d 3d by d gratie godts van England, Scotlant, Franckryk & Ireland, Conig and Beschermer des geloffs, &c. Was getekt

JOHN NANFAN.

pr ordr Van Councill. }
B. Cozens, Sec. Coun }

*B. Cozens Sec. of the Council in a letter to Reyer Schermerhorn, of date 30th Jan., 1701, says "The Govr and Council have given £10 towards the church at Schenectady."—Schermerhorn papers.

six feet north and south, by forty-six feet east and west, Amsterdam measure. The burying ground adjoined the church upon the west side and was fifteen feet wide by fifty-six feet long. Speaking of Schenectady in 1710, the Rev. Thomas Barclay says: "There is a convenient and well built church, which they freely give me the use of." *

Probably it was substantially built of stone, for after its abandonment in 1734 as a place of worship, it was used for some years as a fort. † A wooden building would hardly have been devoted to such a purpose. By the year 1754 it had been removed and the site was successively occupied by a barracks, watch-house and market. ‡

In 1792 the spot being vacant, the Consistory proposed to erect thereon a house at the cost of £170,|| but it is believed this project was never carried out, for in 1794 they resolved to lease it to Arent S. Vedder for building purposes upon condition that it should never be dug up, save so far as was necessary to lay the foundations or to set fence posts—that the foundation should not be laid farther west than where the old church's west wall stood, and that the house built thereon should never be used for *"Tap-drink-of-Vrolyk-huys (so als men deselve gewoonlyk noemt.")*¶ To account for these singular conditions in a deed of conveyance, it is only necessary to remember that this then was looked upon as sacred ground, and that here for sixty years, to 1720, the dead of the village were buried. **

The building above mentioned was never erected. The next year, 1795, the Trustees of the Common lands resolved to make an offer for this lot,†† but if made nothing came of it, for in 1800 the Consistory directed that it "be properly ascertained and marked out," and in 1805 agreed to lease it to Anne McFarlane for $10 per an., but she was not allowed to dig upon it.

---

* Doc. Hist. III, 540
† Act of the Assembly, 1734 (?).
‡ Jno. Mynderse's will in the Ct. of Appeals office. . . and Deeds XII Collins to Van Eps.
|| Consistory minutes.
¶ Consistory minutes
** When the public cistern was built here in 184—the ancient burial ground was encroached upon and many bones were thrown out.
†† Minutes of the Board.

The removal of Do. Freeman was a disheartening event to the church. He had gained the confidence of the people and considerable influence over the neighboring Indians. To obtain another minister from Holland in their present circumstances was impossible. They were not only a small but a poor people, and without aid not in a condition to support a minister.

For the following ten years they were destitute of the stated ministry, being only occasionally visited by the ministers of Albany and other more distant settlements.

Between the years 1705 and 1715 Domines Johannes Lydius and Petrus Van Driessen, of Albany, Petrus Vas, of Kingston, and Gualterus Du Bois, of New York, made 24 visits to Schenectady, baptising 152 children, of whom 19 were Indians. In all this time the records show but one member added to the church. Rev Thomas Barclay, chaplain to the fort in Albany, preached occasionally in Schenectady. In a letter\* dated September 26, 1710, he says: "At Schenectady I preach once a month, where there is a garrison of forty soldiers, besides about sixteen English and about one hundred Dutch families. They are all of them my constant hearers.

I have this summer got an English school erected amongst them, and in a short time I hope their children will be fit for catechising. Schenectady is a village situated upon a pleasant river, twenty English miles above Albany, and the first Castle of the Indians is twenty-four miles above Schenectady. In this village there has been no Dutch minister these five years and there is no probability of any being settled among them. There is a convenient and well built church, which they freely give me the use of. I have taken the pains to show them the agreement of the articles of our church with theirs. I hope in some time to bring them not only to be constant hearers, but communicants."

As early as 1713 the church applied to Governor Hunter for permission to call a new minister and received his license dated July 27, that year. On the 17th day of May, the following year, the Consistory addressed a letter to William Baucker, merchant of Amsterdam, and Rev. Matthias Winterwyck, of Alphen (Dalphin?) Holland, authorising them to procure a minister for

---

\* Letter to the Secretary of the Society for the Propagation of the Gospel in Foreign Parts. Doc. Hist. III, 540

the church, and promising him a salary of £90 to commence on his arrival, a dwelling free of rent, fire wood at the door, a large garden, and free pasture for two cows and a horse. The result of this negotiation was the arrival of Domine Thomas Bronwer in July, 1714.

He probably came from the Province of Overyssell, where he had two brothers living in 1728—the one Gerardus, at Zwoll, and the other, Theodorus, minister at Dalphin.

He made his will* on the 24th of November, 1727, and died on the 15th of January, 1728.† He left £25—one-half to the church and the other for the poor—his gun, pistols, horse, table linen, &c., to various members of the family of Gerrit Symonse Veeder and Johannes Bancker, and his books, best clothing, linen, &c., to his two brothers above mentioned. He speaks of neither wife nor children. During his pastorate of twelve years he married fifty-three couples, baptised five hundred and five children, and admitted one hundred and eight persons to the church.

## CHAPTER V.

1728–36. DOMINE REINHARDUS ERICHZON THE FOURTH MINISTER. THE THIRD CHURCH EDIFICE ERECTED.

The fourth minister of the church was Do. Reinhardus Erichzon. His call, or *Beroepbrief*, was dated 30th march, 1728, two and a half months after the death of his predecessor.

He was probably a native, or at least, a resident of Groningen, North Holland, and before his call to Schenectady had ministered three years to the church of Hackensack, Paramus and Schraalenbergh, New Jersey.

---

* On file in the office of the Clerk of the Court of Appeals.

† He had been disabled by sickness, however, since the month of August, 1723, and unable all that time to perform the active duties of his calling. An assistant was employed to do his work, but the records do not give his name.

The Consistory of Schenectady agreed to give him a salary of £100 ($250), a parsonage house in good repair, a garden kept in fence, pasture for a horse and two cows, and fire-wood at the door.

Sixty or seventy loads of wood was the Domine's annual supply in these early times. For this purpose a *bee* was made usually in the month of January. The congregation then turned out with their teams, and in from one to three days his yard was filled. The Consistory made a bountiful provision for the entertainment of the *bee* makers on these occasions, as appears by the following extracts from the treasurer's books.

| | | |
|---|---|---|
| 16 Jan. 1747¾ to Johannes DePeyster for five gallons of Rum for the Domine's *bee* c 3-6 | | £0–17–6 |
| 19 " to Pieter Groenendyk for ½ gall. wine | | 4–0 |
| 23 " to Metje Fairly for use of the house at the *bee* | | 4–0 |
| 1748, 28th Ap. to Jacobus Mynderse for rum for the Domine's *bee* | | 3–12–2 |
| 1749 Jan. Beer for the *bee* | | 1–14–6 |
| 1751 Jan. 1 for rum and sugar | | 1– 7–6 |
| " 2 for beer | | 0–12–0 |
| " Ap. 28 to Anna Wendell for house hire twice for a *bee* | | – 9–0 |
| to Isaac Abr. Truex for rum and sugar * | | 1–13, 6 |

During the eight years of his pastorate here he married seventy-nine couples, baptised about three hundred and fifty children and received two hundred and six members to the church.

Domine Erichzon left Schenectady in October 1736, having received a call to the church of Freehold and Middletown. N. J., where he remained until "compelled to discontinue his ministry on account of intemperence, whether from an act of suspension by the Classis of Amsterdam or not is not known." The evidence in the case was conclusive. The charge was brought by Mr. Williamson, who had seen him intoxicated upon the pub-

---

* 16 Jan. 1747¾, aan Joh: de Peyster voor 4 gall: Rhum voor D⁰ *bee* a 3 sh- 6 d. .................................................. £0–17–6
19 do. aan Pʳ Groenendyk voor ½ gall: wyn........................ – 4–0
23 aan Metje Fairly voor 't huys gebruyck op de bee ......... – 4–0
1748 28 ap. an Jacobus Mynderse voor rum voor Domᵉ Bee....... £3–12–2
Jan. Bier voor de Bee................................................... 1–14–6

Old church records.

lic road. He remained five or six years in Monmouth, N. J., living in the parsonage, and there is reason to believe (says Mr. Marselis), that he abandoned his evil habits. He and his wife removed to New Brunswick about 1770 and lived with his daughter. Here he probably died.

His widow, it is said, returned to Monmouth. His first wife, Mary Provoost, he married on the 22nd of May, 1726, whilst minister of the church of Hackensack. They had a daughter, Anna, born in Schenectady in 1729, and two sons—William, born in Freehold in 1737, and David, born in 1740. His second wife was Mary Luyster, widow of Rulif Brokaw, and daughter of Johannes Luyster and Lucretia Brower, of Middletown, N. J.

It is not known that Do. Erichzon published anything. The tradition respecting him is that he was a man of learning and of superior pulpit talents.*

His ministry in Schenectady seems to have been a successful one. Since the treaty of Utrecht, in 1713, the country had been at peace, and wealth and population increased rapidly.

Our village was no exception, and before the church erected in 1703 had stood thirty years the population had outgrown its capacity, and it became necessary to erect a larger.

This matter began to be agitated soon after Do. Erichzon became pastor, and instead of appealing to their neighbors for aid as in the former case, the congregation was able not only to build a house which for the times was both substantial and spacious, but also to furnish it with a bell and clock.

As a preliminary step in this new enterprise, a subscription paper was circulated through the town in 1730 by which £322 was obtained, and extending the appeal up the valley into *Maquas Landt*† a still further sum of £33-15 was subscribed in money and wheat.

---

* Taylor's Classis of Bergen, p. 193, and letter of B. W.

Rev. Gerrit C. Schanck, of Marlboro, N. J., has "an old portrait of De. R. Erichzon, painted by Daniel Hendricksen, an Elder in the church and intimate friend of the Domine. He was a farmer, and self-taught artist. The painting is not finely executed." [This painting was procured for the Memorial Exhibition held in the church June 21-24. It has been purchased, and is now in the possession of Dr. Exichzon's descendant, Mr. Daniel Vedder. W. E. G.]

† *Maquaas Landt* was that part of the valley of the Mohawk river lying west of Amsterdam.

## HISTORY OF THE CHURCH.

The following is that portion of this list made up of Schenectady names:—

July, 1730.

List of the voluntary gifts which were promised here at Schenectady, in the County of Albany, for the building of a new church for the behoof of the Dutch Reformed Church at Schenectady *:—

We or I, the underwritten, promise to pay to Arent Bratt, Jacobus Van Dyck, Dirck Groot and Cornelis Vander Volgen and Robert Yates, Jacob Swits, Wouter Vrooman and Jan Barentse Wemp, Elders and Deacons, or to their successors, the sum which we or I subscribe with our hands so soon as the foundation of said church is laid; and failing of the same, we or I promise to pay ten pounds current money, if we or I are negligent in the payment of the sum of money, which I with my hand subscribe, as witness our hands or my hand. †

| | |
|---|---|
| Jellis Vonda | drie pont ‡ |
| Henderick Vooman | fyf pont |
| Capt. Harme Van Slyck | Ses pont |
| Albert vedder | drie pont |
| Abraham Meebie | 4 pont |
| helmis Veder | vier pont |
| John fairley | 3 pont |
| Myndert Wymp | 3 pont |
| Pieter Cornu | 3 pont |
| Barent Vrooman | 2 pont |
| Wyllem Teller | 4 pont |
| Gysbert V brakel | 5 pont |
| John Vrooman | 6 pont |

---

\* 1730 Den July, lyst van de vry Villige gift die belooft wert hierop Schonechtade In de County van Albany tot het ophouwen de *nederduytse gereformeerde gemynte* hier op Schonechtade.

† Wy ondergeschreve of Ick and ondergeschreven beloove to betalen aen Arent Bratt, Jacobus Van Dyck, dirck groot, en Cornelis Vander Volgen, en robbert eets, jacob Swits, wouter Vrooman, en Jan barents wemp, ouderlingen en dyaconen of aen haer successeurs die som die wy of Ick met myn handt hier onderteykene sodra als de gront slag van gemelde kerck gelyt wert en by mankement Vandienso beloove wy of Ick te betalen thien pont corraut gelt Indien wy of Ick nalatig ben om te betalen die som gelt die Ick met myn hant hier onder Schrive, ter getuyge onse hande of myn handt.

‡ The pound New York currency was $2.50.

| | |
|---|---|
| Johannis Van Vorst . | 3 pont |
| Johannis Marselis | . 2 pont |
| Abram groot . | vier stuck van achte. |
| Cornelis Van Slyck | . drie pont |
| Symon Veder . | drie pont |
| Reinhart Erickzon, pred. | 5 pont |
| Arent brat | nege pont |
| Jacobus Van Dyck | . drie pont |
| dirck groot | . vier pont |
| Cornelis van der Volge | . . vyf pont |
| Robbert yets . | vyf pont |
| Yacoep Swits . | . . 2 pont |
| Wouter Vrooman . | twaels (12?) pont |
| Jan Barentse Wemp | 4 pont |
| Abram D Graaf . | 3 pont |
| Cornelis Van Dyck | 3 pont |
| Joha. Sanders Glen . | 3 pont |
| Jacobus Peeck . | . . drie pont |
| Aaernout de Graaf | . vier pont |
| Sander Lanseng . | 3 pont |
| Jacob Glenn . | . acht pont |
| barent hendrickse vrooman . | een pont |
| Joseph Van Slee . | 3 pont |
| Abraham Truax . | 4 pont |
| Sander Van Eps | 2 pont |
| Davet Marinis | . 1 pont |
| Nicolaas Groodt . | 2 £ |
| Daniel Danielse [Van antwerpen] . | 3 pont |
| Symon Vrooman . | 4 pont |
| Johannys ouderkerck . | 2 pont |
| Philip Van Putte . | 1 pont |
| haerme Vedder . | 2 pont |
| Reyer Wempel | . 3 pont |
| Gerret Van Vorst | . 2 pont |
| Johanis Vedder yu. [Jr.] . | 2 " |
| Abraham Glenn . | . 3 " |
| Arent braet, yu. [Jr.] | 4 " |
| hendrick Vrooman, iunier, belofte | . 2 " |
| William Peters . | 2–10 |
| Takel Maerseles . | . 2 pont . |

| | |
|---|---|
| Yacobus Vedder . . . | 2 pont |
| Adryaen Van Slyck . . | 1 " |
| harme m (?) Vedder . . . | 2 " |
| Cornelus Veder . . | 2 " |
| Harmanus Vedder . . | 3 " |

| | |
|---|---|
| 58 . . . . | £195–14 |

| | |
|---|---|
| Joh: Visger . . . | 2 pont |
| Wilhelmus Ryckman . . . . | 2 " |
| lourens Van der Volgen, *Vrywillig* | 6 ', |
| Arent Stevens . . . . | 1 " |
| tierk franse [Van der Bogart] . . | 4 " |
| douwe aukis, geordeneert voor hem of syn erfgenamen . . . . | 3 " |
| Pieter Felinck. 7 stuck 8 of . | £2–8 |
| Johannis Mynderse . | 12 gul |
| Johannis Bleecker . . | 80 guld |
| Sara Luykes | 12 Shil. |
| Pieter Winne . | 1 pont |
| Cornelis pooetman | 3 " |
| Pieter Veder . . | 2 " |
| Jacop Vrooman . . | 2 " |
| Jacop truex . . . | 3 " |
| Gysbert Marselis junior . . | 1 " |
| Gerret (?) Danielse [Van Antwerpen] | 6 betaelt pont |
| Volkle wemp . . . . . | 2 " |
| Jan leenderse . . | 10 shil. |

| | |
|---|---|
| 75 | £229–4 |

| | |
|---|---|
| bartholomewis Vrooman . | 1 pont |
| Jan Vrooman . . . | 1–4 |
| marya Van der Volgen . | 1 pont |
| elysabet van brakel . . | 2 " |
| barent wemp, junior . | 2 " |
| Geertruy mynders | 4 " |
| Sander Glen . . | 3 " |
| Jacop teller . | 2 " |
| antie beck . . | 2 " |
| Jan dellamond . . | 3 " |

| | | |
|---|---|---|
| Capt. bancks [Banks] | 2 " | |
| Jelles Van Vorst | 2 " | |
| Jacobus Van Vorst | 1 " | |
| Douwe Vonda | 3 " | |
| anna lythall | 1 " | |
| Jannyetie Veders | 2 " | Valdaen |
| elyas Post | 1-10 | |
| Jan Baptist Van eps | 6 pont | |
| anna Wendell | 6 shil. | |
| Catrina brat | 6 " | |
| Cornelya brat | 6 " | |
| engelie Symonse [Veeder] | 1 pont | |
| Gerret Symonse [Veeder] | 6 " | |
| William bancker | 2 " | |
| evert Van eps | 2 " | |
| John Dunbar | 2 " | |
| gerret gysbertse [Van Brakel] | 2 " | |
| gysbert Van brakel, junior, | 2 " | |
| Sweer Marselis | 2 pont | |
| Joseph Dance | 3 " | |
| Johannis teller | 3 " | |
| akis brat | 2 " | |
| claes de graef | 6 shil. | |
| daniel degraaf | 6 " | |
| Jacop Schermerhorn | 1 pont 4 S. | |
| Johannis peeck | 2 " | |
| Jan Danielse [van antwerpen] | 2 " | |
| pieter danielse [van antwerpen] | 2 " | |
| Jacop Mebie | 3 " | |
| Pieter Vrooman | 3 " | |
| arent vedder | 2 " | |
| Jacobus Peeck. Junior, | 2 " | en |
| een tonne bier, | | |
| Myndert van gyselingh | 4 pont | |
| Johannis haell | 1-10 | |
| Samuel brat | 1 pont | |
| Wilyem Berret | 2 " | |
| [total] | £322-2. | |

De lyst van de val en maquaaes landt

|   |   |
|---|---|
| De gelt belofte comt | £19–16 |
| het core tege 4–10 pr sch | 13–19 |
| [£355–17] | |

This sum did not amount to quite one third the cost of the church, which was £1167–17–10 [$2,919.73]. The remainder was probably derived from the accumulations of former years and from the sale of lands or leases—the gift of the trustees of common lands.

After thorough preparation the work was begun in the spring of 1732. Hendrick Vrooman was Baas * of the men, of whom seventeen were carpenters, besides masons, glaziers, &c. His wages were seven shillings a day—the others were paid from five to six shillings. The *Preeck-Stoel* † [pulpit] was built by Pieter Cornu for £20, and Gysbert W. Vanden Bergh, of Albany, contracted to do the mason work for £80.

Among the first articles of *hardware* purchased were:

|   |   |
|---|---|
| twee vaten spykers | £18–16 |
| en een oexshoft rom | 13–12 |

and before the close of the year the latter article was exhausted and more purchased. The same liberal supply was made for the year 1733. ‡

This house was dedicated January 13, 1734, on which occasion Do. Erichzon preached in the morning, his text being the third verse of the second chapter of Isaiah. In the afternoon Do. Van Driessen, of Albany, preached from the first and second chapter of the same book.

The following Sabbaths, January 20th and 27th the pastor continued the subject of his first sermon. ‖

---

* This is a genuine Dutch word signifying master or chief.

† In 1761 the pulpit was newly adorned at an expense of £1-14-1 as follows :

| | |
|---|---|
| aan casa Betalt voor 't Bekeeden van de Predickstoel, | £0-3-0 |
| 12¼ elle Swarte Saloen voor Predickstoel te Bekleeden c 2-6 | 1-10-7 |
| Kleyne spikertjes 6d | 6 |
| | £1-14-1 |

—Church accounts.

‡ Church records.

‖ 173¾ Jan. 13.—De Eerste predicatie gedaen in de nieuwe Kerche door heer Doomeny Erichzon uit den Prophet Yesaia het 2 Capittel Vers 3.—Syn inlyding uit Luce 22 verse 32 ent tot besluit gesonge uit psalm 100 vers 3. . . . De twede predicatie gedaen door den Heer domeny Van Driessen uit

This third house was situated in Church street at its junction with Union street, and was eighty feet in length, North and South, and fifty-six feet wide ;* the Trustees of the town conveyed to the church not only this site but also the land around the same ten feet in width, except on the West side, where by reason of the narrowness of the street, it was limited to five feet.† The building material was blue sand stone or greywacke from the quarries east of the village. It had two entrances,—one on the South end, the other on the East side, over which was built a porch with a stair case leading to galleries. The roof was in Mansard style, a few specimens of which still (1860) remain in the city. The bellfry and clock tower stood on the North end. As seen from the East end of Union street it presented a pleasing and imposing appearance. The tub shaped pulpit fixed upon a narrow pedestal and surmounted by a conical sounding board, was built against the West wall in front of which an open space, was railed in called the *Doophuisje*. Here the Domine stood while administering the rite of baptism.

There was a gallery upon all sides save the West, whether built with the church, or at a later day it not known, as no mention is made of it before the year 1788, when it began to be occupied by adult males who could not obtain seats below. In this, as in other Dutch congregations the males and females sat apart :—the former upon raised seats called *gestoelte*, placed against the walls of the church, and the latter in slips or *bancken* upon the floor of the house.

In the year 1809 three family pews were constructed. ‡

---

ded prophet Yesaia 35 capittel vers 1 en 2 en tot besluit gesonge uit 118 psalm vers 1.—20 ditto [Jan.] Den predicatie uit jesaia 2, vers 3 het middel part en tot besluit gesonge psalm 25, vers 22. 27 ditto [Jan.] De vierde predicatie uit jesaia 2 cap. 3 vers laste part, entot besluit gesonge psalm 110 vers 2.—From Simon Volkertse Veeder's Bible, now owned by Mrs. H. J. Bratt.

\* Church charter, Aug. 23. 1734.

† Patentees deed 10 July 1733.

‡ 9 July 1800. Resolved that the two first female seats at your left hand on entering the church by the East door and which are vacant be divided into three or four square pews as the case will permit, and that when finished they be published for sale, reserving, however, one thereof for the minister's family
   Mr. Henry Yates took the *first pew* as you enter the East door.
   The *southeastern pew* was sold to Joseph C. Yates for 50 Dolls.
   The *middle pew* was reserved for the minister.
                                          —Consistory minutes.

## HISTORY OF THE CHURCH.

In the first allotment of seats little regard was had to family relations, nor was there any exchange of sittings, and so long as the yearly rent was paid they were the property of the occupants, but in case of removal or death passed to the nearest relative of the same sex. Only in case of non-payment of the customary rent was a seat forfeited. It was then allotted anew at the discretion of the consistory. Every transfer of a sitting cost the new occupant twelve shillings, beside the yearly rent of five shillings for males and four shillings for females. *

During the eighty years that this church stood but few and trifling changes were made in the slips or *boncken* first erected, and these chiefly by additions to accommodate the increasing congregation. The number of places (*plaatsen*) occupied by adults at different periods were as follows:—

|  | Men's seats. | Men in gallery. | Women's seats. | Total |
|---|---|---|---|---|
| Jn. 1734 | 86 | 0 | 218 | 304 |
| " 1754 | 104 | 0 | 328 | 432 |
| " 1788 | 125 | 35 | 346 | 506 |

From 1788 to 1814 when the old church was removed, new comers could not rent seats without great difficulty except in the gallery, which being chiefly occupied by boys and negroes was not considered quite respectable.

The people worshipped on the Sabbath almost to the beginning of this century, even in the coldest winter weather without any other artificial heat than that derived from foot stoves. The first stoves used in this church were bought in December, 1792, and set up that winter. They were placed upon two platforms elevated to the height of the gallery, and reached by climbing over the balustrade. It is said that the *kloklayer* was accustomed to replenish them at the beginning of the Domine's

---

* Jan. 1, 1747-8. The seats (*plaatsen*) of those that have not paid their dues for a year and a day, shall be sold except paid within 3 weeks, and hereafter seats shall be sold if the occupants refuse to pay for 9 months. Also the seats of those who are deceased shall fall to the church, if within a year and six months after their decease said seats shall not be assigned.

1749, Dec. 31. Each woman's seat (Vrouweplaatse) was rated at four shillings and each man's seat (mans plaatze) at five shillings. The right of succession shall be in the next female and male, and if this fail the seat shall fall to the church.

—Consistory minutes.

See Appendix A.

sermon and to notify to the congregation of the importance of his vocation was particularly noisy in opening and shutting the stove doors. By this arrangement it is said that "the top of the church was comfortable but the people below had to carry foot stoves to keep themselves warm." So unsatisfactory was this first experiment in warming the church that the matter came up and was discussed by the Consistory, and the result was that the elevated platforms were removed and the stoves placed upon the floor of the church.*

The following bill for these stoves is translated from the treasurer's book:

|  | £ s d |
|---|---|
| 1792 Dec. 23. Paid James Murdoch for 2 stoves... | 12–15–8 |
| 29 Dec. To cash for riding stone for the stove floor | 0–13–3 |
| Paid James McWilliams for setting the stoves in the church.................................... | 0–12–0 |
| to a cart to Albany to haul the *gryp* (?) iron for the stoves..................................... | 0–10–0 |
| to 140½ lbs. of iron by Swits for the small work about the stoves................................. | 3–10–1½ |
| to 1 quart of rum for the workmen.............. | 0– 2–5 |
| 1793 Jan. Cash to Maas Schermerhorn paid....... for *set* (?) iron, 25 lbs at 11 pence a pound...... | 1–2–11 |
| Cash paid Walter Swits and Peter Symens for the iron-work on the stoves†.................... | 9–19–6 |
|  | £28–05–10½ |

---

* 25 Dec. 1798. Finding that the stoves in the Church are not placed to the best advantage for casting of warmth to the audience, Resolved

That the Consistory will meet in the church to-morrow and endeavor to place them to more advantage. —Consistory minutes.

† 1792 Dec 23 Aan James Murdoch betalt voor 2 kaghels......... £12-15- 8
29 aen cass voor Roye Stein voor de Caghel vloer ............... 0-13- 8
aen James McWilliams betaelt de kaghels in de kirk te sette 0-12- 0
aen Een wage na Albany voor 't gryp Eyser an de Kakhels te hale........................................................ 0-10- 0
aen 140½ lb. Eyser Door Swits voor clyn werk an de Kaghels 3-10- 1½
aen 1 qart rom an de werk Luyde ........... ............. 2- 5
1703 Jan. cassa aen Maes Schermerhorn voorset eyser betalt 25 lb at 11 pens p pont......... ................. 1- 2-11
Cassa betalt aen Walter Swits in Pieter Symens voor het eyserwerk an Cagels ........................... .......... 8-19- 6

£58-05-10½

## CHAPTER VI.

### 1731-4. THE BELL AND CLOCK. THE CHARTER.

On the 10th February, 1730-1 a subscription was opened for a bell. The heading of this paper is as follows:

*Subscriptions of persons for the bell.*

We the underwritten promise what we with our own hands or by our own orders have here subscribed and promised, to pay for a new bell for the Low Dutch church here at Schenectady & we promise to pay the same to the Domine and Consistory of the Low Dutch church of Schenectady, viz:—to Domine Erichzon, Dirck Groot, Cornelis Vander Volgen, Harmanus Vedder, Abraham Mebie, Jan Barentse Wemp, Wouter Vrooman, Abraham De Graaf and Cornelis Van Dyck, or to one of them, on or before the first day of May next coming. Done in Schenectady the 10th of February 1730-1. *

To this paper are appended 152 names and the amount raised was £45-6-6 ($113.31.)

The bell was procured in Amsterdam and did "good and faithful service for more than a century until it was cracked in 1848." It bore the following inscription:

*De Klok van de Neder-duidsch gemeente van Sconechiade door Haar self bezorght anno 1732. Me fecerunt DeGrave et Muller, Amsterdam.†*

---

\* *Beloften van Personen voor de klock.*

Wy onderschrevenen Belove het Geene wy met onser Igen hant of door onser Igen order hier onder geteckent en Belooft hebben om Een Nieuwe Kloeck te coopen In de Needer Duytsche kerck hier te Schenectady en Belove het selve te Betalen aen De. Heere Domine en Kercken rade van de Needer duytsche kerck van Schenectady by name, Dom. Erichzon, Dirck Groot, Cornels Vander Vollege, Harmanus Vedder, Abra. Mebie, Jan Bar. Wemp, Wouter Vrooman, Abraham De Graaf, en Corns. Van Dyck, of aen Een Van haer en Dat Voor of op den 1 day Van May nu aen staende.

Actum te Schenectady den 10 Feb'y, 1730-1.    —Church papers.

† "The bell of the Low Dutch Church of Schenectady procured by themselves in the year 1732."

"DeGrave and Muller, Amsterdam, made me."

In 1740 the church had a public or town clock purchased, probably at about

Although the church had owned considerable real estate more than fifty years, it had no corporate existence in law, and could neither hold or alienate property save through individuals acting as its trustees. Feeling the precarious nature of such tenure, when the church edifice was finished, the Consistory petitioned the Governor and Council for a charter.*

This application was favorably considered and on the third day of August, 1734, the following Charter was granted under the great seal of the Province.†

George the Second by the Grace of God of Great Brittain, France and Ireland, King, Defender of the Faith, &c. To all to whom these presents shall come, sendeth Greeting:

Whereas we have been informed by the humble petition of our Loving Subjects Rinherdt Erickesen, John Barentse [Wemp], Gerrit Simonse Veeder, Simon Vrooman, Robert Yaats, Sander Lansinck, Abraham Truax, Abraham Glen and Arent Samuelse Bradt, the present minister, Elders and Deacons of the Dutch Protestant Congregation in Schenectady, in our County of Albany, presented our trusty and well beloved William Cosby, Esqr., our Captain General and Governor in Chief of our Province of New York, New Jersey and Territories thereon depending in America, and Vice Admiral of the same and Coll' in our Army, that the said Minister, Elders and Deacons and the rest of the Communicants of the said Congregation have at their own charge built a New Church in the Town of Schenectady aforesaid, and the same have dedicated to the Almighty God, but for the want of being incorporated they are not Capable of Receiving or accepting of such Donations as pious Designed Persons are or may be disposed to give unto them, or of Purchasing any Lands or Tenements for the use of said Church; wherefore in their said humble petition they have likewise prayed our Letters Patent to Incorporate them and the rest

---

the same time with the bell. In 1773 Benjamin Young was paid £5-10 for keeping it in order for one year; and in 1774 £6.

It was the custom to ring the bell three times on the Sabbath, before commencing religious services down to January, 1810, when the Consistory made the change indicated in the following resolution:

*Resolved*, That in future the bell shall be rung twice as usual, previous to the commencement of public worship, and that tolling shall be substituted for the third ringing. It is said the bell was also rung at the close of the service that the servants at home might have the dinner ready on their masters return.

*Col. Mss. LXX, 107.
† Patents in office of Sec. of State at Albany.

of the communicants of the said church, into a body Politick
and Corporate, in Deed, fact and name and Style of the Ministers, Elders and Deacons of the Reformed Protestant Dutch
Church of Schenectady in the County of Albany, and thereby
also to grant unto said Corporation and their successors forever,
the new Church aforesaid and the grounds whereon the same
stands; and also to grant and secure unto them and their successors the free exercise and enjoyment of all their civil and
Religious Rights, and the Liberty of worshipping God according to Constitutions and Directions of the Reformed Church in
Holland, approved and Instituted by the National Synod of
Dort, which Petition we being Willing to grant, and being
Willing in particular favor to the pious purposes of our Loving
Subjects in free Exercise and Enjoyment of all their Civill and
Religious Rights appertaining unto them in manner aforesaid
as our Loving Subjects, and to preserve to them and their suc-
cessors that Liberty of worshipping God according to the Con
stitution and Directions aforesaid.

Wherefore, know ye, that we of our especial Grace, certain
knowledge and meer motion have ordained, Constituted and Declared and by these presents for us, our Heirs and successors do
ordain, Constitute and Declare that they, the said Minister,
Elders and Deacons and the rest of the Communicants of the
said new Dutch Church in Schenectady aforesaid, be and shall
be from time to time and at all times forever hereafter, a body
Corporate and Politick in Deed, fact and name, by the name of
*the Minister, Elders and Deacons of the Reformed Protestant Dutch
Church of Schenectady in the County of Albany*, and them and their
successors by the name of the Minister, Elders and Deacons of
the Reformed Potestant Dutch Church of Schenectady in the
County of Albany, one body Corporate and Politick in Deed,
fact and Name, really and fully We do for us our Heirs and
Successors erect, make, Constitute Declare and Create by these
presents and that by the same name they and their successors
may and shall have perpetual succession, and shall and may be
Persons able and Capable in the Law to Sue and be sued, to
plead and be impleaded, to answer, and be answered,
and Defend and be Defended in all and singular Suits,
Causes, Quarrells, Matters, Actions and things of what
kind and nature so ever: and also that they and their
successors (by the same name) be and shall be forever
hereafter Capable and Able in Law to have, take, accept of,
Acquire and purchase in fee and forever, or for Life or Lives, or
for years, any messuages, buildings, Houses, Lands, Tenements, Hereditaments and real estate, and and the same to
Lease or Demise for one or more years, or to grant, alien, Bar-

gain, Sell and dispose of for Life, or Lives, or forever under certain yearly rents: and also to accept of, take, and possess and Purchase any Goods, Chattels, or Personal Estate and the same Lett, Sell or Dispose of at will and pleasure; and all this as fully as any other our Liege People, or any Corporation and body Politick within that part of our Kingdom of Great Brittain Called England, or this our Province, may Lawfully do:—Provided that such Messuages and real estate as they or their Successors shall have, or may be Entitled to, shall not at any one time exceed the yearly Rent of Two hundred pounds Current Money of our said Province of New York, over and above the Church and ground on which the same is Erected, Built and stands:—And further we do will and grant that they the said Minister, Elders and Deacons and their successors shall and may forever hereafter have a Common Seal to serve and use for all Matters, Causes, things and affairs whatsoever, of them and their Successors; and the same Seal to alter, change, break and make New from time to time, at their will and pleasure as they think fitt: and we have thought fitt and hereby Publish, Grant, ordain and Declare that our Royal will and pleasure is, that no Person in Communion of the said Reformed Protestant Dutch Church of Schenectady as aforesaid, at any time hereafter, shall be any ways molested, punished, disquieted or Called in Question for any difference in opinion in matters of the Protestant Religion, who do not actually disturb the Civil Peace of our said Province, but that all and every person and persons in Communion of the said Reformed Protestant Dutch Church of Schenectady aforesaid, may from time to time and at all times hereafter, freely and fully have and enjoy his and their own judgments and Consciences in matters of the protestant religious Concernments of the said Reformed Protestant Dutch Church, According to the Constitutions and directions aforesaid, they behaving themselves peaceably and Quietly, and not using this Liberty to Licentiousness, or profaneness, nor to the Civil Injury or outward Disturbance of Others, any Law, Statute, usage or custom of that part of our Kingdom of Great Brittain called England, or of this our Province to the Contrary hereof in any ways notwithstanding:—and for the better ordering and managing the affairs and business of the said Corporation and Church, We do for us, our Heirs and Successors Ordain, direct and appoint that there shall be a perpetual Succession of ministers for the service of God and the Instruction of the Communicants and Members of the said Church in the Christian faith, according to the Constitutions and Directions aforesaid and that the present Minister and every other Minister or Ministers of the said Church hereafter to be called, chosen or appointed, shall each of them re

spectively remain and Continue to be a minister of the said
church, so long as the Elders and Deacons of the said Church
for the time being and all those, who heretofore have been or
hereafter shall have been Elders and Deacons of the said Church
or the Major part of them shall think proper:—and further we
will, ordain and by these presents for us our Heirs and Successors do Declare and appoint that for the better Ordering and
managing the affairs and business of the said Corporation, there
shall be four Elders and four Deacons from time to time Constituted, Elected and Chosen out of the Members of said Church
Inhabiting in Schenectady for the time being, in such manner
and form as is hereafter in these presents expressed, which Per
sons together with the Minister or the Major part of them for
the time being shall apply themselves to take care for the best
disposing and Ordering the general business and affairs of and
concerning the said Church and of and concerning all such
Lands, Tenements, Hereditaments, real and personal Estate as
shall, or may be acquired as aforesaid:—and for the better execution of our Royal pleasure herein, We do for us, our Heirs
and Successors Assign, name, Constitute and appoint the aforesaid Mr. Rinherdt Erricksen to be the present Minister of the said
Church, and the aforesaid John Barentse Wemp, Gerrit Simonse
Veeder, Simon Vrooman, and Robert Yaats to be the present
Elders of the said Church, and Sander Lansinck, Abraham Tre-
aux, Abraham Glen and Arent Samuelse Bratt to be the present
Deacons of the said Church, which Elders and Deacons are to
continue in the said several offices respectively until others be
duly chosen to officiate in their rooms, in manner as is herein-
after expressed:—And further we do will and by these, presents
for us our Heirs and Successors do ordain, appoint and Direct
that the minister of said Church for the time being, or in his
absence from sickness or otherwise, the first Elder of the said
Church for the time being, shall and may from time to time,
upon all occasions Assemble and Call together the said Elders
and Deacons of the said Church for the time being, to consult
and advise of the Business and affairs of the said church:—And
further our will and pleasure is and we do for us, our Heirs and
Successors, Establish, appoint and Direct that on the first Saturday in December next the Minister, Elders and Deacons of the
said Church, or the Major part of them shall, at the said church
chuse, nominate and appoint two of the Communicants of the
said Church to serve as Elders of the said church for the next
ensuing year, in the Rooms and stead of Jan Barentse Wemp
and Gerrit Simonse Veeder, and also two other of the said Com
municants to serve as Deacons for the next ensuing year in the
Rooms and stead of Sander Lansinck and Abraham Treaax:

which said two Elders and Deacons so newly chosen and elected as aforesaid shall on New Years Day next ensueing their nomination and election, Enter upon and take their respective places and continue in and exercise their said respective offices, until other fitt persons shall be Regularly Chosen in their respective rooms; And we do for us, our Heirs and Successors Grant, appoint and direct that yearly once in the year forever hereafter, after the First Day of January next ensuing, that is to say on the first Saturday in December in every year, at the said church, the Ministers Elders and Deacons of the said Church for the time being, or the Major part of them shall nominate, appoint and chuse two of the Communicants of the said Church that shall succeed in the offices of Elders, and two others of their communicants that shall succeed as Deacons in the room, place and stead of the two oldest Elders and two oldest Deacons for the year ensuing, which two Elders and Deasons so newly chosen and Elected as last aforesaid shall on New Years Day next ensueing their nominations of Election take their respective places and continue in and Execute their respective offices, from that time until other fitt persons be respectively Elected in their respective rooms and places ;—And if it shall happen that any or either of the aforesaid Elders and Deacons so to be Elected, nominated or appointed as aforesaid, shall dye, or be removed, or deny, refuse or neglect to officiate in the said respective offices of Elders or Deacons before their or either of their time for Serving therein be expired, that then and in every such case it shall and may be Lawful for the Minister, Elders and Deacons of the said church for the time being, or the Major part of them to proceed in manner aforesaid to a new Election of one or more of their communicants in the room or place of such Officer, or officers dying or Removing or denying, refusing or Neglecting to officiate in his or their respective office or offices as aforesaid ;—And further our Will and pleasure is, and we do, for us, our Heirs and Successors, Declare and Grant that the Patronage, Adowson, Donation or Presentation of and to the said church after the Decease or removal of the said present minister, or next avoidance, shall appertain and belong to and be hereby vested in, the Elders and Deacons of the said reformed Protestant Church of Schenectady for the time being and their successors forever, together with all such as heretofore have been or hereafter shall have been Elders or Deacons of the said church, or the Major part of them ;—Provided allways that the succeeding Ministers that shall be by them, or the major part of them presented, called, instituted and inducted into the said Church, shall bear true Faith and allegiance unto us, our Heirs and Successors anything contained herein to the contrary thereof in anywise notwithstanding;—and our will and pleasure is, and we do further by these presents Grant and Declare that the said present Minister and Incumbent and all others, who shall hereafter be Ministers of the said reformed Protestant Dutch church and shall have the care of the Souls of the said members of the said church, shall not nor shall any of them, be removed from the said church or care unless by and with the Direction, consent and Approbation of the Elders and Deacons and all those that have been or shall have been, Elders and Deacons of the Said church, or the Major part of them;— And our farther will and pleasure is, and we do hereby Further Declare that it shall and may be lawful for the Deacons of the said church for the time being, or any other Person Sufficiently Authorized by them, at all and any time or times when the members of the said church, or any of them, meet and Assemble together in the said church for the publick worship or Service of God, to collect and Gather together the free and voluntary alms of the members of the said church, or other persons congregated as aforesaid, which Alms are to be employed by the Elders and Deacons for the time being, or the Major part of them, unto such pious and charitable uses as they and their Successors or the Major part of them at their Discretion shall think Convenient and Needful;—and our will and pleasure further is, and we do hereby Declare that from time to time as need shall require, one or more able Minister or Ministers Lawfully ordained according to the Constitutions and Directions aforesaid, shall and may be Nominated, Elected, Called and Inducted into the said Protestant Dutch Church, (by the same persons, after the same manner and in the same form as is before Directed and Declared, in Case the said Church or Cure (?) should be vacant either by the death or removal of the present Minister or Incumbent), to be a Preacher or Preachers and Assistants to the said Minister and his Successors, in the Celebration of the Divine offices of praying and Preaching and other Dutys Incident to and to be performed in the said Church as shall be required of him by the ministers, Elders and Deacons of the said Church, for the time being, or the Major part of them and shall likewise from time to time Nominate a bell-ringer and Sexton and such other under officers as they shall stand in need of, to remain in their respective Offices so long as the Minister, Elders and Deacons of the said Church for the time being, or the Major part of them, shall think fitt;—And we do of our Further speciall Grace, Certain knowledge and meer Motion, Give and Grant unto the said Minister, Elders and Deacons of the said Church and their Successors forever, that the Minister, Elders and Deacons of the said Church for the time being or the Major part of them shall have and we have hereby given and Granted unto them, full power and authority from time to time and at all times hereafter, to appoint, alter and change such days and times of meetings as they, or the Major part of them shall think fitt, and to Choose, Nominate and Appoint such and so many of our Liege People as they, or the Major part of them, shall think fitt, who shall be willing to accept of being Members of their said Church and Corporation and body Politick, and them into the same to admitt, and to Elect and Constitute such other officer and officers, as they, or the Major part of them shall think fitt and requisite for the Ordering Managing and dispatching the affairs of the said Church and Corporation ;—and from time to time to make, ordain and constitute such rules, Orders and Ordinances for the Good discipline and Weal of the Members of the said Church and corporation, as they or the Major part of them shall think fitt, so that those rules, orders and Ordinances be not repugnant to the Laws of that part of our Kingdom of Great Brittain called England and of this our Province, or dissonant to the principles of our Protestant Religion, but as near as may be agreeable to our Laws of that part of our Kingdom of Great Brittain called England, and Consonant to the Articles of faith and Worship of God Agreed upon by the aforesaid Synod of Dort :—And further know ye that we of our abundant Grace, Certain knowledge and meer Motion, Have Given, Granted, Ratified and Confirmed, and by these presents for us, our Heirs and successors, do Give, Grant, Ratifye and Confirm unto the said Ministers, Elders and Deacons of the Reformed Protestant Dutch Church of Schenectady in the County of Albany and their Successors, all that the said Church and the ground on which the same stands, which said ground is in Breadth from East to West Sixty-five feet, and in Length from North to South Eighty feet, and all benefits, Profits and appurtenances to the same belonging, or in anywise appertaining.—To have and to hold all and singular the premises aforesaid, with the appurtenances, unto them, the said Minister, Elders and Deacons of the Reformed Protestant Dutch Church of Schenectady in the County of Albany aforesaid and their Successors: to their only proper use and behoof forever, to be holden of us, our Heirs and Successors in free and common Soccage as of our Mannor of East Greenwich in our County of Kent, with that part of our Kingdom of Great Brittain called England yielding, rendring and paying therefor Yearly and every Year forever unto us, our Heirs and Successors on the ffeast day of the Annunciation of the blessed Virgin Mary, at our City of New York, the Annual rent of five shillings Current Money of our said Province, in Lieu and Stead of all other rents, Dues,

Services, Dutys, Claims and Demands Whatsoever for the premises;—and we do further will and grant that in case it should happen the said Church, by any accident, happen to be burned, fall down or come to ruin, the Minister, Elders and Deacons of reformed Protestant Dutch Church of Schenectady in the County of Albany for the time being or the major part of them shall and may Build and Erect another Church, in the same or in any other place in Schenectady aforesaid;—And Lastly we do for us, our Heirs and Successors, Ordain and Grant unto the said Minister, Elders and Deacons of the said Reformed Protestant Dutch Church within Schenectady aforesaid and their Successors, by these presents, that this our Grant shall be firm, good, effectual and available in all things to the Law to all interests, constructions and purposes whatsoever, according to our true Intent and meaning herein before declared; and shall be Construed, reputed and adjudged in all cases most favorable on the behalf and for the best benefit and behoof of the said Minister, Elders and Deacons of the reformed Protestant Dutch Church of Schenectady and their Successors, Although Express mention of the yearly value or certainty of the premises, or any of them, in these presents, is not named or any Statute, Act, Ordinance, Provision Proclamation, or restriction heretofore had, made, enacted, Ordained or Provided, or any other matter, clause, or thing whatsoever, to the Contrary hereof notwithstanding.

In Testimony whereof we have caused these our Letters to be made patent, and the Great Seal of our said Province to be hereunto affixed.

Witness our trusty and well beloved William Cosby Esqr., Capt. General and Governor in Chief of our Province of New York and New Jersey and Territories thereon depending in America, and Vice Admirall of the same, and Collonell in our army in, by and with the advice and consent af our Councill of our Province of New York, at our Fort George in New York the twenty third of August in the Eighth year of our Reign Annoq Domini 1734.

       FRED'K MORRIS D. Secy.

## CHAPTER VII.

1749-1752. DOMINE CORNELIS VAN SANTVOORD, THE FIFTH MINISTER. SUBSCRIPTION FOR THE SUPPORT OF THE MINISTER. NEW PARSONAGE.

During the four years succeeding the departure of Domine Erichzon, the church was without a settled pastor, but was occasionally visited by the ministers of Albany—Domines Van Schie and Van Driessen, and others, who in that time married seventeen couples, baptized 164 children and received thirty three persons to the church.

As early as November, 1736, the Consistory authorised Nicholas Schuyler, one of their number, to send to Holland for a successor to Domine Erichzon. The usual salary of £100 and perquisites were promised, to begin from the day he embarked from Holland.

This negociation, after great delay failed, and in November, 1738, the church authorized Levinus Clarkson and John Livingston, during their stay in Holland, to renew the attempt to procure a pastor, but in case of a second failure, resolved to look elsewhere. After waiting about two years longer without success, the church appointed two of their number, Messrs. Vrooman and Feeling, together with Christopher Bancker and Domine Gualterus Du Bois, of New York, to visit and confer with Domine Cornelis Van Santvoord, of Staten Island, with reference to a call from the Church of Schenectady. At this interview his Consistory demanded in case of his removal, a repayment to them of the expense they had incurred in bringing him from Holland to this country, but were told by Messrs. Vrooman and Feeling that they were not authorized to negotiate in relation to this matter. Subsequently, however, a compromise was effected and in August, 1740, he began his ministry in Schenectady. At the time of his settlement here he was 43 years of age, and had been pastor of the Church of Staten Island twenty-two years. His wife, Anna, daughter of John Staats, of Staten Island, died about the year 1744, and the year following he married Elizabeth Toll, of Schenectady, who also died within two years, without issue. He had eight children by his first wife—three sons, Cornelis, Staats and Zeger, who outlived him, and five daughters, two of whom were not living in 1747. In his will he speaks also of a sister, Jacoba, wife of Zeger Hazebroeck, of Leyden, where he was born and received his education under the direction of Prof. John Marck, of the University of Leyden.*

Domine Van Santvoord was a man of good natural parts and fine culture; he preached not only in his native tongue, but also in the French and English; and the sermons which are preserved by his descendants show him to have been a writer of no mean ability.

"He was an intimate friend of Domine Freylinghuysen, of Raritan, sympathising with him in all his trials, while his learning, acuteness and manly independence qualified him to be his advocate. In this character he appeared in a small volume entitled, '*A Dialogue between Considerans and Candidus.*'† He translated Prof. Marck's Commentary on the Apocalypse, adding much to it by his own reflections. He sent it to Holland for approval, and it was not only approved, but adorned with a copious preface by Prof. Wesselius. The high respect entertained and shown by Mr. Van Santvoord for Prof. Marck was but the counterpart of the professor's esteem for him. He declared that Mr. Van Santvoord was one of his most distinguished and apt pupils, and he was honored by the professor's friendship to the end of his life."‡

Under his ministry the church enjoyed a good degree of prosperity. During the twelve years of his pastorate, he married 174 couples, baptized 645 children and received 151 members to the church. His sudden demise at the early age of 55 years was a sad loss to the town. On Christmas day, December 25, 1751, he was well enough to preach: his text was Luke II, 13, 14; seven days after, on New Year's day, he again ascended the pulpit but being too weak to address the congregation closed

---

* There is a *tradition* among his descendants that while living in Schenectady he saw a vision of his sister Jacoba, then living in Leyden. He noted the occurrence and learned afterward that she died at the hour when her apparation was seen by him.

[† This work, a copy of which is now in the possession of the Rev. Talbot W. Chambers, D.D., of New York, has been translated into English by the Rev. W. G. Hamen, of Coxsackie, N. Y. W. E. G.]

‡ Brownlee's discourse.

the service with a prayer and the customary New Year's blessing.* Six days afterward, January 6, 1752, he died.†

For nearly three years succeeding the death of Domine Van Santvoord the church was destitute of a pastor, and only occasionally visited by a minister. Domine Theodorus Freylinghuysen, of Albany, most commonly supplied the pulpit—sometimes a pastor from a more distant church, as Domine Vrooman, of New Paltz, or a divinity student.‡

In this time thirteen couples were married, 119 children baptised and fifty-seven persons added to the church.

Preparatory to calling a new pastor the church opened a subscription, in 1752, for the support of the ministry—the amounts subscribed to be paid yearly and the subscribers, of whom there were 168, also agreeing to increase their seat rent from five to six shillings each and to forfeit their sittings, provided this sum was not paid within six months after it became due.

---

[* See page 22. This ancient form of the New Year's blessing was effectively and beautifully spoken upon the people by Domine Wortman, on Monday evening, June 21, 1880. W. E. G.]

† "1751 Den 25 December heeft Do. Van Santvoort zyn laaste predikatie gedaen op Kersdag en zyn text was uyt Lucas 2 Verse 13, 14, Luydende aldus ;—Ende Van Stonden den was doer met den Engel ean menighte des hemelschen heyrlegers prysende Godt ende seggende &c. Agt [seven] dayen daar na op neuwe year heeft hy de stoel Weder beklommen meer te swak synde omte preek heeft hy syn Dienst voor het laaste besloten met een gebet ende segen sens gewoonelyk op neuwe year, en is 6 dagen daarna te weten op den 6 Januare 1752 in de heere gerust."—Abraham DeGraaf's Bible.

‡ The church treasurer's book shows the following sums paid for occasional supplies during this period :

| | | | | |
|---|---|---|---|---|
| 1752 | April 8. | Dom. Freylinghuysen, | | £3-10- |
| " | Aug. 10. | do do | | 3- |
| " | Dec. 27. | do do | | 3- |
| 1753 | 30 April. | do do | | 3- |
| " | Aug. 13. | do do | | 5- |
| " | 19 Aug. | Dom. Vrooman, | | 5- |
| " | 10 Sept. | do Freylinghuysen, | | 1- |
| " | 18 Dec. | do do | | 3-10- |
| 1754 | Jan. | een Student, | | 1- 4- |
| " | " | Dom. Freylinghuysen, | | 1- |
| " | Mar. 16. | do Vrooman | | 5- 4- |
| | | do Menema | | 1- 4- |
| | | De student Henderikus Freylinghuysen | | 1- 4- |
| | | Goetschius,—Student | | 1- 4- |

The sums subscribed varied from one to thirty-six shillings, and amounted in all to £66–2 ($165.25). This together with the rents from seats, church Mill, Eenkluy's "poor pasture," and the quit rents from farms donated by the Trustees of the Common Lands, made a sum sufficient to meet the current expenses of the church.

The ancient parsonage house on the East corner of Union and Church streets had now stood about fifty years and was falling into decay. It was removed, therefore, in 1753, and a new one, a story and a half high, was erected on the same lot. It was built in the pointed Dutch style fronting Union street, with two rooms in front and a gable above the middle door. This house stood about 60 years until it gave place to the church of 1814.*

## CHAPTER VIII.

1754–1784. DOMINE BARENT VROOMAN THE SIXTH MINISTER.

The sixth minister of the church was Domine Barent Vrooman. He was the first native of the Province and the only one of this city ever called to this sacred office. His great grandfather, Hendrick Meese Vrooman, one of the pioneer settlers of the place, together with his son Bartholomew was killed in 1690, in the sacking of the Village by the French. Among those who escaped was his son Adam, whose wife and child were massacred, whilst his sons Wouter and Barent were carried away captive into Canada, whence they did not return until many years after. Wouter was but ten years old when thus cruelly separated from his parents. On his return he married Marytie Hallenbeck, of Albany, about the year 1708. Thirteen children were the issue of this marriage, of whom nine were living in 1748, when the father made his will. He died Oct. 26th, 1756, aged 75 years.

---

* The bricks used in its construction were made by Jacobus Van Vorst at £1. ($2.50) a thousand. The masons were Gillis Van Vorst, William Hall, Jan Baptist Van Vorst and Ephraim Smith—the carpenters, Nicolaas De-Graaf and Johannes Hall; and the smith, Harmanus Hagadorn.
—Church treasurer's book.

The subject of this notice, the eleventh child of Wouter Vrooman, was born on the 24th of December, 1725. He began his studies for the ministry under the direction of Do. Van Santvoord and finished them with Do. Theodore Frelinghuysen, of Albany. Having received a call to the church of New Paltz, Feb. 4th, 1751, he sailed for Holland soon after to complete his theological studies at the University of Utrecht and obtain ordination. On the 7th of Jan., 1752, he was licensed and on the 7th of Mar., 1753, was ordained by the classis of Utrecht. He sailed soon after from fatherland with three other young clergymen—Johannes Schuneman, Jacobus and Ferdinandus Frelinghuysen, of whom the last two died at sea of the small pox.\*

After visiting his friends in Schenectady he returned to New Paltz, and on the 26 of Aug., 1753, was inducted into his office as pastor of the congregation of New Paltz, Shawangunk and Wallkil. His parish embraced a territory of more than two hundred square miles; and the ancient church whose corner stone was laid by his hands is still used as a house of worship.

The church in Schenectady had been without a pastor more than two years when he returned from Holland, and it does not appear that within this time they had made any attempt to find one, but within one month after Do. Vrooman's Installation at New Paltz they gave him a call here.

These facts seem to show that from the time of Do. Van Santvoord's death they had only awaited his return to make him his successor.

Although his *beroepbrief*, or call, is dated Sept. 18th, 1753, he was not dismissed from his charge at Wallkil until Oct. 29th, 1754.

---

\* "We announce with great sorrow that the Messrs. Freylinghuysen (Jacobus and Ferdinandus) have, while at sea, been removed from this life by small pox, to the great regret of their surviving brethren, and of the Congregations for whom they had been ordained to the ministry, by the laying on of hands of your Reverend Body.

In the meantime, the other two gentlemen, Vrooman and Schunemen, have been installed in their congregations, in the hope that they will be faithful instruments, in the hand of Jesus, for the extension of his gracious kingdom."

Letter of the Coetus to the Classis of Amsterdam 19th Sept. 1753.
—Min. Gen. Synod I, LXXXVIII.

## HISTORY OF THE CHURCH.

Call for the Reverend and Learned Domine Barent Vrooman, minister at the Paltz, Walenkill, &c., in Ulster county, as pastor and teacher of the Low Dutch Reformed Church of Jesus Christ, here at Schenectady, in the County of Albany, in the Province of New York.

Since, God, who rules and orders all things according to the counsel of His own will, in His adorable good pleasure has been pleased to our great grief, to deprive our Church of Schenectady in the Province of New York, of their Reverend pastor and teacher, Cornelis Van Santvoord, who rested in the Lord on the 5th of January, 1752, and since the Consistory of our said church after the death of our aforenamed teacher, Cornelis Van Santvoordt, with the consent and approbation of the Great Consistory, have endeavored under God's Holy blessing, to choose and call here a pious minister; but it has not until now, pleased the Lord that we should make a call; and as it has pleased God, who rules and orders all things to grant your Reverence a safe arrival out of Holland, at your birth place here in Schenectady to your Honored father and friends, where at the request of the Consistory, your reverence has five times preached and proclaimed the gospel to us to the great satisfaction of our whole church; and having seen your pious and praiseworthy gifts, and edifying talents, after mature deliberation, and with the general assent and unanimity of the Great Consistory assembled on the 15th of this month we resolved in the fear of the Lord, to call you, the Rev. Barent Vrooman, as the pastor and teacher of our church here at Schenectady. Wherefore the present Consistory of the Low Dutch Reformed Church of Schenectady, Hendrick Brouwer, John Sanders, Cornelis Van Slyck and Gerret A. Lansignh, elders, and Simon Tol, Johannes Hall, Elias Post and Johannes Van Antwerpen, Deacons, do in our names herewith call the Reverend, pious and learned Domine Barent Vrooman as our public pastor the Holy word purely to preach, the Holy Sacraments" according to the Institution of Christ to administer—to catechise—to exercise ecclesiastical discipline and oversight over this Church; and furthermore all things to do that the office of a faithful servant of Jesus Christ enjoins, according to the rules of the Christain Synod of Dordrecht, holden in the years 1618 and 1619, and in use in the Low Dutch reformed Churches here established. And for your more especial and particular information, it will be your Reverence's duty, when in health, to preach every Lord's day twice, and in the afternoon to treat of subjects from the catechism according to the the order of the Heidelbergh Catechism; and the children twice a week to catechise—that is on Sunday after the second sermon and during the week on the day which your Reverence shall please to elect—on Easter, Whitsunday, Christmas and other festivals to preach, as hitherto among us has been the edifying custom; four times a year the Holy Communion to celebrate; to visit the households of the church twice a year in Schenectady and once a year in the neighborhood, and to baptise and register the Christian children.

And that your Reverence while among us may have nothing to do but to preach in the church, we promise your Reverence in accordance with the power granted us by our great consistory, on the 15th day of this month of September and with the assent of our church, that a yearly salary of one hundred and ten pounds current money of the Province of New York—a just fourth part at the end of every quarter year from time to time during your Reverence's faithful service and ministration here at Schenectady shall be paid promptly by the ruling consistory or by their order; and your salary shall commence from the day of your dismissal from your church of the Paltz, Waalenkil, &c.

Moreover your Reverence shall have a good house belonging to us rent free and kept in good repair, a good garden kept in fence, also free pasture for two cows, and a horse if your Reverence be pleased to keep one, and sixty loads of fire wood delivered at the door yearly.

All this we promise you by virtue of the beforementioned order and resolution of our church, for the making up of a sufficient salary; and for the precise performance of the same, we bind and obligate ourselves and our successors, as Elders and Deasons of our church for the time being.

This then being our affectionate and final call to you, the Reverand, pious and learned Barent Vrooman in the name of our church of Schenectady, it is our persistent desire that you (considering the necessities of our church in respect to its much desired edification and the upbuilding of the same in the most holy faith) will please to accept, with hearty inclination this our

Christian call, in the name of the Lord—in our behalf and in the name of the whole church promising to hold your Reverence in such esteem, love and honor as is due to an upright teacher in a Reformed Church.

We likewise request the honored bretheren, the elders and deacons of the church of the Paltz, Waalenkil, &c., and those to whom this our call shall be offered, as speedily as possible, to dismiss the Reverend Domine Barent Vrooman from his service at the Paltz, Waalenkil, etc., to which end the church of Schenectady recognize the justice of their sharing with the aforesaid church of the Paltz, Waalenkil, &c., in the expense to which they were put in sending Domine Vrooman over to Holland to be ordained.

Finally, we pray the great Shepherd of the sheep this our call to follow with his divine blessing, that the same may redown to the magnifying of God's holy name, the upbuilding of his church and the winning and salvation of many souls. Amen.

Thus done by us, the present Consistory of the Low Dutch Reformed Protestant Church at Schenectady, and with the seal of our church ratified the 18th day of September *Anno* 1753.

Signed and sealed with the seal of our Church in the presence of us, Isaac Vrooman, John Fairley.

hendrick Brouwer, Elder
John Sanders, "
Cornelis Van Sleyk, "
Gerrit a Lansing, "
Seymon Tol,
Johannis Hall,
Elias Post,
Johannis V. Antwerpen.

Domine Vrooman arrived in Schenectady on the first day of November, 1754, and on the third day preached his first sermon.*
On the 17th he was installed, Domine Frelinghuysen, of Albany, preaching the sermon on that occasion.

The expense and trouble of calling a minister 100 years ago is very imperfectly understood by those of the present day. All candidates in theology were obliged to spend more or less time at a University in Fatherland, and after their ordination they

---

* Nov. 1 1754, Domine Vroman heir gekomen.
Nov. 3, syn eerste text Jesaias III, 10, 11. Segget den regtveerdigen dat het hem wel gaan sal, &c.
—Abraham De Graaf's Bible.

returned at the expense of the churches calling them. In case of a subsequent removal it was customary for the church making the call to pay a portion of this expense.

The call of Domine Vrooman cost the church of Schenectady $563, nearly half of which was paid to the three churches of New Paltz, Walkil and Shawangunk.

The various items of expenditures are shown in the following statement drawn up by the Consistory:

" A memorandum of expenditures made by the Consistory in calling Do. Vrooman from New Paltz:*

| | |
|---|---|
| 1753. To Cornelis Van Slyck and Isaac Vrooman to tender the call.............................. | £5-12-0 |
| 1754. To Joseph R Yates for his horse 12 days for Philip Reylie to make inquiry concerning his coming ............................. | 1- 4-0 |
| Sept. To Gerrit H. Lansing and Joseph R. Yates, by order of the full Consistory, sent to New York to request Do. Vrooman's dismission by the Cœtus there, in the presence of Do. Vrooman, which was found fruitless............ | £6- 8-0 |
| To the Skipper for bringing up some goods from New York and for riding the same from Albany for Do. Vrooman....................... | 1-13-0 |
| To Abraham Mebie and Isaac Vrooman to fetch the Domine from his station at New Paltz and satisfy those churches—for their expense and trouble having been gone 16 days with their horses........................... | 12- 0-0 |
| To Claas Van Patten for shoeing a horse.......... | 2- 6-0 |
| To three ministers who gave the Domine his dismission there and wrote the call—for their trouble ................................ | 10- 0-0 |
| For a sloop hired to bring up the Domine's goods from Sopus ................................ | 4-10- |

---

\* Een memorie van de koste die de Kerkenraat Gedaen hebbe voor Dom: Vrooman te beroepe van de pals in als volght vizt:

| | |
|---|---|
| 1753. An Cornelis V. Slyck En Isack Vrooman voor het Beroep hem an te biede................................................................. | £5-12-0 |
| 1754. An Joseph R. Yates voor 12 Dage van zyn paert met Philip Reylie om Een ondersack to Doen van zyn komst............ | 1- 4-0 |

| | | |
|---|---|---|
| For traveling expenses of Abraham Mebie and Isaac Vrooman | | 2– 7–2 |
| To £50 in satisfaction for a horse from the churches for Do. Vrooman | | 50– 0–0 |
| To £19–14 as a payment to the church of New Paltz | | 19–14–0 |
| 1756, May 22, To £66–6 as a payment to the church of Do. Vrooman at Shawangunk and Walkil | | 66– 6–0 |
| | | £182–0–6 |
| To the Consistory of New Paltz" | | 43 |
| Total...........[$563] | | £225–0–6 |

In 1774, and for several succeeding years he officiated occasionally at Caughnawaga, for which he received an additional compensation of £25 yearly from his Consistory. The depreciation of the currency during the revolutionary war compelled the church to raise the nominal salary of their pastor. Thus, in 1770, by reason of "*de scaarse tyden*," they agree to add to it £12 quarterly.

On June 25, 1779, the church paid a half year's salary in the following sums:

"To Domine Vrooman 500 dollars Continental at 5 for one," ............... £200– 0–0
"To ditto in hard money .................. 5– 0–0
and £10 in corn from the mill," * .......... 10– 0–0

On 10th of September, a quarterly salary was paid as follows:
"To Domine Vroomon 462 Dolls and 1-6,"........ £184–17–6
"And in hard money ............................ 3– 6–6
"at 10 for one the money being so bad." †

Domine Vrooman's final sickness commenced about 1780, from which time he was frequently aided by his clerical brethren from abroad—Rev. Elias Van Benschoten of Schaghticoke, Rev. Theodoric Romeyn of Hackensack, N. J., Rev. Jacob R. Hardenburgh of Marbletown, Rev. Nicholas Lansing of Living-

---

* Aen Domine Vrooman 500 Dolders Contenenteel en 5 voor een... £200–
Aen ditto Vrooman aen hart gelt...... .................................... 5–
ande £10 aen koren uyt de meulen voor een half yaer tractament.

† Aen Domine Vrooman 462 Dolders en 1-6.......... ............ £184–17–6
ende aen hart gelt............................................,........... 3– 6–6
Voor ¼ yaer tractement tegen 10 voor een het gelt so sleght te syn.

ston Manor, and others. For these occasional services the consistory usually paid from £3–5 to £4 (8 to 10 Dolls.) for each Sabbath's services, which sum seems to have included travelling expenses. In the spring of 1784 his condition became hopeless, and on March 11th the consistory resolved to call another minister to be co pastor with him, who, they say, "has now for a long time in God's Providence been visited with a dangerous palsy in his right side, which has afflicted his Reverence to that degree as wholly to incapacitate him for the performance of Divine service." *

On the 4th of April the Consistory came to an understanding with him, by which he was to continue to receive his salary of £110 and £10 yearly for the rent of a house, and if he recovered was to officiate half the time in the church with Do. Romeyn, whom they had called on that day. He lived to see his successor installed and died on the 13th of Nov. 1784, at the age of 59 years.

He was married to Alida, daughter of David Vander Heyden, of Albany, on the 12th of January, 1760. She survived him nearly 50 years, dying in 1823, aged 99 years. The fruit of this marriage was three children,—David, Maria Dorothea and Walterus. The last two lived to mature age. Maria married John Louis Victor Le Tonnelier, by whom she had one son, the late Dr. John Samuel Le Tonnelier of New York. David left no descendants.

The following notices of Do. Vrooman and his people are taken from the Essex (Mass.) Institute Historical collections :

1758. "Dined with Domine Vrooman Predikant in Schenectady—in height 6 feet 4 inches and ½, and everyway large in proportion; preaches without notes with little premeditation. Explains a text A. M., and preaches Divinity in ye afternoon, as he has bin pleas'd to inform me several times. The People here attend their Publick religious exercises with great Devotion."

[Extracts from Rev. Daniel Shute's Journal.]

---

\* \* \* \* die nu alvoor langh tydt, onder het Vreymatige der Godelyke Voorsienigheidt besoght is gewest, met eene gevaarlyke Beroerte in syn reghte syde welke syn E. dermaten heeft aangetroffen dat syn E. gansch onbekwaam is ter Waarneminge van den Evangelie Dienst.

—Consistory Minutes.

1758. "Tuesday [June] 20th, this day tarried at Schenectady, took some view of the town, which is very pleasantly and compactly situated; according to my judgement it is large as Charlestown, near Boston; they have a stone chh, or meeting-house; the minister is a Dutchman and so are the generality of the people."

22. "Thursday. We attended prayers and then supped at our new lodgings, having dined with Domine Vroom[an] the Dutch minister of Schenectady."

24. "Saturday. At prayers this evening I made a speech of some length to the Regiment as they were to march the next day early; there were present many of the towns people, both men and women. The people of the town are very sorry that we must march from them.

The People of Schenectady were quite a civil and they have quite a good sort of a man to their Minister."

[Extract from the journal of Rev. John Cleveland, Chaplain of Col. Jonathan Bagley's Regiment in the French war of 1758].

During his pastorate of 30 years Do. Vrooman married 386 couples,* baptised 3,521 children and received to the church 453 members.†

Time has destroyed most of the traditions of his ministry; it is stated, however, by one who knew the fathers of this church in the early years of this century, "that Domine Vrooman had more heart than Doctor Romeyn, and did more to gain the hearts of the people—was more familiar and social. The latter was elevated and perhaps distant—had far more learning, was more intellectual and theological, but not so popular."

* From June 25th, 1775, to June 9th, 1775, no record was made (or if made has been lost) of any marriages, and only three for the year 1766.

† From October, 1772, to July 19th, 1783, no members were received according to the record. Do. Romeyn's complete list, however, made in 1785, soon after his arrival, shows that 18 members were then living who were received in 1773, but that in the nine years intervening between 1773 and 1783 none were admitted to the church.

## CHAPTER IX.

1784–1804.   DOMINE ROMEYN THE SEVENTH MINISTER.   AGITATION OF THE CHURCH ABOUT ENGLISH PREACHING.

With the waning century passed away many of the ancient church customs inherited from Fatherland. Domine Romeyn was the last of that long line of ministers who had from the days of Thesschenmaecker conducted the entire services of the church in the Dutch language. His active spirit infused a new influence into the church and little community; an influence which is felt to this time in the educational institutions of the city.

He was born in Hackensack, N. J., the youngest child of Nicholas Romeyn and Rachel Vreeland. The rudiments of his education he acquired partly under the tuition of his brother, the Rev. Thomas Romeyn, then minister of the Reformed Dutch churches on the Delaware, and partly under that of the Rev. Doctor Johannes H. Goetschius, pastor of the Reformed Dutch churches of Hackensack and Schraalenbergh, N. J. In 1763 he became a member of Princetown College, then under the care of President Finley, and was graduated in 1765.

"At the early age of nine years it pleased God, as he hoped, to make him a subject of his special grace. He made a public profession of his faith in the Lord Jesus either at the close of his 16th or at the beginning of his 17th year. Contemplating the work of the ministry from the time when it pleased God to call him by his grace, he combined the acquisition of theology with that of human knowledge. In consequence of this he was early qualified to offer himself for the ministry to the Reverend Coetus of the Reformed Dutch Church. That body, after two days of examination, sustained his trials and admitted him into the ministry. He was ordained by the Rev. John Schureman and the Rev. Johannes H. Goetsching, as pastor of the united churches of Marbletown, Rochester and Wawarsinck, on the 14th of May, 1766. In 1775 he accepted a call from the united congregations of Hackensack and Schraalenbergh in New Jersey, and was installed pastor of the same by Rev. Samuel Ver bryck. Here he remained throughout the Revolutionary war, preaching whenever he could, suffering with his people and encouraging them by his word and example." *

In 1778, six years before Do. Vrooman's death, this church invited Do. Romeyn to visit Schenectady, apparently with the intent of calling him to be their assistant minister. †It was not, however, until April, 1784 that the formal call was tendered. After due deliberation it was accepted on the 26th of August, ‡ and on the first Sabbath of November he was installed by the Rev. Dr, Westerlo, of Albany. ‖

The salary promised in this call was £140 ($350), with free house rent, garden, pasture for two cows and a horse, and seventy loads of fire wood delivered at the door. In 1796 this was raised to £200 with the promise of a pension of £30 to his widow in case of his death, and in 1797 £100, and in 1798 and 1799 £50 were added to his regular salary on account of the high price of provisions. **

Among his first labors in Schenectady was an attempt to improve the schools and establish an Academy and seminary. †† The result was a charter for Union College, which institution he lived to see commence its prosperous career under the management of Doctors John Blair Smith, Jonathan Edwards and Jonathan Maxey. ‡‡

For some years after his settlement here this was the only Dutch Reformed church within the ancient limits of the town, and as a consequence the congregation then quite numerous, was much scattered, and the pastoral care laborious. In a communication to the Consistory made in 1793, Do. Romeyn states that the accountable members of the church amounted to a few

---

\* Alden's Epitaphs, IV, 223.
† Letter dated Mar. 14, 1778.
‡ Letter.
‖ Alden's Epitaphs IV, 223.—Do. Westerloo was paid for his services on this occasion, £9-6-8.
\*\* Church books.
†† 17th May, 1785. The Reverend President [Romeyn] reported in the village of Schenectady some disasters relative to the school to be established at that place had prevented the scheme from being carried into effect: wherefore the matter of a Seminary at that place is further intrusted to the gentlemen appointed on the Committee.        —Min. Gen. Synod, I, 135.
‡‡ Appendix B.

less than 600, who were so scattered that it was impossible for one minister to look after them. Whereupon the Consistory took into consideration the calling of a second minister, and resolved to call a meeting of the Great Consistory to deliberate on this matter.

On the third of September the Great Consistory approved of the project, but counselled the acting consistory to increase the subscription for a second minister, to £150.* Acting in accordance with this advice, on the 1st day of October, 1794, three persons were proposed from whom a choice was to be made, viz. :

Rev. Nicholas Van Vranken, of Fishkill, Rev. James Van Campen Romeyn, of Greenbush, and Proponent Jacob Sickels.

The first named was chosen, and on the 7th of Nov., the consistory resolved to pay him a salary of £200, sixty loads of wood free pasture for a horse and two cows, or £25 yearly instead and one-half the perquisites of the office.

March 16th 1795, Do. Van Vranken answered that he would perhaps accept the call provided a house were furnished him—a condition which was not complied with, for on the 27th of April he declined the call and the consistory thereupon appointed Mr. Jacob Sickels, then a student of theology. He came to Scheuectady in October, 1795, and remained nearly two years, leaving in the summer of 1797.

After his departure Do. Romeyn remained sole minister of the church for five years with the exception of the occasional assistance of a *Catechiser* for the children. †

—————————————————

—*Consistory minutes.

† 25 Dec. 1798. The Consistory, considering the propriety of appointing a person to catechise the youth and others of this congregation in the country, recommended to the succeeding consistory the appointment of Mr. Harmanus Van Vleck as suited to this work.

4 June, 1799. Agreeable to the recommendation of the 25th December last, the consistory proceeded to appoint H. Van Vleck "to catechise the youth of this congregation for six months ; one week on the North and the other on the South side of the river nnd so on alternately ; and that he attend two or three days in the week at such places as the consistory shall recommend, and that he receive for such service at the end of six months the sum of £25."

—Consistory minutes.

And though the duties required of him in maintaining the oversight of so large and scattered a congregation was a severe tax upon his physical power, his first serious illness did not occur until the summer of 1801,* when the church granted him a much needed vacation, and at the beginning of the following year set about in earnest the procuring a coadjutor. †

By the middle of the year 1802 he became permanently incapacitated for the full performance of his ministerial duties and agreed to relinquish all claims upon the church under his call and to accept instead a salary of $520. He was required to preach but one sermon on the Sabbath—in Dutch. ‡

In October the church called the Rev. John Hardenburg Meier, of New Paltz, as an assistant minister, and in the spring following he entered upon his labors. Dr. Romeyn survived nearly a year and closed his labors on earth on the 16th of April, 1804, at the age of 60 years.

He married Elizabeth, daughter of Wessel and Catharine (Dubois) Brodhead, of Ulster county, June 11, 1767.

Two children arrived at maturity—John Brodhead Romeyn, who died 22d of February, 1825, in his 47th year, pastor of the Cedar Street Church, New York, and Catharine Theresa, wife of Caleb Beck, of Schenectady.

Mrs. Romeyn died at Schenectady Jan. 27, (?) 1815, aged 74 years, 7 months and 11 days.

During Dr. Romeyn's ministry in Schenectady, he married 945 couples, baptised 3541 children, and received to the

---

* 3d Aug. 1801. "Dr. Romeyn, our Pastor, having been visited with indisposition such as requires relaxation and exercise, therefore requested leave of absence for a time to recover his health."

"Resolved that leave be given him accordingly in confidence that he will resume his service as soon as he is able."  —Consistory Min.

† 1st Mar. 1802, the Consistory called a meeting of the Great Consistory to consider the state of the church, &c., and in view of Dr. Romeyn's age and growing infirmities, "Resolved that it is expedient to call a second minister."
—Consistory Minutes.

‡ 30th Aug. 1802. The nature of Dr. Romeyn's disease is shown in the preamble to the resolutions passed by the Consistory on this occasion.

"Whereas it has pleased Divine Providence to afflict this congregation by a visitation of his faithful servant, the Rev. Dirck Romeyn, our worthy pastor, with an infirmity apparently partaking in its nature of the palsy, &c."
—Consistory Minutes.

church 248 members. In the beginning of the year 1785 he made a complete list of the members living, which amounted to 414.

Doctor Romeyn* was a man, who lived not for himself, but for God and his fellow-creatures. To his exertions the public are indebted, first for the Academy, which formerly existed in Schenectady, and afterward for the establishment of Union College in that place. In 1797 the General Synod of the Reformed Dutch Church elected him one of their Professors of Theology."

"He was blessed with a vigorous mind. His passions were strong but they were controlled by reason and grace. His literary, scientific and professional acquirements were so respectable as to entitle him to a rank among the first of his brethren in his own or any sister church. He was open and frank in his disposition, affable and unassuming in his manners. He was possessed of a noble independence of spirit, and few have ever displayed an equal liberality of conduct.

In the discharge of his duty he exhibited the zeal of the primitive disciples of Jesus, and he never knew what it was to fear the face of any man upon earth. His boldness of address like that of Paul, was not unfrequently sufficient to make a Felix tremble. He was solemn in his rebukes, tender in his expostulations and pursuasive in his instructions. The style of his preaching was bold, plain, pungent, intelligent, sometimes pathetic and always eloquent. His sermons, the fruit of deep investigation, were replete with the most important and most interesting instruction, and they were uniformly delivered in the most natural and impressive manner; yet the Great Head of the church did not see fit to grant him that extensive visible success, which often attend the labors of those who to human appearance, are greatly his inferiors as to ministerial abilities and graces. It was in reference to this fact that his son added the scriptural passage which forms a part of his monumental inscription. The rest of the epitaph was written—except the dates and those parts depending upon them—by Doctor Romeyn himself.

The subject of this article was an able counsellor, a sincere friend, an honest man, a dignified and affectionate husband and parent.

---

* The following estimate of Dr. Romeyn's character is taken from Alden's Epitaphs, IV, 223.

He was but once married and left two children, a son and a daughter."

"The late Rev. John H. Meier, colleague and successor of the venerable Doctor Romeyn, delivered a sermon, occasioned by his death, from the manuscript copy of which the following characteristic sketch is here preserved."

"Perhaps no period of his life was filled up with more affecting and trying incidents than during his stay among that people (his first charge). For the space of seven years he was in a state of continued exile by means of the war, and subject with his family to all its painful calamities.

"In all his perils and sojournings to and fro, a merciful God preserved his servant in his way and gave him once more, upon the return of peace, to return to his home and his charge in peace and safety.

"Since his advent to this place the details of his life are better known to you than to me. They are doubtless still fresh in the memory of you all. Besides others of an ordinary nature, he has uniformly had in view the prosecution of two peculiarly favorite and highly interesting objects. From the moment he arrived among you he contemplated the establishment of a college, nor did he lose sight of his object, until by uninterrupted exertions and the co-operation of others he compassed his wishes and gained his purpose. It is perhaps but justice to declare that to his more than to the exertions of any other person we are indebted for the present Institution. The other object equally near and more dear to his heart, for which he labored with equal zeal and perseverance, was the extension of the Church. Much praise is due to him for his unwearied and unremitted exertions in this respect. They were crowned with success, and the wilderness is glad in consequence thereof. Whilst in this quarter of Zion he has yielded his church and its interests the most essential services, may these be duly appreciated and rightly acknowledge.

"He has been particularly successful in training young men for the ministry. Appointed at first by the judicature of his church to the office of a teacher and afterwards in 1797, to the office of professor of theology, he continued to discharge the incumbent duties with honor to himself and to the benefit of others till the close of this life. The pupils of his care lift up their voices in the cities and instruct in the wilds. As an evidence of the high respect he commanded in society he was twice honored with the offer of the Presidency of Queens [now Rutger's] College, and received at her hand, as a tribute of respect due to his merit, the degree of Doctor of Divinity.

"He maintained through life a conspicuous and elevated standing, was respected and revered, and departed this life with a high and well-earned reputation. After having run well and served his God in the Gospel for the space of thirty-eight years, he finished his course in the sixty-first year of his age on the 16th day of April, 1804.

"The Rev. Doctor Romeyn was of manly stature, tall and portly, dignified in his mien and commanding in his manners and address. He, moreover, possessed a mind strong and energetic and more than ordinarily comprehensive, capable of viewing thing in their natures, their connexions, their dependencies and ends. His apprehension was quick, his understanding clear and informed. His judgement was sound and mature and his memory remarkably retentive. In the application of these powers of mind he was chiefly bent upon his professional studies. In these he most delighted and labored the most of all to excel. He, however, had also a thirst for the Pierian Spring, and pressed forward to the scholar's goal. He was well versed in the circles of general science, well read in history and had made no mean attainments in the philosphy of the human mind. In this latter his talent perhaps was most improvable. To him the name of scholar and divine was not misapplied.

"In the discharge of his ministerial functions he proved himself an able minister of the New Testament—a watchman that needed not to be ashamed. As he had loved the doctrines of Grace and had experienced their power and influence on his own heart, so also he insisted upon them in his public ministrations. His theme universally was Christ and him crucified. His manner was bold, intrepid and daring. In the execution of his duties he was neither daunted nor moved. He was the Boanerges of the day. When he reproved the sinner trembled. When he pronounced Ebal's curses against the wicked, it was like the thunders of Sinai. He was, however, not incapable of the pathetic. He could at times move the heart and melt the audience into tears. His discourses were solid and interesting.

ofttimes enlivened by historical anecdotes. In the introduction of these he was peculiarly happy. He always entered deep into his subject. His delivery was animated and unaffected, without ostentation and becoming his subject. He aimed at nothing but what was perfectly natural.

"In his intercourse with the world he supported a becoming dignity. Independence of action marked his path through its busy rounds. He knew not how to dissemble. He was polite to all, familiar with few. This rendered the circle of his intimates contracted and the number of his confidential friends small. In his conversation he was interesting, always instructing. His family, in him, have lost an affectionate relative, a watchful guardian, and a great example; the church a pillar, and society an ornament.

"He was an ardent advocate of religious and civil liberty. This he evinced by resisting the pretentions of the mother church in Holland, and by his firm attachment to the principles of the Revolution."

During the ministry of Dr. Romeyn the church was seriously disturbed on the subject of English preaching. Thirty years before, in 1764, this innovation had been first made, in the Dutch church of New York city, by the Rev. Dr. Archibald Laidlie.

English had been the official language of the executive and legislative branches of the government, as well as the judiciary of the Province, from the time of the surrender by the Dutch in 1664, and before the close of the last century was better understood, perhaps, by the youths of the villages and cities than their native Dutch.

In 1794, when the agitation commenced, there were two churches in Schenectady—the Episcopal and Presbyterian, in which weekly services were held in the English language.

To prevent the members of the Dutch congregation from being enticed away from their own church, on the 6th of February, 1794, Messrs. Joseph Yates, Abram Oothout, Dirk Van Ingen and Stephen N. Bayard, leading members of the church, appeared before the Consistory and called their attention to the necessity of calling a second minister and to the increasing of the religious services in the English language, "to the end that the church be not scattered." *

---

* ten eynde de Gemeente niet verstroyt werde."

Dr. Romeyn read to them the action of the Consistory and Great Consistory, of the 27th of August and 3d of September last, and the Consistory again resolved to use their best endeavors to increase the subscription for a second minister.

To carry out the suggestion made by these gentlemen, one week later, to wit: on the 13th day of February, 1794, the Consistory resolved:

1st, That for all coming time so long as there are twenty families in the church, who attend Divine Service in the church of the village, who contribute from time to time with others their just proportion for the maintenance of Divine Service, and who declare that they can be better instructed in the Dutch than in any other tongue, so long, either the forenoon or afternoon sermon in the church of the village shall be delivered in the Dutch and the other in the English tongue. *

2d, The Consistory say that when a second minister shall be called, there shall be a Sunday evening service in Dutch, so long as it shall be well attended, but if it be neglected they will make such other arrangements as shall be best for the prosperity of the church.

3d, That the catechetical exercises shall be in a different language from the evening sermon.

4th, That when the church shall have two ministers, one shall preach once a fortnight in the *Woestyne*. †

And the weekly evening lecture shall be in a different language from the Sunday evening sermon. ‡

It is quite evident the above concession was anything but a peace offering and that it carried too much English and too little Dutch, for on the 17th day of June, 1794 the Great Consistory were called together again to confer respecting English

---

* 1, Dat in all toekomende tydt zo lange 'ez twentig famelien zyn in de Gemeente die den Godsdienst bywonen in de kerk van het Dorp, Die haar gereghtigd deel van den order haud der Godsdienst van tydt tot tydt neffens andere toe brengen ; en die verklaren bieter gestight te kunnen werde in de Duytsche dan in eenige andere Taal, Dat zo lange 't zy de voor of namidags Predikatie in de Kerk van het Dorp door een der Predikanten in het duytsh zal geddan werden, de andere zal in de Engelsche taal geschieden.

† The westerly part of the town (now county) was called the *Woestyne* or Wilderness.

‡ Consistory Minutes.

preaching; and they advise in respect to Article 1, of the resolutions of the 13th of Februray, that it would be best to change it and that for the present a sermon be preached in the English tongue in the village every other Sunday, instead of every Sunday, either in the forenoon or afternoon, and in regard to Article 2, that the Sunday evening service be in the English language. *

By this change one sermon every two weeks was to be preached in English, and if a second minister were called the Sunday evening lecture was to be in the same language.

On the 2d of October, 1795, Rev. Jacob Sickels was called as assistant minister to Dr. Romeyn, and remained two years.

Nothing in the Consistory minutes would lead one to suppose that the matter of English preaching was seriously agitated again until the year 1798, soon after Do. Sickles left.

On the 19th of March, 1798, the Consistory took into consideration the necessity of preaching in the English language more than has hitherto been done, that the rising generation may be preserved from connecting themselves to other denominations, and came to the following resolution:

* * * * That it be recommended to Dr. Romeyn to preach one sermon in English on every other Lord's day afternoon, until consistory shall find it necessary to increase the English service.

Resolved, Also that the clerk be directed to procure at his own cost, an English clerk to be approved of by the consistory to perform the duties when worship is carried on in English.

And on the 21st of February, 1799, it was moved and seconded that the board [consistory] procure English bibles for the use of the consistory, when it was

Resolved, that eight English Bibles be purchased accordingly and that Mr. Yates purchase the same as soon as convenient.

On the 13th of May, 1799 it was moved in consistory by Mr. John S. Glen and seconded by Mr. Henry Yates, that in future

---

* De oudt Kerkenraadt adviseerde om trent Art. I, van den 13 Feb. dat 't best zoude zyn dit te Veranderen an te stellen dat voor het tegenwoordige om de andere zondag in plaats van elke zondag de voor of namiddag Predikatie in het Dorp in de Engelsche taal te zullen geschieden : en omtrent Art. 2, Dat de zondag Avondt dienst in het Engelsch Taal geeschieden.
—Consistory Minutes.

Divine Service in the Dutch Reformed Church be done one-half in the Dutch and the English language. *

Again on the 2nd of July, 1799, the motion for preaching half the time in English was once more taken up, and after mature consideration it was

Resolved, unanimously, That in future one-half of the service on every Lord's day be done in the English language.

22 November, 1799. Messrs. Abram Fonda, Zeger Van Santvoord, Jellis Fonda and Cornelis Van Santvoord, requested that the consistory would alter their order respecting English preaching—and the consistory took this request into consideration.

30th November, 1799. The consistory finding from information given that some uneasiness prevails amongst a few of the older class of their people, on account of the present order in respect to English preaching, and desirous at all times to pursue that which may work for peace and edification,

Resolved, Therefore, that their resolution of the 2d of July last be altered to read thus, viz. : That it be recommended to the minister of our church to preach in English as frequent as the consistory shall from time to time direct.

Thereupon, Resolved, That it is hereby recommended and directed that the Rev. D. Romeyn do in future preach one Sabbath out of three entirely in Dutch, and the other two, one-half of the service to be in the English language and in the afternoon in each, and that until consistory shall direct otherwise. †

This last compromise closed the long agitation. The battle of the tongues here closed, and when Domine Romeyn's long and honored ministry terminated in 1804, stated Dutch preaching ended in the church of Schenectady.

— * Consistory minutes.
— † Consistory minutes.

## CHAPTER X.

1795 – 1869.   REV. MESSRS. SICKLES, MEIER, BOGARDUS, VAN VECHTEN, TAYLOR, J. R. SEELYE, E. E. SEELYE AND WORTMAN.

*Rev. Jacob Sickels the Eighth Minister.*

Mr. Sickles was born at Tappan, in 1772, graduated at Columbia College in 1792, studied theology under Doctors Froeligh and Livingston, and was licensed by the Classes of New York in 1794.

He was called as assistant minister of this church on the 2d day of October, 1795, being then a divinity student. His salary was £200 ($500).

At the end of two years he received a call to the church of Coxsackie and Coeymans, and announced to the Consistory September 21, 1797 that he had concluded to accept the call.

He remained pastor of these churches until 1801, when he accepted a call from the church of Kinderhook, where he continued until his death in 1845.

" His field at Kinderhook was very extensive, embracing the present area of several churches. His labors were greatly blessed, the numbers professing their faith under his ministry averaging twenty a year for thirty years. As a pastor he had many excellencies. He was noted for uniform and sincere affection and his proverbial prudence. *

His first wife was Catharine, daughter of Hon. Henry Glen, of Schenectady, whom he married August 1, 1797. She died within a year after marriage.

*Rev. John Hardenberg Meier, the Ninth Minister,* 1803 – 1806.

The Rev. Mr. Meier, son of Rev. Harmanus Meier, of Pompton Plains, N. J., was born on the 19th day of October 1774. He graduated at Columbia College in 1795, studied theology under Doctor Livingston, and was licensed by the Classis of New York in 1798.

---
* Corwin's Manual.

His first pastoral charge was the Church of New Paltz and New Hurley, where he was installed minister in 1799. In October, 1802, he received and accepted a call from this church as assistant minister to Do. Romeyn, whose physical disabilities demanded some relief. His salary was $662.50, with house and lot of ground 140 ft. by 100 ft., Amsterdam measure, the rent of which was estimated at the low rent of $87.50, which being added to his salary made his compensation $750 or £300 New York currency.

The following is the call of Mr. Meier:

To the Rev John H. Myer, minister of the gospel at New Paltz, [L. S.] &c., in the County of Ulster, and State of New York. Grace, mercy, and peace from God our Father, and Jesus Christ our Lord.

Whereas the Church of Jesus Christ, in the City of Schenectady, and in the County of Albany, from its extensiveness and numbers, together with the increase of years upon our present Pastor, the Reverend Dirck Romeyn, and the incidents peculiar to an advanced state of life, stands in great need of increasing the stated preaching of the word and regular administration of the ordinances; and being desirous to enlarge the means of Grace, which God has appointed for the salvation of sinners through Jesus Christ his son, by the calling of a second minister to and with our present minister the Rev. Dirk Romeyn aforesaid:—

And, Whereas the said Church are from information well satisfied of the Piety, Gifts and Ministerial Qualifications of you, John H. Myer, and hath good hope that your labors in the Gospel will be attended with a blessing. Therefore we, the Minister, Elders and Deacons of the Reformed Protestant Dutch Church, in the City of Schenectady aforesaid, with the advice and approbation of a respectable number of the members and people of this Church have Resolved to call, and we do hereby solemnly and in the name of the Lord call you the said John H. Meyer, to be our pastor and teacher, to preach the word in truthfulness, to administer the Holy Sacrament agreeable to the Institution of Christ, to maintain Christian Discipline, to edify the Congregation, and especially the youth by Catechetical Instruction, and as a faithful servant of Jesus Christ to fulfil the whole work of the Gospel ministry agreeable to the word of God, the excellent rules and constitution of the Reformed Dutch Church, established in the last National Synod held at Dordreght, and ratified and explained by the judicature under which we stand and to which you upon accepting this Call must with us remain subordinate.

In fulfilling the ordinary duties of your ministry it is expressly stipulated that beside preaching from such texts of scripture as you may judge proper to select for our instruction, you also explain a portion of the Heidelbergh Catechism on the Lord's days, or Lord's days evenings, either in the Dutch or English language, as you and the consistory may judge most beneficial for the Congregation, agreeable to the established order of the Reformed Dutch Church, and that you further conform in rendering all that public service which is usual and has been in constant practice in our congregation. The particular service which will be required of you is that you shall be held to preach twice on every Lord's day in the Dutch and English languages as aforesaid, that is after our present minister shall have preached one sermon in the Dutch language at least, if he is able, and that in our said Church in this city. You shall also with Dr. Romeyn, our present minister, or if need be without him, dispense the Lord's Supper four times the year at our said Church in this City, each of which occasions shall be preceded by a preparatory discourse suited to the occasion, done in either of the above languages as the consistory with you shall determine.

As also, you shall once in every year visit the families belonging to our Congregation, at least if judged practicable, or otherwise as frequent, and such parts of the Congregation as the Consistory shall from time to time deem necessary; and to observe the weekly Catechises of the children and adult persons as frequent as the interest of Religion shall appear to require.

And finally do and perform, as God shall enable you, every duty, matter and thing which you and our Consistory shall from time to time judge necessary for the advancement of the prosperity of our said Congregation and the promotion of saving knowledge and holiness of life among the members thereof.

To encourage you in the discharge of the duties of your important office, We promise you in the name of this Church all proper attention, love and obedience in the Lord. And to free you from discouraging worldly cares and avocations, while you are dispensing the gospel and ordinances to us, We the Minister, Elders, and Deacons of the Reformed Protestant Dutch Church of the city of Schenectady, do promise and oblige ourselves to pay to you the sum of six hundred and sixty-two dollars and fifty cents, together with a house, and lot of one hundred and forty feet in depth and one hundred feet in width all Amsterdam wood measure, the rent of which is estimated at the low rate of eighty-seven dollars and fifty cents per annum, which being added to the foregoing makes the whole to amount to the annual sum of seven hundred and fifty dollars, or three hundred pounds New York money—the six hundred and sixty-two dollars and fifty cents to be paid yearly, and every year in four equal and quarterly payments as long as you continue to be the minister of this church; the first payment to be made three months after the first sermon which you shall deliver in our said Church in virtue of this call; and the consistory will also bear the expense of your removal to this city, and on your arrival will provide you with a good dwelling house until we can deliver you the house above referred to, which will be within a year from this date.

For the performance of all which we do hereby bind ourselves and our successors firmly by these presents.

Done in Consistory; sealed with our corporate seal and signed by us respectively, this —— day of October, in the year 1802.

Done and executed under the Presidency and with the approbation of D. Romeyn, V. D. M., and resident minister of the Gospel at Schenectady.

Nicholas Vedder,
Jesse D. DeGraff,
Abr'm Oothout,
Nicholas S. Vedder,
Jacob Swits,
Jelles A. Fonda,
John N. Marselus,
Jacob Schermerhorn.

The above call having been laid before the Classis for approbation, the same was approved of as in order.

J. BASSET, Pres't.
JOHN DEMAREST, Sect'y.

Done in Classis of Albany, Dec. 17th, 1802.

In the following May (1803) he was installed by the Rev. John Basset, of Albany, and Rev. Jacobus V. C. Romeyn, of Hackensack, N. J. The latter preached the sermon.

Less than a year from this event his venerable colleague was removed by death and he became sole pastor of the church, an office which was again vacated two years after by a like sad event. He died of consumption on the eleventh day of September, 1806, in the 32d year of his age and in the eighth year of his ministry. The funeral services were held at Schenectady,* but he was buried in the Dutch Church burying ground at Albany. †

Mr. Meier was of medium height, agreeable manners and deservedly popular with his congregation and the people generally. During the period of his pastorate subsequent to Dr. Romeyn's death, he married 118 couples, baptised 283 children and received 10 members to the church.

"As a man Mr. Meier was amiable, possessing a peaceable disposition, fond of social intercourse and desirous of the happiness of others. As a minister of the Gospel he was greatly esteemed by all who knew him, being blessed with a sound judgement and devoted to the services of the sanctuary.

---

\* James Lighthall, sexton of the church, was paid on this occasion two dollars for " wringing " the bell, and two dollars for notifying the Great Consistory ; also two dollars for the sextons of the other churches. [Episcopal and Presbyterian].

—Consistory minutes.

† The following is the inscription upon his grave stone :
"Under this stone are interred the mortal remains of
John Hardenberg Meier,
late minister of the Reformed Dutch Church in the city of Schenectady. He adorned the Doctrines of God his Saviour, displaying uniformly his attachment to them and their influence over him.

As a minister of the Gospel he was greatly esteemed by all who knew him, being blessed with a sound judgement, devoted to the service of the sanctuary from principle, loving the Glorious Redeemer, desirous of winning souls to his dominion.

In the midst of his days he was called hence and left this world with faith and patience for the blessed appearance of the Great God and our Saviour Jesus Christ.

He was born Oct. 19th, 1774, and died Sept. 11th, 1806, aged 31 years, 10 months and 23 days, having been engaged in the service of Jehovah Jesus almost eight years, of which he spent better that three in Schenectady."

—Annals of Alb., VI, 166.

"His talents and acquirements were of the useful kind and very respectable. Being cautious in his disposition and reserved in his manners he displayed fewer mental resources in his intercourse with men than he really possessed. The native benevolence of his heart always rendered him a welcome and acceptable companion to his acquaintances. He was esteemed as a preacher but more especially as a member of the several church judicatures with which he was connected. He was rising in reputation and his sphere of usefulness was enlarging when it pleased a holy God to take him to himself.

"His education having been strictly religious, he had from his earliest years a deep reverence for divine things. His liveliest impressions of religion were when he was at the Academy at Flatbush about the year 1793.

"Before he finally left his home, which was in the beginning of August, he did not calculate on a recovery. He had accordingly arranged his temporal concerns. He spoke of his death and gave directions about his funeral with the utmost composure. His covenant Father gave him desirable support and comfort. He died without a struggle or a groan."\*

1808-12. *Rev. Cornelius Bogardus the Tenth Minister.*

For two years after the death of Do. Meier the pulpit was supplied temporarily by ministers from the neighboring churches.

From the many candidates recommended as his successor the choice fell upon Rev. John Brodhead Romeyn, son of the their late pastor. His call was dated July 8th, 1807. The salary named was $1,000, with house and firewood, and he was required to preach twice each Sabbath, in Dutch and English, as he and the consistory might think proper. For some reason this call was not accepted, and after further deliberation for a year Mr. Cornelius Bogardus became the successful candidate.

He was born Sept. 26th, 1780, studied theology, under Livingston, was licensed by the Classis of New York in 1808, and was ordained and installed pastor of this church on the 27th November, 1808, being then in his 29th year. The sermon on this occasion was preached by Rev. John Basset, of Albany.

\* Albany Gazette, 15th Sept. 1806.

During his short pastorate of four years the church was greatly increased in numbers—157 members having been admitted in that time. He married 117 couples and baptised 444 children. He died of consumption on the 15th of December, 1812, aged 32 years.

Mr. Bogardus was in stature above the medium height and of commanding presence. As a preacher he had more than ordinary power and was considered a rising man, bidding fair to take a prominent position in his profession. *

1815–1849. *Rev. Jacob Van Vechten, D. D., the Eleventh Minister.*

The longest pastorate of this church was that of the Rev. Jacob Van Vechten, its eleventh minister. He was born at Catskil and baptised September 7th, 1788, the fourth of nine sons, children of Samuel Van Vechten and Sara Van Orden.

The first settler of the name—Teunis Dirkse Van Vechten, *alias* Poentie, came over to New Netherlands in 1638, in the *Arms of Norway*, with his wife, child and two servants, and in 1648 occupied a farm in Greenbush. He is referred to in 1663 as an old inhabitant here. In 1700 he had at least three sons living—Dirk, the eldest, Cornelius and Gerrit, besides a daughter, Pietertje, wife of Myndert Frederickse, of Albany.

Dirk Teunis Van Vechten, son of Teunis Dirkse, settled in and bought land at Catskil, made his will April 4th, 1687, proved March 30th, 1703, and died November 25th, 1702. He married Jannetje Michielse, [Caljer?] and mentioned the following children in his will: Jannetie, born 1660; Wyntje, born 1662; Michiel, born 1664; Neeltja, 1665; *Johannes*, born 1667; Teunis, born 1669; Annatie, born 1671; Fytje, born 1672; Samuel, born 1673; Sara, born 1675, and Abraham, born 1679.

Johannes Dirkse Van Vechten, of Catskil, married Elizabeth ————, and had at least two sons, *Teunis* and Dirk, and perhaps others.

---

* The first application made for the use of the church for a 4th of July celebration was made June 24th, 1811, when the consistory granted the request, "provided no instrumental music shall be used and nothing be said in the oration to wound the feelings of any political party."
—Consistory Minutes.

*Teunis* Van Vechten, of Catskil, married Judikje Ten Broeck. Among others he had a son, *Samuel*, who was baptised in Catskil, October, 1742, and became the father of the Rev. Jacob Van Vechten, as before stated.

Doctor Van Vechten's early education was pursued first at Catskil and afterwards at the Kingston Academy. The teacher who fitted him for College was the Rev. Alexander Miller, who had been pastor of the Presbyterian Church at Schenectady prior to 1790. He entered the Freshman Class of Union College in 1805, with his class and room-mate, Gideon Hawley, of Albany, and graduated A. B. in 1809. Soon after leaving College he entered the law office of his uncle, Abraham Van Vechten, of Albany, as a law student, with the intention of making the law his profession.

"In October, 1809, he united with the Reformed Protestant Dutch Church in Catskil, and abandoning his first choice of a profession turned his attention to the Gospel ministry, for which he prepared himself by a course of study in the Theological Seminary of the Scotch Church, under the care of the Rev. Doctor John M. Mason," of New York, in 1813, and in the New Brunswick Theological Seminary in 1814, when he was licensed to preach by the Classis of New Brunswick. As early as August 1st, 1814, the consistory of this church resolved to call Mr. Van Vechten as their minister, but it was not until June 8th, 1815, that he was ordained and installed pastor. On this occasion the Dr. John M. Bradford, of Albany, preached the sermon.

The year following he married Catharine, daughter of his venerated preceptor, Dr. Mason; she died in 1820, and two years later he married Maria, daughter of Abraham Van Dyck, of Coxsackie. "Of nine children from these two marriages he lost six in their youth or prime."

"His health was delicate in early manhood from pulmonary tendencies and rheumatic affection for which he went to Europe in 1823. He returned after a year's absence improved in health, but made permanently lame at Paris from a surgical accident in operating upon his rheumatic knee." He received the degree of Doctor of Divinity from Williams College in ———. At the time of his death he was Senior Trustee of Union College, to which office he was elected in 1837.

He resigned and was dismissed from the pastorate of this church on the 6th of March, 1849, after a service of more than 34 years, during which time 910 members were received into the Church.

"On retiring from his charge he did not seek another but preached as opportunity offered; and employed his leisure in literary labors, among which was a Biography of his late father-in-law, Dr. John M. Mason.

In 1851 he removed to Albany, and from thence, in 1868, to Auburn, where he resided in the family of his son-in-law, Professor Huntington, until his death, which occurred on the 15th of September, 1871.

The following letter was received from Doctor Van Vechten in answer to a request for some facts in the history of the church during his pastorate.

AUBURN, OCT. 21ST, 1869.

DEAR FRIEND: —
Your project of *historising* (a new word) the good old Dutch town of Schenectady with its institutions * * I hope will not be relinquished.

Dr. Romeyn was the last pastor of the Dutch Church who preached *statedly* in our native language. I never saw him. Meier was minister when I entered College [1805]; often heard him preach in English, *very seldom*, if at all, in Dutch.

Mr. Bogardus, my predecessor, was a worthy man—gave us good plain sermons, altogether in English—gathered in a large number of communicants; aimed, though rather feebly, to raise the standard of *spiritual* as opposed to formal religion. In less than four years his health gave away and shortly afterwards he died.

An interregnum of about two years intervened before my settlement. The history of my labors can not easily be given by me. From the very beginning I encountered great difficulties from the innovations, or as I prefer to call them, *reformations*, which I endeavored to introduce. The people had been accustomed to the baptism of *all* children who might be presented. I thought the Bible limited it to Christian children. Members had been received at a certain age, or at least on reciting the catechism. I thought more experimental qualifications necessary. An honest account of such matters would still be attended with delicacy and perhaps bad feeling.

I can inform you further in this direction when we meet ; till then I will leave your request. At present I have no leisure to proceed further.

I have reminiscences which are interesting to myself, but cannot say that they would be so to others.

With high respect and esteem,
    Your sincere friend,
        JACOB VAN VECHTEN.

1849–1852. *Rev. William J. R. Taylor, D. D, the Twelfth Minister.*

He is the son of Rev. Benjamin C. Taylor, D. D., of Bergen, N. J., and Anna Romeyn his wife, and was born in Schodac, Rensselaer co., N. Y., July 31st, 1823.

He graduated at Rutger's College in July, 1841, and the Theological Seminary of the Reformed (Dutch) church at New Brunswick, N, J., July, 1844, and was ordained to the gospel ministry at Hackensack, N. J., in August, 1844. The following have been his pastoral charges—all in the Reformed (Dutch) Church : —

| | |
|---|---|
| New Durham, Hudson co., N. J., | 1844–1846. |
| Van Vorst. (Jersey City), N. J., | 1846–1849. |
| Schenectady, N. Y., | 1849–1852. |
| Jersey City, (3d) | 1852–1854. |
| Philadelphia, (3d) | 1854–1862. |
| Corresponding Secretary of the American Bible Society at New York city, | 1862–1869. |
| Newark, N. J., | 1869——— |

Dr. Taylor was installed pastor of this Church Nov. 18th, 1849. During the winter and spring of 1852 the church "enjoyed a gracious revival of religion."

Through over exertion at this time, a long and dangerous illness was brought upon him, from which he barely recovered with his life. It was during his ministry and chiefly through his exertions that the Second Reformed Church of Schenectady was formed.

Doctor Taylor has published several Thanksgiving Sermons, public addresses, etc., besides discourses in memory of Rev. Henry G. Livingston, pastor of the Third Reformed Church of

Philadelphia, Rev. Dr. John Ludlow, Provost of the University of Pennsylvania and Professor of the Theological Seminary at New Brunswick, N. J., Rev. George W. Bethune, D.D., Rev. Samuel A. Van Vranken, D.D., Professor of Didactic Theology in the Theological Seminary at New Brunswick, N. J., and the Hon. Theodore Frelinghuysen, * &c., &c.

1853–1858, *Rev. Julius H. Seelye D. D., the Thirteenth Minister.*

He was born in Bethel, Conn., September 14th, 1824. At the age of 15 years he entered his father's store, remaining there until he was twenty-one. He entered the Freshman Class of Amherst College at the beginning of the second term, January, 1846, and graduated in 1849.

The same year he entered the Theological Seminary at Auburn, N. Y., and at the end of his three years course, in 1852, visited Europe remaining nearly a year, the greater portion of which was spent at Halle.

On his return, in 1853, his first sermon was preached at Schenectady, May 22nd; on May 31st, he received a unanimous call as pastor of this church; June 14th, accepted the call, and August 10th, was ordained and installed by the Classis of Schenectady; Dr. Hickok, Vice-President of Union College, preaching the sermon on this occasion. On the 23rd of October, 1858, he married Elizabeth James, daughter of Rev. William James, D.D., of Albany.

Having resigned the pastorate of this Church to accept the professorship of Mental and Moral Philosophy in Amherst College, he was dismissed by the Classis August 30th, to take effect September 14th, 1858, his 34th birth day, and the completion of five and a quarter years of his ministry.

During his pastorate he attended 136 funerals, solemnized 80 marriages, baptised 30 infants and 11 adults, and received as members of the church on profession of their faith 110 and by letter 31. No communion service passed during his ministry

---

\* For a complete list of the writings of Dr. Taylor and additional facts concerning the living and deceased ministers of the Reformed Church, see Dr. E. T. Corwin's Manual of the Reformed Church in America, 3rd edition. [W. E. G.]

without the reception of some members to the church on a profession of faith.

The contributions of the church for benevolent purposes were as follows:

| | |
|---|---|
| 1854, | $415. |
| 1855, | 453. |
| 1856, | 545. |
| 1857, | 808. |
| 1858, | 939.51. |

Professor Seelye's mercantile experience was a good preparatory discipline and the business habits thus acquired were of great benefit in his subsequent career. Having decided to acquire a liberal education late, his preparatory course for College was short; nevertheless during the latter part of his College course he stood among the best of his class in scholarship. His Theological course was distinguished for depth, soundness, thoroughness of investigation and controlling influence among the students and in the surrounding religious community.

While abroad, he profitted largely in acquaintance with leading men, and attendance upon University lectures, and added greatly to his philosophical and theological knowledge. His pastorate with this church, though his first, was eminently successful, not only in gaining for him the hearts of his people by his kind and genial manners, but also in commanding the respect of the best minds of the community by his sound and edifying discourses.

In 1875–6 Prof. Seelye represented his district in Congress, and in 1877 was elected President of Amherst College.

1858–1864.   *Rev. Edward E. Seelye, D.D., the Fourteenth Minister.*

The Rev. Edward E. Seelye, the fourteenth minister of the Church was born in Lansingburgh, September 24th, 1819. He entered the Sophomore Class of Union College September 9th, 1836, and graduated A. B. in July, 1839.

During his connection with the College he became a member of the Presbyterian Church, and in 1840 entered Princeton Seminary, from whence he graduated in 1843.

"At the completion of his course of study he became pastor of the Presbyterian Church at Stillwater, where he labored with fidelity and success for seven years, until 1850. He was then called to the Presbyterian Church at Sandy Hill. During the later years of Dr. Seelye's ministry at Sandy Hill he preached statedly at Fort Edward, and there founded a Presbyterian Church, which has grown into a large and prosperous congregation.

Dr. Seelye was twice called by the Reformed Church of Schenectady—once previously to the settlement of Professor Julius H. Seelye and again after he left. The first call was declined under the advice of the Presbytery in view of the wants of the Church he was then serving. But when a second time this Church pressed him to become their pastor, he accepted their invitation.

In 1858 he removed to Schenectady, and on November 1st was installed pastor. In this, his last charge, he was called to meet some peculiar difficuties. In 1861 the church edifice was destroyed by fire, and for the two years following that event the Church had no more convenient place of worship than the lecture room of the Presbyterian Church, kindly furnished for that purpose, the edifice of the second church not being then in possession of that people. In addition to the disadvantages of such contracted accommodations, all the labor and anxiety of adopting plans and carrying forward the great enterprise of erecting a new, large and costly church building, involving in its progress the obliteration of private claims on pews, and more important still, the absorption of a valuable church property, was thrown upon the Consistory and necessarily to some extent upon the pastor. Yet Dr. Seelye lived to see that two years' work, so delicate and momentous in character, fully and peacefully accomplished, and had the satisfaction and honor, on the 6th of August, 1863, of preaching the dedication sermon."

"Physically, he was robust, a little above the medium height, with a compact, well-knit frame." His last was the only sickness of his life.

In August, 1864, he left home "for his annual vacation for a few weeks in the fresh air and the free woods which he loved so well," and was suddenly taken ill at Sandy Hill, the place of his former charge, where he died August 10th, 1864.

[The facts for the following sketches of the lives of the three pastors of the church who succeeded the Rev. E. E. Seelye, are taken mainly from Dr. E. T. Corwin's "Manual of the Reformed Church in America," a book which is invaluable for officers and members of the Reformed Church.

The Rev. Dennis Wortman, D.D., was graduated from Amherst College in 1857, and from the New Brunswick Theological Seminary in 1860, and was settled over the church at South Bushwick, L. I., for three years. Accepting a call from the Third Reformed Church in Philadelphia, he succeeded Dr. W. J. R. Taylor, and labored two years, when he was called to Schenectady. Here, in the midst of his duties most faithfully performed, his health failed; nor did a trip to Europe (during which he attended the sessions of the Evangelical Alliance at Amsterdam, Holland,) restore him fully to health, as he had hoped. He resigned his charge in 1870, greatly to the regret of the people, by whom he was greatly loved. Since 1870, he supplied vacant churches; but in 1880, feeling his health sufficiently established, he accepted a call to the Reformed Church at Fort Plain, N. Y. Of Dr. Wortman's labors in Schenectady, and of church life during this period, one may form an impression by his own modest words of reminiscence in his address on Monday evening, June 21st, 1880.

"With grateful hearts, dear friends, we scan the six years we spent together here. Much there was in it very delightful—while there was that of sorrow in it to give a proper chastening to our souls. Truly I was with you in weakness and in pain and in much trouble, and my speech and my preaching was not with enticing words of man's wisdom, but it was in demonstration of the Spirit and of power. And to-night I testify alike to your helpful affection, and to the strengthening grace of God. Yes, we did have some good times together here, in that consistory room, helping one another in our prayers to God, in this sanctuary studying the word of God, and welcoming from the world the new found friends of Christ. One especially precious season we enjoyed when 27 united at the same time in their avowal of the love of Christ. Immediately after my leaving you, also, and before a successor had been called, there was a powerful, though very quiet work of grace, and a larger number even than that was gathered in, of whom I affectionately think as somehow—if God so will—my own children in the Lord. Indeed there was during the whole period of our union not so much a revival, but a constant living interest in spiritual things. Yet while it is given us to praise God for his mercy in accepting and blessing our poor labors, we must be very careful to attribute to him not part but all, all, the praise and all, all, the love! Very pleasant times we had together. You began right—paying off in close connection with your call to me a debt of $11,000.* Then let me see, the time is short, I can but hasten on the memorandum of those years. The great civil war well nigh at its ending. Before my installation in May, Lee had surrendered, and the fanaticism of Booth had illustrated the madness of the enemies of freedom, and immortalized Abraham Lincoln as the martyr President. It was for us then to gather up the lessons of the fearful strife, to calm the turbulence of passions, to reconstruct a christian loyalty, to guard against the terrible reaction after the war, to welcome back to peaceful industries our gallant soldier host—and turn the thoughts of men again to the labors of peace, and the virtues of love. I must not forget to thank you that in a season of weakness you permitted me, without expense, to make that long tour in Europe; during which, besides seeing so much of the old world, I had so glorious a foot tour through the Eastern Alps with Dr. Hurst, one of the new and most honored bishops of the M. E. Church, and to attend and participate in the meetings of the first Evangelical Alliance in Holland, in 1867. During that absence you provided yourself with the spiritual and poetic strong preaching of one who since then as the author of "All About Jesus," has gained an American and an English reputation.† During that absence of your pastor, also, you signalized your interest in the church and your desire to fence off offending intruders on sacred ground by putting around this fine lawn of yours the beautiful iron fence, which well befits the beauty of this noble structure. I call up the names of men and women with us then who have since entered to their rest. I cannot name all, only a few. Elder Nicholas Van Vranken, for 30 years the honored treasurer of this church, has gone to his rest. There

---

* Subscribed, but paid only to the extent of $8,500. [W. E. G.]
† Rev. Alexander Dixon.

was Groot, there was Clute, there was Angle, there was Dr. Fonda, there were the Veeder's and Swits's, and Yates's and others, there was one dear brother Cain, (to whom, primarily, with the warm co-operation of the brethren in this and other churches, we owe the Y. M. C. A. Hall), McNee, the always faithful, Judge Mitchell, there was the beloved physician, whom the whole city honored, Dr. A. M. Vedder. There were honorable women, not a few who have entered their rest, well represented and led by Mrs. Dr. Vedder, Mrs. Myers, Miss Fuller, who with others were indeed faithful ministers to your pastors. Then the massive head, with the long grey locks hanging venerably down, sitting yonder near the Banker Screen, deafening gradually to the voice of the human preacher, all the more intent on listening to Him that speaketh from above; the gentle and strong, the humble, the scholarly and wise teacher, writer, lover of Christ. There should be somewhere in this building a memorial of some kind erected by us who loved him so, to the memory of Tayler Lewis! Will not some one see that they who would so love to do, may be led into the privilege?"

The Reverend Ashbel G. Vermilye, the sixteenth pastor of the church, is the son of the Rev. T. E. Vermilye, the senior of the College of Pastors of the collegiate church in New York city. He was born at Princeton, N. J., in 1822, and was graduated from the New York University in 1840. His pastoral charges from 1845 to 1871 were at Little Falls, N. Y., Newburyport, Mass., and Utica, N. Y. He preached his first sermon in the church August 6th, 1871, the anniversary of the burning of the old and the dedication of the new (fifth) edifice. Dr. Vermilye contributed a masterly sermon on " The Huguenot Element Among the Dutch," for the Volume of *Centennial Discourses* published in 1876; a work which well illustrates the genius and characteristics of the Reformed Church in America. He was also one of the three editors of the " Hymns of the Church." Dr. Vermilye's labors ceased by resignation in December, 1876. He accepted the charge of the Marine Chapel for one year at Antwerp, Belgium, in 1878, and after doing a good work there among the American sailors and residents, began the execution of a long cherished plan to travel in Europe and the East. See his letter on page 24.

The present pastor was born in Philadelphia, Pa., on the 17th day of September, 1843, and entered Rutgers College in 1865. After graduation, in 1869, he traveled in Europe for a few months, entered the New Brunswick Theological Seminary for a year, and in December, 1870, went to Japan to engage in the Government Educational service. After spending one year in Fukui, province of Echizen, he was called to the capital, Tokio, where, as Professor in the Imperial University, he remained until July, 1874. He studied two years in the Union Theological Seminary of New York—1875-1877. While in the Senior Class he was invited to preach in the church at Schenectady, on Sabbath, April 22nd, 1877. He received a unanimous call to be pastor May 1st, 1877. He accepted and was ordained and installed May 31st. A large number of ministers assisted in the ordination, among them the venerable Abram J. Swits.

The chief events in the church during the last three years have been the increase and improvement of the Sunday School Library; the publication of a Manual and Directory of the Church; considerable reform in the matter of Sunday funerals; payment of a large portion of the debt which has existed since the erection of the present edifice; the completion of the work of removing the remain's from the old neglected burial ground on Green street, which had been partially carried on for over twelve years, to Vale Cemetery; putting in complete repair, both outside and inside, the church edifice at a cost of $700; the addition of several decorative and memorial features of permanent interest, such as inscriptions and tablets; laying the corner-stone of Prospect Hill Mission School building; the celebration, in befitting style, of the bi-centennial anniversary, and the publication of the History of the Church.]

The editor may be permitted to add that other enterprises which await the future for their execution are the erection of a Sabbath School room, either in a separate building, or better, attached to the church edifice; the erection of a baptismal font; a new carpet and improved ventilation; the chanticleer of Saint Nicholas on the spire, as the weather-vane; a large fire-proof safe or vault for the safe-keeping of the archives; a building for the Water street Mission School; and, when the next pastor comes, a parsonage, according to the old custom of the church.

All these, or the best of them, under God's providence, the people willing, will doubtless come in due time.

It behooves the citizens of Schenectady, without distinction of creed or descent, to erect at the end of Church street, on State— the old "Street of the Martyrs"—a monument in honor of Van Curler and the founders of the city; in memory of the first two generations of the first settlers, including the victims of the massacre in 1690; and in witness to the site of the first two church edifices of the oldest institution still in existence in Schenectady. Shall this monument be erected?

## CHAPTER XI.

### THE CHURCH OF 1814—ORGAN AND CHANDELIER.

As early as the year 1805 the congregation began to agitate the question of repairing the old church, and on the 23d of March, 1810, the consistory appointed a committee to draw a plan and report upon the feasibility of building a new one. On the 11th of June, finding this project impracticable, another committee was appointed to estimate the expense of repairing the old house. This effort also failed, and an attempt was again made on the 10th of August to build a new church by authorizing the circulation of subscription papers. In this manner the consistory hesitated for more than two years, sometimes inclining to one scheme, then to the other. Finally on the 4th of April, 1812, the Great Consistory being called together, decided that "if good subscriptions to the amount of $4,000 shall be obtained within 6 weeks a new church should be built, otherwise to repair the old one." The result of this advice was a subscription of $3,379.50 in money and 243 days work.

To provide further means for the building, the consistory resolved, on the 30th of October, 1812, to sell to the city their two church sites (the one at the junction of Church and State streets, the other at the junction of Church and Union streets,) for 200 acres of land worth at least ten dollars an acre, provided these two lots shall never be used for private purposes, but be left open in the streets for public convenience.

On the 3rd day of December, 1812, contracts were signed for the construction of the new house—for mason work and materials with David Hearsey and Thomas McCully, to be commenced as early as May 1st, 1813, and finished by September 1st, but by consent subsequently extended to December 1st—and for carpenter's work, painting, glazing and materials with Gerrit Bensen and Joseph Horsfall, to be completed on or before October 15th, 1814, and extended afterwards to April 15th, 1815.

The masons received $4,570 and the carpenters $5,800 for their respective contracts.

The dimensions of this building were 57 feet by 96 feet, exclusive of the tower projections, with walls of brick 28 feet high above the foundations. *

It was situated on the church site on the East corner of Union and Church streets, which up to this time had been used for the parsonage. It was a neat, plain, well-proportioned building with a tower and cupola on the South front. The bell of the old church was hung in the belfry. Besides the middle entrance through the tower there were two side doors, all in front, and corresponding to the three aisles.

In the arrangement of seats the separation of the sexes was no longer kept up, but the English plan was adopted of sittings in families. The pulpit was built against the North wall opposite the main entrance. There were 24 family pews along the walls and 72 slips or benches on both sides of the middle aisle.† The side galleries were reserved for the miscellaneous audience; the front gallery for the choir, organ and colored people. About 800 persons could be comfortably seated in this house.

In the autumn of 1814 the new house was so near completion that it could be used for worship, and on the 20th of November

---

* 17th April, 1813 : "To paid the masons for laying the last stone," [for grog,] 37½ cents.
         —Treasurer's book.

† See Appendix C.

the last services were held in the old building;* on which occasion Dr. Andrew Yates preached in the morning and afternoon from the 132nd Psalm, 3rd, 4th, 5th and 6th verses.† On the following Sabbath, November 27th, the new house was dedicated, and Dr. Eliphalet Nott preached twice from the 4th verse of the 27th Psalm. It was used as a house of worship 47 years, until the 6th of August, 1861, when it was destroyed by fire.

The increase of this congregation has doubtless been much retarded by the want of seat room. This was felt many years before the church of 1734 was removed. In view of this fact it is singular that the church of 1814 should not have been built larger. It could accommodate but a few more persons than its predecessor. ‡ Indeed it may be said that from 1734 to 1862, a period of 128 years, the church accommodations of this congregation remained substantially the same. In the meantime the little hamlet grew into a village and the village into a city of respectable dimensions. It had but few competitors in the field, and though it became the mother church of this region, with one exception all her colonies were sent out some years subsequent to 1814.

Before closing this short account of this house it may be proper to mention the honored names of Nicholas Vander Volgen and his wife, who were considerable benefactors to it.

Many of the congregation remember the huge brass chandelier and pleasant organ of the old church. These were their gifts; the former in 1792, the latter in 1797.

---

* The old church was sold to the contractors for 450 dollars, and they were about to remove it in the spring of 1813, when on a remonstrance being made to the consistory against thus depriving the congregation of a place of worship while the new house was building, the contract was annulled, and it was left standing until 1814.

In the remonstrance allusion is made to the desecration of the old church by lawless persons breaking the seats and pews, and it was advised to prosecute the marauders.

—Consistory Minutes.

In the Treasurer's book is the following entry under date 5th July, 1814: "To paid for liquor when the old spire was taken down, 37½ cents. Nov. 30th, 1814. Charles Kane and Henry Yates bought the old church for $442.50.

†Abraham Fonda's Bible.

‡ The dimensions of the church of 1734 were 80 feet by 56 feet, those of the church of 1814 were 86 feet by 57 feet.

The great chandelier (*groote kroon*) had eighteen lights, besides which there were seven lesser ones (*kleyndere kroonen*) of six lights each, costing altogether £67-10 New York currency.

The money for the organ was given in 1797, and suffered to accumulate until 1826(?) when an instrument was obtained from Henry Erben, of New York, at the cost of 1,000(?) dollars. This was consumed with the church in 1861.

The action of the consistory in regard to these donations may be seen in the following extracts from their minutes:—

Sept. 17th, 1792. "Mr. Nicolaas Vander Volgen and his wife Sarah Vander Volgen have presented to the church of Schenectady a great chandelier of 18 lights and seven lesser chandeliers each of 6 lights; the sum given therefor by them was £67-10. Wherefore the consistory in the name of the church heartily and solemnly thank Mr. N. Vander Volgen and his wife for this handsome donation for the accommodation of the evening service, praying the Lord that they with the church may for a long time enjoy the use thereof in peace and good health. The consistory were

D. Romeyn, Pastor loci.

| | |
|---|---|
| Nicholas Hall, | Abram Oothout, |
| Gerrit S. Veeder, Jr., | Thos. Brouwer Bancker, |
| Nicholas Veeder, | Abram Swits, |
| Simon J. Van Antwerpen, | Frederick Clute, |
| Deacons. | Elders. * |

---

\* Sept. 17th, 1792. Dan heeft de Heer Nicholas Vander Volgen en syn huysrevrouw Sarah Vander Volgen Veeringe gemaakt aen de kerk van Schenectady Een groote Kroon van 18 lichten en seven Kleyndere Kroonen Van elk 6 lighten de kosten door hun E. geeven was de Somma van £67-10.

Den E Kerkenraadt heeft daarop de Heer N. Vander Volgen en zyn huysvrouw uyt naam van degemeente hertelyk en pleghtilyk bedankt Voor dese aanzienlyke Donatie, tot gereyvinge Van den Avont godsdienst met nevens gaande Toebiddinge dat de Heere hun E nog lange tydt het nut daor van met de Gemeente zal doen genieten in Vreede en Welvaaren.

Kerkenraadt Waaren.

D. Romeyn, Pastor loci.

| | |
|---|---|
| Nicholas Hall, | Abram Oothout, |
| Gerrit S. Veeder, Jr., | Thos. Brouwer Bancker, |
| Nicholas Veeder, | Abram Swits, |
| Simon J. Van Antwerpen, | Frederick Clute, |
| Diaconen. | Ouderlingen. |

April 3d, 1797. Mr. Nicholas Vander Volgen, Elder of the Consistory, having made known through Do. Romeyn that his Honor had laid aside out of his estate £150 for the providing of an Organ for our Church, hoping that the Consistory would raise the rest of the money required for the purchase of such an organ as may be suitable for our Church building—the Consistory is very sensible of the favor of this charitable gentleman, and thank his Honor cordially for this gift. Furthermore,

Resolved, That means be taken at once to raise money to be added thereto for the purchase of a good organ for our church. *

9th May, 1797. Resolved, That a subscription be opened at once for the organ, and presented to every householder belonging to our church for subscriptions—the Consistory shall at once promote this project, each elder and deacon taking his own neighborhood. †

May 26th, 1797. Received by the hand of Derick Van Ingen, as executor of the last will and testament of Nicholas Vander Volgen, the sum of one hundred and fifty pounds for the purchase of an Organ.

7th April, 1800. "As the late Mr. Nicholas Vander Volgen some years ago made an additional donation to the chandeliers

---

\* Ap. 3th, 1797. Mr. Nicholaas Vander Volgen, Ouderlingen der E. Kerkenraadt bekent gemaakt hebbende door D. Romeyn dat zyn E £150 uvt zyn goederen dfgelegen hadde tot verzorginge van een Orgel in onse kerke wenschende dat den E Kerkenraad de overige Verevschte gelden daar by Willde doen tot Verkryginge van sulke Orgel als ons kerk gebouw sal Voegen.

De E Kerkenraad is zeer gevoelig Van de gunste van deze goedadige Heer, on bedankt zyn E.. hertgrondiglyk voor dese gifts. Voorts. Besloten,

Ten eersten middelen aante wenden tot Verkryginge van Penningen Welke hier toegevoeght moeten werden all ook tot Verkryginge van een goede Orgel voor ouse kerk.
—Consistory Minutes.

† 9th May, 1797. Besloten, Eene subscriptie Voor de Orgol ten eerste te openen en by zeder huys tot onse gemeente behoorende aan tebieden ter teekkinge, sullende de kerkenraadt dit ten eerster bevorderen elk der Ouderlingen er. Diaconen haare buert daartoe nemende.
—Consistory minutes.

May 26th, 1797. Aen Gelt ontvang By hande van Derick Van Inge als Voght van het Leste will and Testement van Niechs Vander Volgin Die Somme van Een Hondert en Vifttg Pont Vore het Gebruyck van Ecn Orgel.
—Church acct. book.

given by him sometime before, for the purpose of enabling the board to procure an Organ for the use of the Church, which donation amounted to £150, and which has accumulated by interest to something more than £180; and as the Consistory wish to obtain an organ for their Church as soon as may be,

Resolved, Therefore, that a committee of three be appointed out of their congregation, who are hereby requested to call upon the Collector of this board and select out of the obligations belonging to this Board, now in the hands of their Collector, an amount equal to £200, and that such committee attend to the annual interest with precision, and continue from year to year the said £200, by interest and private donations, until said sum shall amount to £400, unless the Consistory should call for a return of said obligations at any time before, and that said Committee report annually to the Board their progress when called up. That the Committee be Messrs. Gen. A. Oothout, Joseph C. Yates, Esq., Mayor of this city, and Dirk Van Ingen, Esq., who are hereby also authorized, when the money aforesaid shall have accumulated to a sufficient amount, with advice of any five members of this Board, three of them being Elders, to purchase such organ, and place the same in the church for the use of the Congregation.

Jan. 1st, 1806, a Committee was appointed to enquire respecting the fund bequeathed by Mr. Vander Volgen for an Organ. * * * They report that the money was paid to the Church and blended in the General Fund. *

Finally April 3d, 1817, the Consistory acknowledged the receipt of £150 from the Heirs of Nicholas Vander Volgen. And about 1826 this bequest and its accumulations were invested in an Organ."

---

*Consistory minutes.

## CHAPTER XII.

### THE CHURCH OF 1863.

On the 6th day of August, 1861, a destructive fire occurred on the river bank near the Mohawk bridge. Owing to the strong northerly wind prevailing many buildings were destroyed before the fire could be subdued. The burning shingles were carried to all parts of the city. One of these alighted upon the belfry of the Church, which was several hundred feet south of the conflagration. Before it was discovered the flames had made such headway that no human aid could save the building— in one hour nothing was left of this beautiful house but the bare walls and the smoking embers.

For some years the congregation had been straitened for room and, as in 1810, the question of enlargement had been long agitated. Even the formation of the Second Church had not materially relieved the pressure.

After the fire, a portion of the congregation advocated enlargement and rebuilding upon the old walls, which were still sound. Wiser counsels, however prevailed, and it was resolved to build anew from the foundation.

In carrying out these views the Consistory committed the designing of the new House to Edward Tuckerman Potter, Esq., of New York, who in his "statement of the considerations influencing the design of this church" says. "The first point to be considered, in making this as every design, was the wants to be provided for—the second how to provide for them at the least cost and at the same time to secure a pleasing result. The congregation desired a Church building capable of seating about eight hundred persons—a consistory room, which should also be used for a Sunday School room, and a tower and spire. The lot being on the corner of two principal streets, the problem, which I set for myself was, how to place these required buildings on it so as to produce the best effect for the sum to be expended. Some of the Congregation proposed a Consistory room placed on one of the streets, but separate from the Church as the old one had been; but this would have made one contrast ill with the other, and would have cut up the lot to a disadvantage, and have thrown away that important element of architectural effect—mass. It seemed better therefore to group them so as to make one architectural whole. Again it was proposed to place the Church in the centre of the lot, with the Consistory behind it and the tower in front—a common plan. This would have left no grass or place of any kind in front, but merely two strips of grass on the sides."

"These considerations suggested the arrangement of the present plan, which combined all the buildings in one group,—a group convergent or pyramidal in its lines—the tower and spire from every point of view forming always the centre of the picture. In addition to this the building so arranged left the unemployed space on the lot where it would most tell; and by placing the group of buildings somewhat back from the open sides of the lot the space for the greensward was further enlarged, so that it is common to hear the remark that the church is fortunate in having such a fine site and so much open space about it, when in truth it was the planning the Church which gave the open space which is admired, and which as we have seen would not have existed if the plan first proposed had been followed."

"It was originally my intention to choose the style in which many of the Dutch Churches of the state were at one time built; such as the North Dutch Church, Fulton street, New York, Dr. Wyckoff's Church, Albany, &c. But the steep Dutch gables of Schenectady, and the views which had been preserved of the churches erected in the early days of the Dutch Colony pointed to an older and more picturesque style, and one more suited to the site, the character of the building and the reminiscences which I wished to preserve."

"The material to be used also had necessarily much to do with the choice of a style. A more beautiful and economical material, or a more durable one when properly used than the purple greywacke of Schenectady, it would be hard to find. The builders in the Fatherland, however, had no such material, and their great churches, though built in the pointed style, as were early Dutch Churches on this Continent, have a meagreness and an absence of distinctive features, which afford little that is noticeable or that can be copied. And except the great use of

20

the richly stained glass, the frequent introduction of armorial bearings and texts of Scripture as ornaments, the use of corners, painted arches, high pitched gables, &c.,—features, indeed, which are not the exclusive property of the pointed style of any time or country, though introduced on this Continent from Holland—there was little to be found in the Church architecture of the Fatherland, sufficiently distinctive to serve as a model; and the architect was left to use his material, a more beautiful one, as has been said, than that used in Holland,—in the way to which that material was best suited. Moreover as economy was a prime consideration, it was necessary, both externally and internally to do every thing which must be done, in such a way as to add to the general effect—to cover up nothing merely to hide it,—and to spend what little money could be devoted to ornament on one or two points, instead of frittering it away over the whole building."

The following brief description was published in the *Christian Intelligencer* some time after the dedication of the Church in 1863.

"One of the first things that strikes a stranger is the fine site of the Church. It stands on a corner of two of the principal streets, two wide, shady, pleasant and not too busy streets the lot is one hundred and forty-one feet six inches, by one hundred and eighty-nine feet." *

"The Church faces Union street, the Consistory room faces Church street. The end of the Consistory abuts against the side of the Church forming an inverted angle so formed stands the tower surmounted by a spire. * * * * The whole building, including butresses, measures outside one hundred and thirteen feet from North to South and one hundred and sixteen feet from East to West; and it is one hundred and seventy feet from the ground to the top of the spire. It is built of stone and roofed with slate. The color of the stone used for the walls is a beautiful purple grey, varied by the introduction of stones of other colors, principally Con-

---

* The Church lot was originally one hundred by two hundred feet, Amsterdam measure, or about ninety-three by one hundred and eighty-seven English feet. Deeming this too narrow, the Consistory, in 1861, purchased the adjoining lot on the East, of the heirs of Isaac Riggs, thus increasing the width of the site forty-six feet. The price paid was $2,605.

necticut brown stone. The tracery of the large Rose Window over the entrance is of Caen Stone. The main entrance is enriched with polished shafts of red granite, with bases and capitals of Nova Scotia stone, the latter carved with representations of the principal productions of the Mohawk Valley, such as oats, broom corn, hops, &c. The text of Scripture carved over this door it the following ": " I have brought the first fruits of the land, which thou O Lord hast given me." Deut. 26 : 10.

"One of the side entrances is called in accordance with an old Dutch Custom the *Brides door*, and over it is a little triplet window with shaftlets of polished white marble, whose capitals are filled with orange blossoms carved in stone."

The legend over this door is the following text of scripture:—
"His banner over me was love,"* Canticles II : 4.

[The eastern side entrance named " Forefather's Door," contains the scripture passage from 1 King's 8 : 57 "The Lord our God be with us as he was with our fathers."]

"These beautiful passages † from the word of God take the place of those symbols sometimes seen in painted architecture, the use of which is by our Catechism forbidden."

"The dimensions of the interior are as follows: the church is sixty by one hundred feet : the Consistory fifty by thirty feet and the tower about sixteen feet square. In the latter a book case is recessed in the wall for the Sunday School Library. The Church and Consistory have open timbered roofs, the former being fifty-eight feet and the latter forty-four feet high from floor to ridge. There are no galleries except one at the entrance end of the Church. A space for the Choir is provided in connection with the organ behind the pulpit. By thus placing the organ behind the pulpit, and so grouping the representatives of the preaching, prayer and praise which make up our worship, that barrenness of the pulpit end of the interior, which in so many of our churches makes itself painfully felt, is here avoided. The Consistory room that feature peculiar to us, is also made to add greatly to the effect of the building, both externally and internally. The screen which divides it from the Church is composed of carved black Walnut and plate glass—is thirty

---

* [ Carved in May, 1880.  W. E. G. ]
† [five in number, three of which are in gold, W. E. G.]

feet wide and over forty feet high, and by an arrangement of weights * in themselves ornamental can be opened or closed. The advantage of this was shown on the occasion of the dedication when the Consistory room was filled by the overflow of the congregation, who were thus enabled as well as those in the Church, to see and hear and take part in the Services. The windows are so managed that while there is no glare to the eye, a softened light falls from above on the faces of both preacher and people. One of the principal windows bears the arms of the Dutch church and its mottoes; *Nisi Dominus frustra: Eendracht maakt macht.* The windows of the tower (which open into both Church an Consistory by large archways) contain views of four of the different churches which have succeeded each other during a period of nearly two hundred years. In other windows may be seen the Coats of Arms of some of the Dutch families of Schenectady. * * * One of the pleasant things connected with the building of this church is the generosity which has been called forth. The organ, † a beautiful instrument in every sense; the pulpit of carved black walnut enriched with costly marbles; the screen before spoken of; ‡ and all the windows, are gifts to the church, some of them by persons not residents of Schenectady, but who thus give evidence that they have not forgotten that they are her children."

"All the windows are filled with stained glass. A good deal of color has been introduced in the interior decoration. All the construction is in sight and made serve a decorative purpose. The building is equally well finished in every part. No imitations have been used; stone, wood, iron and plaster, all showing for just what they are." ‖

---

* [these weights were removed several years ago, after an accident, and the windows are now raised by concealed pulleys like ordinary window sashes. [W. E. G.]

† the gift of the late Abraham Doty, a former officer of the church. [W. E. G.]

‡ the screen and pulpit were the gift of Mr. Gershom Bancker. [W. E. G.]

‖ For a full and detailed description of this church reference may be had to the architects " statement of the considerations influencing the the design of the First Dutch Reformed Church, Schenectady, N. Y.," published in 1868.

For a plan of this church see appendix D.

Every one of the upright windows and the two large rose windows of the church were presented by friends or members in their own name or in memoriam of relatives. The North rose window, representing in stained glass, Faith, Hope and Charity, was presented by the daughters of the late Andrew Yates, a former professor in Union College. The South rose window, presented by the members of the Vedder family, contains the coat of arms of the House of Orange with the added motto of the Dutch Church, and is set in Caen Stone. The four triplet windows at the North and South angles of the Eastern and Western walls were presented by John McNee, Jacob V. Vrooman and Nicholas Van Vranken. The windows in the South and North and West walls of the church are the gift of Henry Rosa, Albert Ward, Martin DeForest, Mrs. Amelia Klein Groot and Casper F. Hoag. The East wall is pierced by five windows. The first is the gift of P. W. Holmes, in memory of his grandfather, Volkert Douw Oothout. The second is in memory of Helen Ann Consaul. The third is the gift of Julia T. Doty, and the fourth of William H. Helmer. The fifth is in memory of Jonas Holland, born March 10th, 1784, died March 25th, 1839. The uninscribed tower window of black walnut and plate glass was given by Peter B. Yates. The windows in the tower room are the gifts of Aaron Barringer and Chauncy Vibbard. In the Consistory room, the South window was given by Thomas B. Mitchell. Of the North windows, one is in memory of Abraham A. and Marie Truax, and the other two contain the coats of arms of the Cuyler and Clute families. Of the five windows over the entrance door, the central one is the gift of Nicholas Cain, and the others of Thomas H. Reeves, Daniel Vedder, Charles N. Yates and Charles E. Angle. Since the church was erected, eight or more of the donors have died, so that several of these windows are already *in memoriam* of the departed friends, whose names they bear. The tablet set in the niche in the eastern wall, reads as follows :

TO THE
# GLORY
OF
## ALMIGHTY GOD,

IN HONOR OF THE FOUNDERS OF THIS CITY

### A. D. 1662.

AND OF THIS CHURCH

### A. D. 1680.

IN PITIFUL REMEMBRANCE OF THE MARTYRS WHO PERISHED IN THE MASSACRES,

OF

### FEBRUARY 8th 1699, AND JULY 18th 1748.

IN REVERENT MEMORY OF THEIR FOREFATHERS.

IN GRATITUDE TO THEIR BENEFACTORS,

### HANS JANSE ENKLUYS, DEID 1683.

AND

### NICHOLAS VAN DERVOLGEN, DIED 1799.

AND IN TESTIMONY OF THE FAITHFUL LABORS OF THEIR

PASTORS.

| | | | |
|---|---|---|---|
| Petrus Taschenmaecker | 1684-1690 | John H. Meier | 1803-1806 |
| Bernardus Freeman | 1700-1705 | Cornelius Bogardus | 1808-1812 |
| Johannes Lydius | 1705-1709 | Jacob Van Vechten | 1815-1849 |
| Thomas Brouwer | 1715-1728 | William J. R. Taylor | 1749-1853 |
| Reinhardt Erichzon | 1728-1736 | Julius H. Seelye | 1853-1858 |
| Cornelius Van Santvoord | 1740-1752 | Denis Wortman | 1865-1870 |
| Barent Vrooman | 1754-1784 | Ashbel G. Vermilye | 1871-1876 |
| Dirck Romeyn | 1784-1804 | Wm. Elliot Griffis | 1877—— |
| Jacob Sickles | 1794-1797 | | |

THE PEOPLE OF THIS CHURCH CELEBRATE THEIR

200TH ANNIVERSARY.

AND

ERECT THIS MEMORIAL

JUNE 21st, 1880.

This edifice was dedicated to the purpose of worship and praise on the 6th day of August, 1863,—the anniversary of the destruction of the former house two years before. The sermon on this occasion was preached by Rev. Doctor Edward E. Seelye, his text being the fifth verse of the seventh chapter of Luke. "For he loveth our nation and he hath built us a synagogue." The following tablet set into the niche reserved for it on the western wall of the church, to the right of the pulpit was erected in 1878.

## THE REFORMED PROTESTANT DUTCH CHURCH

OF

SCHENECTADY.

FOUNDED A. D. 1680.

This edifice, the corner-stone of which was laid May 29th, 1862, was dedicated

TO THE WORSHIP OF ALMIGHTY GOD

August 6th, 1863.

EDWARD E. SEELYE, *Pastor.*

| | |
|---|---|
| SIMON C. GROOT, | H. V. V. CLUTE, |
| MARTIN DEFOREST, | ABRAM DOTY, |
| CASPER F. HOAG, | THOMAS B MITCHELL, |
| ABRAM VROOMAN, | CORNELIUS THOMPSON. |

*Building Committee.*

EDWARD TUCKERMAN POTTER, *Architect.*

Ponsonby and Magin, Mastor Masons.   Peter Van Dyck, Master Carpenter.

## CHAPTER XIII.

### THE VOORLEZER, VOORSANGER AND KLOKLUYER; BURIAL CUSTOMS AND PLACES.

*Voorlezer.*—The duties of *Voorlezer* and *Voorsanger* were usually united in the same person and defined in the following resolution of the consistory:—

January 8th, 1810, "Resolved that in future the clerk of the church shall commence the public service in the morning with the reading of the ten commandments, a chapter of the Bible * and Psalm or Hymn at discretion, and in the afternoons, with the reading of the articles of the Creed together with the chapter and Psalm or Hymn." In addition to the above he had "the right and emoluments of burying the dead of the congregation." Next to the minister he was the most important officer of the church.

According to tradition the first *Voorlezer* of this church was Harmen Albertse Vedder, and the second his son Albert. They were succeeded by the following persons:—

Jan Dellamont, 1735–49, with a salary of £7 to £12.
Philip Riley, † 1750–57,          "      "    £8–10 to £14.
Johannes Van Sice, 1758–66,      "      "    £12.
Daniel Price, 1768.
Pieter Van Benthuysen, 1768–70, "      "    £12.
Cornelis DeGraaf, 1771–1800,    "      "    £20, or $50.
Simon J. Van Antwerp, English
       clerk, 1798–1801,         "      "    £10.
Cornelius Van Vranken, 1801,     "      "    $50.
Cornelius Zeger Van Santvoord, 1802.

---

\* 1759 aen Johannes Vedder voor een Voorlezeri Byble.  £200.
—Church acct. book.

† Philip Ryley was *Catachisatie Meester* (and probably *Voorsanger* & *doodgraver*) of the church of Albany in 1761; in 1767 the church of Schenectady complained that he had taught unsound doctrine, and he was called upon by the Church of Albany to recant, refusing to do so, they deprived him of his office of *voorlezer, doodgraver* &c., and ordered him to vacate his house.
—Albany Church minutes.

John J. Van Antwerp, 1803.
Arent A. Vedder, * 1804–8.
William R. Bogardus, 1809–13.
Abraham Swits, 1814.
Eliud L. Davis, 1815–22, (?) with a salary of $75.

To improve the Psalmody of the congregation, on the 13th of February, 1794, the Consistory took the following action:

"The Consistory taking into consideration the defective condition of the Dutch Psalmody in the public worship of this church,

Resolved, That Cornelis DeGraaf, the Chorister, shall use his endeavors, in each family of this village and elsewhere, to obtain pupils in singing, on condition that each shall pay one shilling and sixpence a month, the Consistory also adding thereto for each scholar for the term of six months, one shilling and six pence a month; provided a certificate be shown to the Consistory signed by Mr. DeGraaf that each scholar has diligently spent his time as he ought. Also Mr. DeGraaf in singing shall try to observe the measure of the half notes and soften his voice as much as possible."

If tradition tells the truth respecting Mr. DeGraaf's singing the advice last given was by no means inappropriate. It is said that while sitting on the "back stoop" of his house then standing upon the site of Mrs. Abel Smith's house in State street, he beguiled the evening hours in summer by psalm singing and that his voice could be clearly heard two miles up the river in a straight line.

*Klokluyer.*—The sexton of the church was called the *Klokluyer*, or bellringer and his duties seem to have been not only to ring the bell, but to keep the benches and seats in proper order and to dig and fill the graves. The earliest mention of this officer by the church records is the following:—

"At a Consistory held this 1st July, 1696, it was resolved that Simon Groot senior, for rigning the bell and arranging the benches and stools in the church, shall receive annually out of the income of the church, or out of the deacon's money, the sum

---

* 1778, Feb. 6th. Arent A. Vedder was *Voorlezer* of the Church of Albany.
—Consistory minutes.

of 60 guilders, seawant, [$7.50], to begin on this 1st July. Thus done in Schenectady this 1st July, 1696." *

Simon Groot senior mentioned in this resolution was the first of the name, who settled at Schenectady and the ancester of all the Groots found in this vicinity. He and his five sons were carried away captive in to Canada by the French and Indians in 1690.

The salary of the sexton down to 1735 was 60 guilder or $7.50. This year Hendrick Vrooman filled the office and was succeeded by Joseph Van Sice until 1747 at a yearly stipend of £6 or $15.

Margarita Veeder, † widow of Symon Volkertse Veeder, held the office during the years 1718–9 for £3–10 or $8.25.

From 1750 to 1758 Sara Marselis was *klokluyer*, the duties being performed for £4 or $10 "*by haar neger Sees.*"

In 1759 Isaac Quackenbos' *neger* rang the bell :—and "Peeter Seesar" (Caesar) from 1760 to 1766, for £6 *per. an*.

Jacobus Van Sice was sexton from 1771 to 1791, at a salary of £10 and was succeeded by his son Gysbert, who was dismissed from office in 1799 for an unfortunate indiscretion, as will appear from the following extract from the Consistory minutes :—

"October 25th, 1799. A complaint having been delivered in against G. Van Sice, the Sexton, that he had delivered the scull of a corpse to the house of Doctor Anderson; being sent for and interrogated, he finally confessed that he had taken a scull out of the burying yard and delivered it to Mr. Hagaman, student of medicine with Dr. Anderson."

"Resolved, That Van Sice without fail return the scull tomorrow morning and deposit it in presence of one of the members of this board in the place whence it was taken."

"Resolved, Moreover, that said Van Sice be and is hereby dismissed from his service as Sexton."

---

\* KerkenRaad gehouden desen 1en July, 1696. Is geresolveert dat Simon Groot d' oude voor het Klokluyden, bank en stoelen setten in de kke, jaarlyx uyt d inkomsten der kke of uyt de kasse des diaconye jaarlyx genieten sul de some van 60 gl zeewant welk syn aanvang desen 1en July nemen sal. Aldus in Schenechtade desen 1en July, 1696.

† she lived on the north corner of Union and Church streets,

"26th Oct., 1799. Mr. Lighthall was appointed Sexton in the place of G. Van Sice removed." He continued in office until 1829, and was succeded by John TenEyck.

It would appear from the following resolution of the Consistory, that it was the duty of the Sexton to preserve order in Church during public worship, and it is presumed that the ears of not a few of the worthy burgers of Schenectady will tingle as they read this extract and remember the faithful services of those ancient worthies Lighthall and Ten Eyck, in carrying out the behests of their superiors.

"June 8th, 1880, Resolved, That the Sexton is authorized by this board to maintain due order in Church during public worship, and that he shall be indemnified against any legal process, which may arise in consequence of correcting or turning out of church, the unruly and refractory : provided he do not essentially injure, or scandalously abuse any person."

*Funerals.*—At funerals "no woman attended the body to the grave, but after the corpse was borne out, remained to eat cakes and drink spiced wine. They retired quietly before the men returned, who resumed the feast and regaled themselves. Spiced wine, and cakes and pies were provided, and wine and cakes were sent to the friends of the family. The best room in the house was specially appropriated as the "dead room" and was rarely opened but to be aired and cleaned. Wealthy citizens in anticipation of a death in their families, were accustomed to procure a cask of wine during their lifetime and preserved it for this purpose." \* When the coffin was removed from the house it was placed upon a bier at the door and covered with a pall of black cloth. † The bier was then borne upon the shoulders of the bearers to the grave followed only by invited guests. The chief direction of the funeral ceremonies was taken by the *Voorlezer* assisted by the *Klokluyer*, and all their charges were regulated by the Consistory. The following is a list of prices established in 1771.—

---

\* Annals of Albany I 129.

† The church owned two palls, which were always used on these occasions ; for the use of the *great pall* a charge was made of three shillings ; for the *small pall* nine pence.

"Rules for Cornelis DeGraaf, appointed Sexton the 18th of November, 1771, in regard to what he is at liberty to take for inviting [the friends] and burying [the dead]:

"For a person of 20 years and upwards, - - 16s. to 20s.
For a person of 15 to 19 years, - - - 15s. to 19s.
For a person of 10 to 14 years, - - - 14s. to 18s.
For a person of 5 to 9 years, - - - 13s. to 17s.
For a person of 1 to 4 years, - - - - 8s. to 12s.
For an unbaptised child [infant] when the bell
    shall be rung once, - - - - - 6s. to 10s.
For ditto when the bell shall not be rung; - 3s. to 7s.
For the Great Pall, - - - - - 3s.
For the Little Pall, - - - - - -9d.

All thus when he is obliged to invite [the friends] within the Village; but when he likewise is obliged to extend the invitations without, he may ask 4 shillings [altered to 6 shillings] more each; this is to be understood, as far as Claas Viele's, [upper end of Maalyck,] or this side; but when he is obliged to extend invitations further—to Syme Vedder's, [Hoffman's Ferry,] or this side—then he may ask yet 3 shillings [altered to 6 shillings] more. The prices in the above standing rules are increased by reason of the hard times."

"Regulations for Jacobus Van Sice, appointed grave-digger and bell-ringer for the dead, on the 18th November, 1771, in respect to what he may take for grave digging and bell-ringing:
For a person of 7 up to and above 20 years, for a grave, 3 shillings, and for the bell 3 shillings.
For a child of 1 to 6 years, for the grave 2 shillings, and for the bell 3 shillings.
For an unbaptised child when the bell shall be rung once, for the grave 2 shillings, and for the bell 2 shillings.
For tolling the bell he may likewise ask 1 shilling more.

The above mentioned Jacobus Van Sice shall, at his own expence, keep proper tools for making and filling graves, likewise proper cords, &c."

The following is a list of persons for whose burial the Church Pall was used by Arent A. Vedder, Clerk and Sexton of the Church. He was obliged to pay to the Church three shillings each time he used the Pall for grown persons and nine-pence for small children:—

| | | | |
|---|---|---|---|
| 1803, Sept. | 8. | Fred. Reese's child, | £0–0–9 |
| " | 9. | Adam Van Slyck, | 0–3–0 |
| " | 22. | William DeGraaf, | 0–3–0 |
| Nov. | 7. | Myndert A. Wemple's child, | 0–9 |
| " | 21. | Jacob Van Guysling, | 3–0 |
| Dec. | 5. | Sister's child, | 0–9 |
| " | 26. | Abm. Schermerhorn's wife, | 3–0 |
| " | 31. | Catharine Bradt, | 3–0 |
| 1804, Jan. | 6. | Wm. J. Schermerhorn's wife, | 3–0 |
| " | 22. | A child of Esq. Wilkie, | 0–9 |
| " | 23. | Caty Barhydt, dau. of Jno. B. | 3–0 |
| " | 24. | James Rosa's wife, | 3–0 |
| Mar. | 10. | Folkey Swits, | 3–0 |
| April | 10. | a child of Corn. Van Antwerp | –9 |
| " | " | a child of Saml. Jones, | –9 |
| " | 18. | Domeny Romeyn, | 3–0 |
| June | 7. | Christopher Ward's son, | –9 |
| " | 18. | a dau. of Jno. R. Vrooman, | 3–0 |
| July, | 9. | a child of Harm. Van Slyck, | –9 |
| " | 19. | Nicholas Van Patten, | 3–0 |
| " | 27. | a child of Jacob Van Antwerp, | –9 |
| Aug. | 4. | a child of James Rose, | –9 |
| " | 10. | a child of Mr. Tyms, | –9 |
| " | 11. | a child of Mrs. Mackentire, | –9 |
| " | 25. | a child of James Van Sice, | –9 |
| " | 30. | Michael Tyms, | 3–0 |
| Sept. | 9. | Folkert Veeder, | 3–0 |
| " | 12. | John Toll, | 3–0 |
| " | 19. | a child of Corn Bradt, | –9 |
| " | 25. | Folly Wemple, | 3–0 |
| Oct. | 1. | Dau. of Johannes Vedder, | 3–0 |
| " | 3. | Andrew Truax, | 3–0 |
| " | 4. | Christina Moyston, | 3–0 |
| " | 7. | Joseph Carley's child, | –9 |
| | | | £3–8–3 |
| " | 9. | Alida Fonda wife of Jacob F. | 3–0 |
| " | " | a child of Richd. Waldrum, | –9 |
| " | 10. | a child of Mr. Williams, | –9 |
| " | 11. | a child of James Wood, | –9 |

|  |  |  |  |
|---|---|---|---|
| " | 21. | John S. Bradt, | 3–0 |
| Nov. | 17. | a child of Nich. N. Marselis, | –9 |
| Dec. | 12. | a child of Jno. Bpt. Clute's wife's dau. | –9 |
| 1805, Feb. | 9. | Marta Frank's child, | –9 |
| " | 15. | Abraham Fonda, | 3–0 |
| Mar. | 6. | Susan Truax, | 3–0 |
| " | 13. | Elizabeth Visger, | 3–0 |
| " | 17. | Gerardus Quackenbos' wife, | 3–0 |
| " | 26. | John Vrooman—hermitage, | 3–0 |
| June | 2. | Emetje Veeder, | 3–0 |
| " | 21. | Richd. Waldrum's wife, | 3–0 |
| July | 13. | Jno. Baptist Van Eps, | 3–0 |
| " | 18. | Andrew McMartin, | 3–0 |
| " | 21. | John S. Bardydt's wife, | 3–0 |
| " | 23. | Jno. F. Clute. | 3–0 |
| " | 24. | a child of Mr. Cole, | –9 |
| Aug. | 8. | a child of Mr. Jno. C. Barhydt. | –9 |
| " | " | Harmanus Van Slyck, | 3–0 |
| " | 10. | a child of Rev. Nich. Van Vranken, | –9 |
| " | 15. | Jacob Winne, | 3–0 |
| " | 17. | Mr. Olsaver, | 3–0 |
| " | 24. | Mr. Carpenter, | 3–0 |
| Sept. | 5. | a child of Wm. H. Peters, | –0 |

|  |  |  | £6–8–0 |
|---|---|---|---|
| Sept. | 12. | Rykert Van Vranken, | 3–0 |
| " | 16. | a boy of Thos. Clinch, | –9 |
| " | 24. | Abraham Groot, | 3–0 |
| " | " | a child of Thos. Clinch, | 3–0 |
| Oct. | 1. | John W. Truax, | 3–0 |
| " | 27. | a dau. of Mr. Jno. Mynders, | 3–0 |
| Nov. | 4. | a child of Jno. Lambert, | –9 |
| " | 18. | Albert Vedder, | 3–0 |
| Dec. | 23. | a dau. of Dav. Vander Heyden | 3–0 |

|  |  | £7 10–6 |
|---|---|---|
| Wid. Eve Bradt and son, | | 6–0 |
| Myndert Wemple's child, | | –9 |
| Christopher Ward's son, | | –9 |
| Danl. Peck—2ce the small one, | | 1–6 |

|  |  |
|---|---|
| Arent Van Antwerp, | 3–0 |
|  | £8–5–9 |
| Sarah Wid. of Isaac Marselis, | 3–0 |
|  | £8 8–9 |

Rec'd. Pay. 19th Feb., 1806.

Prior to the year 1800 there had probably been no hearse in the village; in all funeral processions the bier and pall were used; hence, as it was not convenient to carry the dead great distances in this manner, the people in the country buried upon their own lands.

At a meeting of the Consistory held April 7th, 1800, it was

"Resolved, That a hearse be procured as soon as convenient for the use of carrying the dead of this Congregation to the burying ground, and also for the use of the public, under such regulations as this board shall afterward prescribe."

And again December 3d, 1800, having obtained a hearse it was

"Resolved, That the hearse and harness be kept by the Sexton in some convenient place as near the burying ground as possible, to be provided by the Consistory; and that whenever any of the citizens may want it, application be made to him, and that it be his duty to collect the fees." * * * * *

*Burial places.*—The earliest public burying ground * in the village was on the West side of the first church at the junction of Church and State streets. After this plot of ground had been used for this purpose about 60 years another was selected without the palisades,—the grave yard lying between Front & Green streets.

In 1705 this spot together with all the land lying west of it to the Fort, then covered with woods was granted to Philip Schuyler for £18 N. Y. currency, or 45 Dollars. Two years before, Ryer Schermerhorn the sole living patentee had granted

---

* It was not uncommon for persons residing without the village to bury their dead upon their own lands : Many of these enclosures are still found on the old homesteads along the banks of the Mohawk. The only private burying ground known to have been within the village was that of Adam Vrooman. This was on his pasture lot on the North side of Front street, on lot now numbered 42 ; its dimensions were 46 feet in depth by 9½ feet in width.

4 morgens of wood land lying to the Eastward of the present burying grounds to Thomas Williams of Albany, who conveyed it, April 7th, 1709, to Arent Van Petten from whom it passed to his son Frederick.

The following are abstracts from conveyances of the burial ground made to the Church:—

August 1st, 1721. The Patentees of Schenectady conveyed to the Dutch Church a lot, " for a Christian burial place for all the Christians of the town of Schenectady and adjacent places":
\* \* \* \* " lying Eastward of the fort of Schenectady, the South side butting the roadway [Green street] opposite over against Dirk Groots' pasture ground 160 feet,—on the West side 240 feet, and on the East side [end] 338 feet long, butting the lot of Arent Van Petten:—and on the North side [on Front street] is 195 feet long." \*

This conveyance was confirmed by another conveyance to the Church made March 1st, 1733-4, by Jan Wemp and Arent Bradt, the surviving trustees of the Common lands.

\* \* \* \* \* "A lot of land and burial place lying to the eastward of His Majesty,s fort, in Schenectady, and on the East side of a lot belonging to Benjamin Van Vleck—being bounded as follows: On the South by a road leads to Symon Groot's bridge, † [Green Street,] on the North by the road that goes to Jellis Fonda's, [Front Street,] and on the West by the lot of Benjamin Van Vleck:—Beginning from the Northeast corner of the lot of said Van Vleck [on Front Street] and running East 217 feet to a *stack* put there unto the ground for a mark; then South 330 feet to another *stack* put up there for a mark, [on North side of Green Street]; then West 155 feet to the South-east corner of the Lott of Benjamin Van Vleck; and then North along the lot of said Van Vleck 232 feet to the place of beginning—all Amsterdam measure—for a Christian Buriall Place for all Christians in the said town and places adjacent that are now, or which from time to time and forever hereafter shall be." \*

On the 7th of August, 1765, Frederick Van Patten, for the sum of £125, conveyed to the Church a parcel of ground for an

---

\* See old deed among Church papers.

† Symon Groot's bridge over *Symon's kil*—now College brook—was within the yard of the Locomotive Works, and in a line with Pine Street.

addition to the East side of the burial grounds, which parcel is described as follows: —

"All that parcel of land on the East side of the town on the South side of a street that comes out of said town and leads by Jacob Fonday's to the *Aelplaas*, * [Front street], and also on the North side of a street [Green] that comes out of said town and leads back of his Majestys' fort by the house of Jacobus Van Vorst and Jeronimus Barheydt—being *putted* and bounded as followeth:—On the North the Highway leading by Jacob Fonday's to the *Aelplaas* aforesaid; on the West the Church yard or burial place; on the South the Highway that leads back of the Fort by Jacobus Van Vorst aforesaid:—On the East by a lott of ground [which the said Frederic Van Petten reserves for himself] laid out between the lott of Myndert Wemple and the here in above recited land, which lot is to contain in front along said street [Green] fifty feet and in *rare* [rear] along the lot of Zeger Van Santfort 53 feet all woodmeasure, and the above rented ground is also bounded on the East by a lot of ground heretofore sold to Zeger Van Santfort." †

A great majority of the people buried their dead in the common burying ground, but for those who coveted the honor or sanctity of a grave in the church, this privilege could be bought for about twenty times the price of a common grave. The following were the rules for burying the dead in the Church in 1759:

For persons of twelve years old and upwards there shall be paid three pounds. For graves of children of four years to twelve, forty shillings. And for the grave of a young child up to four years of age, four & twenty shillings. ‡

*Monuments.*—No head stones are found at the graves of the first settlers; the graver's art did not then exist among them and the marble and granite had not then been quarried.

---

* The *Aelplaas* was above the State dam at the Aqueduct.

† It is believed that this lot of Zeger Van Santvoord, fronting on Front St. was subsequently acquired by the Church and added to the burial ground.
—See church papers.

‡ Regelatie voor Graften in de kerck van Dooden als Volght:—Van Twalf Jaaren out tot dat sy out syn sullen daar Voor Betalen Drie Pont,—En voor de Graften van kinderen van vier Jaar out Tot Twalf Jaaren out Veertigh Schellinge,—En voor Een graft van En Jonck kint Tot vier Jaaren out vier en Twentigh Schellinge.

The oldest gravestone found in the city was a few years since taken from a cellar wall into which it had been built, having been used evidently as a whetstone many years after it had served the purpose of a funeral monument. It was a fragment of the blue stone, found in the quarries East of the City; its dimensions were fourteen by seven inches and four inches thick and bore the following inscription rudely and slightly cut:—

Anno 1690
Den XX8 May
is myn soon in den
Here gerust
Hendrick Jansen
Vrooman,
Jan Vrooman.

[Translation.] "On the 28th of May, in the year 1690, my son, Hendrick Vrooman, rested in the Lord. Jan Vrooman."

The oldest grave stone in the Church burying ground was set up in 1722, and is of the same material as the above mentioned stone.

## CHAPTER XIV.

### ENDOWMENTS.

Probably no church in the State, outside of the city of New York, was so munificently endowed as that of Schenectady. In 1740 she owned fully 12 square miles of land in this county, which, had it been conveyed by long leases and not in fee, would have been worth to her now from $300,000 to $500,000. All this magnificent estate has passed away, and fortunately at this time she possesses barely a fine house of worship and the lot upon which it stands. I say fortunately, for it seldom happens that great wealth in a church conduces to growth of piety among her members.

Several reasons may be assigned for the dissipation of this large property. Inasmuch as the pew rents covered but a small part of the current expenses of the church, this deficiency was supplied from time to time by the sales of the patent lands, which were held of little account except for pasturage and timber and were sold therefore at a low figure. Moreover, if tradition be correct, large portions also of this fair domain were frittered away in gifts to the relatives and friends of influential members of the congregation, under cover of conveyances, with a mere nominal consideration. Only a brief description can be given here of the chief pieces of real estate that have been owned by this church.

1. *Church sites.*—The first in order of time was the old site at the junction of Church and State streets. It must have been reserved for this purpose from the first laying out of the village, before the year 1664, which accounts for the great width of Church street. Its dimensions North and South were 56 feet, East and West 46 feet, Amsterdam measure, together with a strip of 15 feet wide upon the West side for a burying ground. Subsequently it was extended South 84 feet towards the creek— the rear line being 44½ feet.* On this extension now stands the house which belonged to the late Gerardus Q. Carley.

After having been used for various public purposes the Consistory resolved, in 1785, to build their new Academy upon it ; afterwards, to erect a dwelling house upon it ; and finally to convey it to Arent S. Vedder for the same purpose. But all these projects failed because it was manifestly unsuitable for a building site (saving the rear on Mill Creek) and especially that portion which had been used for more than 50 years as a village burial ground.

Finally when the Church began their new House of Worship, in 1812, the Consistory resolved to sell this lot together with

---

* About fifty years after the village was laid out the church first received a formal conveyance of their House of Worship and lot from the Patentees of Schenectady. This is dated 3d October, 1715, and on the back is this endorsement made doubtless at a later daty :

"Wood measure" [11 inches to the foot.]
"The front is 60 [feet]
"behind 44½
"Deph 140

their other church site at the junction of Church and Union Streets to the City for 200 acres of land, worth at least $10 an acre: "Provided that these two lots shall never be used for private purposes, but left open in the street for public convenience."

2. *De Arme Wey or Poor Pasture.*—Of all the ample domains of the Church *De Arme wey* was the longest held and the last sold. The title deeds of this property are lost if any ever existed; even tradition is at fault, and the donor's true name has utterly perished from the remembrance of those who have been benefitted by it.

The story has been told that Jan Rinckhout gave this property to the church reserving simply "a small spot on which he erected a hut partly under ground," and there lived a hermit life.

Rinckhout was a baker in Albany, but about 1670 removed to Schenectady, having leased his house and bakery to Antony Lespinard, "with privilege of baking for Christians and savages." He was living in Schenectady as late as 1704, when his son, Jurriaen, dying, made provision in his will that his wife, six children and father, Jan, should be maintained out of his real and personal estate here and in New York. It is certain that the Church owned *De Arme Wey* seventeen years prior to this date. These facts therefore render it quite improbable that Jan Rinckhout was the donor.

Discarding tradition and romance the evidence is clear that the true benefactor of "the poor of Schenectady" was Hans Janse Eencluys, an ancient servant and soldier of the Dutch West India Company. He early came to New Netherland, and was sent by Governor Van Twiller, in 1632, to erect the arms of the States General at a spot called *Kievits Hoek* [Saybrook] at the mouth of the Connecticut river.

On the occasion of Governor Stuyvesant's visit to Rensselaerswyck, in 1648; he was employed to clean the Heer Patroon's cannons and to fire the salutes. As early as 1668 he was an Inhabitant of Schenectady, where he continued to reside until his death, in 1683, after which event the Deacons of the Church, Johannes Pootman and Sweer Teunis Van Velsen, petitioned the Court of Albany for authority to administer upon his estate, saying that on the 7th day of March, 1674–5, he [Hans Janse Eenkluys] had made over to the poor of Schenectady his plantation, upon condition that he should be maintained in his old age and weakness, and that on the 2nd of May, 1680, he had made the Deacons of the Church administrators of his whole estate. They aver, also, that thirteen years ago [1670] he began to be very weak, that they had given him support while living and had paid the expenses of his funeral.

This petition to the court of Albany—the only clue to the Church's title to this valuable property—is as follows:—

Aende E. Achtbr Heeren
Commissarissen Van Albany
Colonie rensselaersw: etc.

Verthoonth met behoorelyke reuerentie Johannes Pootman ende Sweer Theunissen diaconen van Schaenhechtade, hoe dat eenen Hans Janssen op den 7 meert 1674-5 heeft ouergedraegen aende aermen van Schaenhechtade zeecke zyne plantage mede gelegen aen Schaenhechtade onder conditie dat hy in zynen ouderdom ende Swackheyt daer voor zoude onderhonden werdden, blyckende by zyne handt teeckeninge op Dato Voor *de* het is nu soe dat de supplianten Voor *&c* den seluen eenigen tydt Volgens zyne Vahnacht in den dato den 2 May, 1680, onderhoudt hebben gegeuen, ende mitsgaders zyne begraeftenisse bekosticht, ende dat op den thoon beginnen to Komen seer Swacke reckeningen wel Van dertien Jaeren geleden, d' welcke den supplianten doet bedencken hierinne niet to administeeren Sonder UE. Achtbr notitie Versoeckende derhaluen hierinne to moden genieten het beste benefitien Voor den aermen Volgens zyne begeerte waerop haer Verlaeten blyuen

UE. Achtbr diensten
onderdaenen
Johannes Pootman
Sweer thoonissen Van Velsen. *

[Endorsed upon this paper is the following:]

Haer E vand Gerechte Ravvoyerden C Supplianten aen D Commiss. Van Shinnechtady. Actum in Albany op den 1 May, 1683.

Pr. Cur.
Pet. Livingston, Seer.

request voor de Diaconen van Schaenhechtade.

---

* See Church papers.

This *Plantation* is first mentioned in the Church books in 1687, when it was leased to Symen Groot, Barent Wemp and Gysbert Gerritse Van Brakel for 82 guilders ($32.80) per an. The rent was paid chiefly in wheat at five skipples the beaver, or 80 cents a bushel. About this time it began to be called *De Wey*, *Hans Janse's Wey*, and *De Arme Wey*.

In 1742–8 it was leased to Gillis Fonda for £19–7 (48.38).

To Cornelis DeGraaf it was leased in 1781 for £36, or $90. 1784 for £48, or $120. 1785 for £40, or $100.

1789 to Jacob Fonda for £48, or $120.

The *Poor Pasture*,\* in its original condition, consisted of Eighteen morgens (about 36 acres) of the finest Mohawk flats, and was bounded by the river on the North, the River road (a continuation of Front Street) on the South, the "Fonda Place" on the West, and the "Hansen kil" (now College brook) on the East, by which it was separated from the *Boght*. This latter parcel of land, consisting of 16 acres, was purchased of Harmanus Van Slyck, in 1806, for $1,750.

Several attempts were formerly made by the Church to dispose of this property but without success.

In 1795 the Consistory "Resolved to sell the *Arme Wey* for not less than £800, ($2,000), at which price no purchaser was found; but in 1863 it was disposed of, including the *Boght*, at auction for about $11,000, and the avails were mingled with the general funds of the church.

Thus passed away Eenkluys' gift "to the poor of Schenectady," after having been in the possession of the Church nearly 190 years. Long ago the old soldier's name was forgotten, but the results of his benefaction are perpetuated to this day; not indeed in the direction which he had indicated, but in that beautiful structure lately dedicated as a house of worship. Among the honored names there emblazoned and curiously carved is there no room for that of *Hanse Janse Eenkluys?*

---

\* A memorandum made by Do. Van Santvoord makes mention of the conveyance of *The Pasture* by Gov. Lovelace (*Groot vief t in de weide by Gov. Lovelace*) as among the important papers of the Church. This was probably the Governor's patent to Eenkluys, and must have been dated about 1670. It is no longer among the church papers.

3. *Church Mill and Mill Pasture.*—This fine property, the bequest of Sweer Teunise Van Velsen, (*alias* Van Westbrook,) the town miller, consisted of six acres of land, bounded Northerly by State Street, Southerly by the *Sand kil,* (latterly called Mill Creek), Easterly by Dock Street, and Westerly by the lot of Douwe Aukes Defreeze, which latter lot, 140 feet front on State Street, (Amsterdam measure), was on the Westerly corner of mill lane and State Street, opposite the late Schenectady Bank building.

Defreeze was an inn keeper, and next East of his lot probably stood Van Velsen's house, his grist mill being in the rear on the Creek. Both houses were burned in the massacre of 1690 by the French and Indians, at which time Sweer Teunis with his wife Maritie Mynderse perished in the flames. As he left no heirs his property passed to the children of his wife by her first husband, Jan Barentse Wemp. It was understood, however, before his death, that he had made a will devising the half or third of his estate to the Church; but no such instrument was ever found. Nevertheless his step-children, to carry out his wishes, released to the Church the Mill and six acres of land above described.

The Church took possession of this property soon after Van Velsen's death, and within about thirty years disposed of the entire front upon State Street for building lots.

That portion between Ferry and Dock streets was divided into ten parcels varying in width from 45 to 53 feet (Amst. meas.). The lowland in the rear called the *Church parture* was retained until 18—, when it was sold to Archibald Craig and *
* * * *

The *Church Mill* stood upon, or near the site of the old brick mill now standing in Mill Lane. It was usually leased for about £50 New York Currency. After holding it for 120 years the Church sold it in 1800 to David Burt and John J. Peek for $2570. In 1813 it was turned into a Cotton Mill by Dr. Archibald Craig, who built the present brick building.

4. *The Sixth Flat.*—On the 20th May 1714, Ryer Schermerhorn, the only surviving Patentee of Schenectady, conveyed to the Dutch Church,—" A lot of land on the North side of the Mohawk river about 7 miles above Schenectady, called the *Sixth Flat*, containing about seven morgens or fourteen acres ;"

—"Also 10 morgens, or 20 acres of Wood land behind said Sixth flat and so going up to a creek called by the Indians Toggutchero,—in English named "Color Creek [in Dutch *Verfkil*], at the East end of the "Seventh flat," and so on North behind the said Flat into the woods as far as the bounds of the said town."

From a petition presented to the Trustees of the town, on the 16th January, 1716, by Jacobus Van Dyck, in behalf of the Consistory, it appears that these parcels of land had been purchased, but an account of pressing debts and urgent need they are asked to remit the purchase money. How long the Church retained this farm and how or when they disposed of it is not known. *

5. On the 25th January, 1715, the trustees of Schenectady conveyed to the Dutch Church a piece of woodland, "in the East end of the town, bounded North by the highway, [river road to the Aqueduct]—South by the common woods; West by the wood land of heirs of Hendrick Brouwer, and East by the land of Claas and Tjerk Fransen [Van de Bogart]. This land lay opposite to and this side of the, lower, (late Freeman's) bridge on the river road and was still in possession of the Church in 1734. How or when it was disposed of is not known.

6. *Leases.*—The Patentees and Trustees of Schenectady usually conveyed the common lands by perpetual leases, reserving a small quit rent either in money or more commonly in wheat.

On the 6th day of October, 1716, Ryer Schermerhorn, Jan Wemp, Johannes Teller, Arent Bradt and Barent Wemp, the Patentees of the town, assigned to the Church, all the leases which they then possessed, conditioned that the Consistory should pay the annual quitrent of 40 bushels of wheat due to the Province of New York.

The number and value of these leases does not appear.

Again on the 30th of December, 1747, Jan Wemp and Arent Bradt, then the only surrviving Patentees, assigned another batch of 29 leases "for the behoof of the Church Wardens"; and on the 26th of May, 1750, Pieter Felinck, the village schoolmaster, made out a list of all the leases then belonging to the Church, with the amounts due yearly on each. They were

---

* See Church papers.

found to be 46 in number, on which the rents amounted to 95 skipples of wheat,, £3-2-9 in money and 20 boards. *

7. *The Burial Lot.*—As has been before stated the earliest burial place used by the founders of Schenectady was on the West side of the old Church at the junction of State & Church streets. Some were buried *under* the Church, especially such as could afford to pay for this privilege.

The first mention made of the present burying ground between Front & Green streets is in the deed of this plat given by Patentees of the town to the Church, dated August 1st, 1721. †

8. A lot of ground " to the Northeast of the town and lying at the Northwest corner of Cornelis Slingerland's land upon the East side of Barent Vrooman's land, &c. This parcel was probably on the *Kalleberg* road.

9. *The Princetown Patent so called.*—This property consisting of 3870 acres exclusive of roads and 500 acres heretofore granted to Arent Van Petten and Jan Dellamont, was first surveyed and laid out for James DeLancey and John Chambers, who on the 7th November, 1737, released their claim to Arent Bratt and Jan Wemp, patentees of Schenectady.

Under date of the 16th of December, 1737, Bratt and Wemp received a patent for this tract, which was described as " beginning at the South west corner of the township of Schenectady and runs thence along the bounds of said township South 40° East 296 chains, and South 55° 30' East 149 chains, and South 74° 15' East 32 chains, then West 343 chains, then North 322 chains to the place of beginning."

On the 27th day of December the Elders and Deacons give a contract to said Bratt & Wemp, in which they promise to give a bond to pay them £500 for the above land and quitrent reserved on the same of 2-6 the 100 acres, within 14 days after they shall have received their new Church seal according to charter. ‡

10. *The Niskayuna Patent.*—This tract lay to the East and South of the Schenectady patent and extended from the *Ael Plaats* South to the North line of the Manor of Rensselaerswyck

---

* See Appendix E.
† For a description of this parcel of ground see Chapter XIII.
‡ Groote Schuld Boek.

In 1711 Capt. Philip Schuyler of Schenectady purchased these lands of the Indians, and in 1723 obtained a warrant for the survey of the same, but the justices of Schenectady objecting, he failed to obtain a Patent, because they were needed by the inhabitants "for a common or drift for cattle and for firewood." Again in 1738 Wouter Vrooman purchased a portion of this tract for " three blankets of strouds and three pairs of stockings," but failed of getting a conveyance from the Governor on account of the opposition of the citizens. *

On the 5th of August, 1738, a patent was obtained for this land by Arent Bradt and Jacob Glen in trust for the Reformed Protestant Dutch Church of Schenectady ; it was then estimated to contain 2,500 acres, but owing to an error in measurement rectified in 1788, fell considerably short of that amount. †

The West line of this church patent was the East line of the Schenectady patent, the starting point for which line at the *Ael-Plaats* had been fixed by the citizens at the mouth of *Jan de Laggers kil*. ‡ The Consistory claimed & rightly too, that this point should be at the mouth of the *Ael-plaats kil*, thus claiming a strip of land from the East bounds of the town, of more than 1200 acres. This controversy was finally determined in favor of the Church and Arent Bratt, only surviving Patentee of the town on February 5th, 1754, gave them a deed of Conveyance of the property. The whole number of acres conveyed to the Church by these conveyances was 3,621.

11. It appears also from a memorandum on the cover of the old Church Ledger, of dates 1790 & 1801, that the Consistory owned lots Nos. 18 and 26 of 200 acres each in Vrooman's Patent North of Jerseyfield.

---

\* Land papers, XII. 99, 123.

† The cost of this patent was £130-8, as appears by the following entry in the Church Ledger : —

‡ *Voor de patent tusс onse Nistagioene en de patrons lyn all de coste* £130-8.

‡ *Jan De Lagger's kil* is a small brook or rill emptying into the Mohawk river from the North side near the Aqueduct and many rods Easterly from the *Ael-plaats kil*; by assuming this as the starting point of the South Easterly line of the town patent the area of the town lands was increased at the expense of the Church, whose lands adjoined them on the South East.

## CHAPTER XV.

#### FINANCES.

In early times the Dutch churches often acted as guardians of widows and orphans; they provided for the poor and kindly looked after the aged and infirm, who had no natural protectors; and it was not unusual for the latter to place their property in the hands of the Consistory from whom they received from time to time such support as their wants required. The Consistory were the Almoners of the Church; every Lords day a collection was taken of the free will offerings of the people for this and certain other purposes, and this duty was not omitted even though there were no present objects upon whom their bounty might be bestowed.

In the outset the little community of Schenectady seems to have had few or no poor people; with the exception of a "shirt for a captive Frenchman" it does not appear from the accounts that the Deacons gave a stiver to any person during the years 1687–9. As the funds accumulated they were loaned on bond at 6% interest to citizens. Thus in the audit of 1689 obligations to the amount of nearly 3,000 guilders were included in the assets of the Church. Moreover the Consistory traded with another portion of these funds, buying and selling brass kettles, nails, linen, thread, baize, coverlets, &c. This seeming perversion of the funds given for a more sacred purpose was simply a temporary necessity of the times and ceased altogether when private enterprize provided for the wants of the people.

Among the permanent sources of income, were *de wey* or "Poor Pasture", originally given by Hans Janse Eenkluys "for the poor of Schenectady";—the Church Mill and Mill pasture given by Sweer Teunise Van Velsen:—leases received from the Trustees of the town * ;—seat rents and burial fees.

Besides the payment of the Domine's salary and the Voorlezer & Klokluyer's Stipends, out of these funds the bread and

---

* See Appendix E.

wine and sacred utensils for the Lord's Supper were purchased; the Church was cleaned, and incidental repairs to the Parsonage were made, such as glass for windows, posts, nails, &c., for the fence. *

A knowledge of the domestic habits and Church customs of a people is most difficult to be learned after a lapse of two centuries;—even uncommon events were seldom recorded, how much less likely then that social manners and every day occurrences should become matter of history. Particularly unfortunate has it been for Schenectady that the flames of 1690 spared almost nothing of her early records;—with the exception of a few leaves of the Deacons' account book all is blank.

As something however may be learned even from such unpromising materials as these, both in respect to the customs and finances of the Church, the following extracts are subjoined:

During the year 1686-7 the Church accounts were kept by Deacon Johannes Sanderse Glen and are quite legible.

[Translation.]

1686, 20th Oct. Jan Brouwer, Dr.

to 14 ells of linnen @ 7 ells the beaver † . . . 16 gl.

Maria Klein, Dr.

| | |
|---|---|
| ditto to 6 ells of linnen @ 7 ells the beaver, . . | 6–8 |
| to a coverlet @ 10 guild. . . . . | f. 10–0 |
| to 6 ells baize, . . . . . . . | 8– |
| to 4 lbs. nails, . . . . . . . | 2. |
| to 7 ells linen @ 7 ells the beav. . . | 8. |
| to 2 skeins thread, . . . . . . | 0–5 |

---

\* 1735 By een predicatie Bock. £1-4-0.

1777 December, the Church paid "Voor een gifte aan afgebrande menschen van dese plaats."

13th September, 1794 Bey Cassa voor een groten Engelsen Beybel.

5th September, 1815, The Consistory resolve to refund to the deacons enough to buy 4 silver mugs and one metal flaggon. [The present Communion service W. E. G.].

—Church, acct. book.

† The guilder, or florin, beaver was worth about 38 or 40 cts.—the guilder seewant, or wampum, was equal to one shilling N. Y. Currency or one-third of the former;—the beaver skin being considered the specie of the Province. These accounts are kept in guilders & stivers, partly seewant and partly beaver.

## HISTORY OF THE CHURCH. 181

|  |  |
|---|---|
| 15th Septem.  Johannes Potman, Cr. | |
| 11 days work on the church @ 7 guilders a day, | 25 |
| ditto Isaac de Trieux [Truax.] | |
| to 6 lbs. nails, | 3– |
| 20th Nov.  Adam Vrooman, Dr. | |
| to 9 lbs. nails, seawant, 14, | 4. |
| to 2 lbs. nails, beaver, | 1. |
| ditto Sander Glen, Dr. | |
| to 9 lbs. nails, | 4. |
| 1686, 30th Sept.  Johannes Glenn, Dr. | |
| to 42 lbs. nails @ 20 lbs. pr. beaver, | 17– |
| to 34 lbs. nails @ 20 lbs. pr. beaver, | 13–15 |
| to skiples of wheat, | |
| 1689, 30th Oct.  Cr. | |
| 2 beavers in silver money | 16– |
| one beaver, | 8. |
| also by settlement. | 6–15 |
| 8th Oct.  Domine Thesschenmaecker, Dr. | |
| to 14 ells of linnen @ 7 ells pr. beaver, | 16– |
| Walter Vrooman, Cr. | |
| for a place [seat] for his wife,* | 36– |
| ditto Barent Wemp, Dr. | |
| to 14 ells of linnen @ 7 ells pr. beaver, | 16– |
| 1689, Oct.  Cr. | |
| 2 beavers in silver, | 16– |
| ditto Sweer Teunisse [Van Velsen], † Dr. | |
| to 14 ells linnen @ 7 ells per beav. | 16– |
| to 7 ells linnen fetched by his maid Jannetie, | 8. |
| Nov. 1.  Cr. | |
| to silver f. 26.– beaver; | 26. |
| 10th Oct.  Daniel Janse Van Antwerpen, Dr. | |
| to 26 ells linnen @ 7 ells pr. beaver, | 29–15 |
| 1688, 20th Aug.  Cr. | |
| to 89–5 sewant, | 29–15 |
| 1686, 10th Oct. Abraham Groot, Dr. | |
| to 14 ell, linnen @ 7 ells beav. | 16– |

\* It would seem from this that a single seat in the church at this time cost 36 gl., or $4.50.

† The town miller, killed in the massacre of 1690.

|  | 1688. | Cr. |
|---|---|---|
| two beavers by Barent Janse [Ditmars] on a reckoning of Domine Thesschenmaecker, | | 16– |
| ditto. Andries Arentse [Bradt] Dr. | | |
| to 17½ ells linnen @ 7 ells pr. beav. | | 20. |
| ditto. Jan Van Rotterdam, Dr. | | |
| to 12 guilders seawant in an action which he had with Hendrick Meese [Vrooman], | | 4– |
| 6th Mar. to 12 guilders seewant in the contest which he had with Hendrick Lammerse, | | 4– |
| ditto. Hendrick Lammerse, Dr. | | |
| to 12 guilders seewant in the contest which he had with Rotterdam, * | | |
| 10th Oct. The Commmissaries. † Dr. | | |
| to 20 lbs. nails, | | f. 8. |
| Account of Sales. | | |
| 10 lbs. nails, | | 4– |
| 40 lbs. nails sewant, | | 40– |
| 1½ ells linnen, | | 5–3 |
| 8 skeins thread, | | 2–16 |
| 3 lbs. nails for the Church, | | 4–10 |
| Out-go. | | |
| 6th Nov. for the little pall, ‡ | | f. 108. |
| for the sewing [same], | | 1–6 |
| 5th Dec. for the wine for the Lord's Supper, | | 25– |
| for freight of a tub of nails from the *Fuyck*. ‖ | | |
| 4 lbs. nails, | | 6– |
| for glass for the Church, | | 30– |
| 1687, 28th Mar. | | |
| to Ryer Jacobse [Schermerhorn], | | 600– |
| and 47 skiples of wheat @ 5 skiples pr. beaver, which he has received of Sweer Teunisse [Van Velsen]. | | |

---

\* Did the Consistory act as a court of Justice imposing and collecting fines, or were the fines collected by the Magistrates handed over to the Deacons for the poor?

† The magistrates of the Village.

‡ The "little pall" owned by the Church was used at the funeral of children.

‖ A name given to that part of Broadway, Albany from State St., to Steuben street.

also through Simon Groot 12½ skiples of wheat.
also through Gysbert Gerritse [Van Brakel] 16 skiples of wheat.
also through Barent Wemp 11 skiples of wheat, all @ 5 skiples per beaver.

| | |
|---|---|
| 4th Sept. also to wine for the Lord's Supper, | 30– |
| also for linnen 4 ells, | 7–6 |
| also a shirt for a captive Frenchman, | 8– |
| also 2 skiples of wheat bo't. | 10– |
| also for wine for the Lord's Supper, | 15– |
| also 27 guilders sewant to Potman as is to be seen by his settlement. | 27– |

A. D. 1687, 5th Dec. in Schenectady.

The Consistory, minister, elders and deacons,—have received an account of the cash and all other things from John Sanderse [Glen] and delivered the same to Claes Lourentse Purmerent [*alias* Van der Volgen] as follows:—he has in seawant [wampum] and silver money. . . . g. 697–2
and he is to receive in outstanding debts for linnen, 423 f.
Purmerent has sold according to his book, 249½ lb. nails
in his book yet unpaid, . . 128 lb. "
also Purmerent has in his house, 149 lb. "

total. . . . 528½ "

Petrus Thesschenmaecker.
Meyndert Wemp.

The accounts for 1688 were kept by deacon Claes Lourentse Purmerent [Vander Volgen]. The sales being similar to those of the year preceding but few extracts will be made.

1687, 15th April.

Simon Groot, Barent Wemp and Gysbert Geritse (van Brakel) are indebted for a year's hire of the plantation,* guilders, . . . . 82.

---

* The *plantasie* here mentioned for the first time in these accounts, but afterwards called *de wey* and *de arme wey* was the 18 morgens of land bequeathed "for the poor of Scherectady" by Hanse Janse Eenkluys. This parcel of ground was known later as the *Poor Pasture*.

1688, 15th April.

Simon Groot, Barent Wemp and Gysbert Gerritse [van Brakel] are still in debt for a year's hire of this plantation, . . . . . . . 82.

f. 164

1689, 15th April.

Simon Groot, Barent Wemp and Gysbert Gerritse [van Brakel] debt for a year's hire of the plantation, . . . . . . . . . f. 82.

1687, 28th March. Simon Groot, Cr.
to 13½ skiples of wheat @ 4 skiples the beaver, . 20.
Gysbert Gerritse (van Brakel, Cr.
to 16 skiples of wheat @ 5 skiples pr. beaver, . 25–12
Barent Wemp, Cr.
to 11 skiples of wheat @ 5 skiples pr. beaver, . 17–12
1688. Gysbert Gerritse (van Brakel), Cr.
10 skiples of peas @ 5 skiples pr. beaver, . . 16.
Dirk Bradt, Cr.
15 skiples of wheat, . . . . 24.
by Jan Roeloffse * (De Goyer), . . . 6.

109–4

1688. The diaconate, Dr.
66 lbs. nails on the fence and 39½ lbs. nails on the House, † . . . . . . . . .
1688. The diaconate, Cr.
66 lbs. nails, . . . . . . . .
sold 34 skeins of thread, at 6 stuivers pr. skein, .
the skeins come to . . . . . . . f. 10–4
Cr.
For the selling of thread, . . . . . 10–4

[Audit for the year 1688.]

A. D. 1688, Nov. 1st, in Schenectady.

The Consistory of Schenectady—ministers, elders and deacons—have received from Claas Lourentse Purmerend [alias

---

* Son of Anneke Janse by her first husband, Roeloff Janse.
† Parsonage house and fence.

Vander Volgen] an account of the cash, and at this date have delivered over the same to Adam Vrooman in the following items:

| | |
|---|---|
| An obligation against Hendrick Meese [Vrooman] of the year 1681, April 23. | f. 600. |
| An obligation of Bennony Arentse [Van Hoeck] of the year 1686, August 2nd. (Except the interest.) | 336–1 |
| An obligation against William Abrahamse [Tietsoort] of the year 1697, November 28th. | 600. |

An obligation against Reyer Jacobse [Schermerhorn] of the the year 1687, 28th March, f. 1008– except the interest.

Sundry sums from the pasture land of the year 1688, April 15th, . . . . . . . . 164–8
From Gerrit Bancker for the pasture land, . . 44–
Freewill offerings of Barent Ditmars, . . . 24–
⅜lb. thread, . . . . . . . .

                     Sum. . . . f. 3369–16–

The which we witness—

        Petrus Thesschenmaecker, preacher.
        Sweer Teunise Van Velsen,
        Reynier Schaets,
        Meyndert Wemp,
        Claes Lourentse [Vander Volgen],
        Adam Vrooman.

This is I C ⟅ the mark of Isaac Swits.

Deacon Adam Vrooman was treasurer of the Diaconate for the year 1689. The following are some of the expenditures.

                    1689, 6th January.

Paid to Elisabeth Von Trich [Tricht *] for Hans Janse [Eenkulys], . . . . . 57–12

                    February.

to myndert Wemp paid 7 skiples of wheat, . . 28.

                    March.

paid for wine for the Lord's supper, . . . . 17.

---

\* daughter of William Teller and wife of Abraham Van Tricht of Albany.

| | | |
|---|---|---|
| paid to the guardians of Peter Kruyns, | | 144 |

1689, 30th May.

| | | |
|---|---|---|
| also to Ludovicus Cobes lent upon interest, | | 132 |

23rd July.

| | | |
|---|---|---|
| also paid for 4 days work in the pasture of Hans Janse [Eenkluys], | | 16. |

30th October.

| | | |
|---|---|---|
| also paid for wine for the Lord's supper, | | 17–10 |

3rd September.

| | | |
|---|---|---|
| also to Teunis Karstense lent upon interest, | | 120. |

[Audit for 1689.]

A. D. 1689, Nov. 26th, in Schenectady.

The consistory—Ministers, Elders and Deacons—have received from Adam Vrooman an account of the cash, debts, obligations and [dues] for the [Poor] Pasture, and delivered the same to Isaac Swits at this date in the following items:—

| | |
|---|---|
| In cash seawant, | gl. 245–14 |
| The Poor Pasture is indebted, | 212–11 |
| | 458–5 |

Obligations Debit.

| | |
|---|---|
| Hendrick Meese [Vrooman], | f. 451–5 |
| Bennoni Arentse [Van Hoeck], | 396–1 |
| Ryer Jacobse Schermerhooren, | 1128. |
| Willem Abrahamse [Tiotsoort], | 612. |
| Ludovicus Cobes, | f. 132. |
| Teunis Carstense, | f. 120 |
| Carel Hansen [Tol], | f. 120 |
| | f. 2959–6 |

Book debts.

| | |
|---|---|
| John Brouwer, | f. 54. |
| Maria Cobes, | f. 45–19 |
| Isaac De Triex [Truax], | 16–10 |
| Alexander Glen, | f. 15–15 |
| John Glen, | f. 32 15 |
| Jacob Van Laer, | f. 3. |
| Philip Philipse [DeMore], | 27–12 |
| Jan Joncker [Van Rotterdam], | f. 24. |
| Hendrick Lammerse, | 12 |

## HISTORY OF THE CHURCH. 187

| | |
|---|---|
| Andries Bradt, | f. 24 |
| Willem Abrahamse [Tietsoort], | f. 30 |
| Douwe Aukes [De Freeze], | 31–1 |
| Jan Mebie, | f. 13–10 |
| Joris Aerssc [Van der Baast], | 12. |
| Jesaias Swart, | f. 12 |
| Bennoni Aerssc [Van Hoeck], | 33–10 |
| Gerrit Bancker, | 44–8 |
| Barent [Janse] Van Ditmars, | 24 |
| | 527 |

f. 3944–11

Petrus Thesschenmaecker, preacher.

Myndert Wemp,  
Frans Harmense, } Elders.  
[Van Der Bogart].

Adam Vrooman,  
This is the I C ⌒ mark of Isaac Swits, } These four  
Willem Appel, Deacons.  
This is the B W mark of Barent Wemp.

For many years after 1689 the treasurer's accounts no longer exist, only yearly audits of the Consistory are shown below.

| Years. | Receipts. | Expenditures. | Balance at close. |
|---|---|---|---|
| 1691 | | | 97 gl. 16 stiv. |
| 1692 | 368–12 | 110–5 | 258–7 |
| 1693 | 779–7 | 240– | 539–7 |
| 1694 | | | 462–1 |
| 1695 | 1480–5 | 998–12 | 481–13 |
| 1696 | 1719–10 | 1617–5 | 102–5 |
| 1697 | 972–10 | 857– | 115–10 |
| 1698 | 1915– | 1757–19 | 157–1 |
| 1699 | 1967–6 | 1988– | |

The credit for the years 1705 to 1713, inclusive, made in one statement by Domine Van Driessen, of Albany, showed receipts of more than 13,000 guilders.

| Years. | Receipts. | Disbursements. |
|---|---|---|
| 1736 | *£241-12-02 | £267-19-09 |
| 1738 | 282-03-00 | 314-17-10 |
| 1739 | 45-04-11 | 45-12-00 |
| 1740 | 58-15-00 | 58-04-00 |
| 1741 | 54-04-07 | 61-11-02 |
| 1743 | 145-11-11 | 135-02-05 |
| 1744 | 111-00-00 | 120-16-00 |
| 1745 | 121-19-04 | 123-04-03 |
| 1746 | 131-09-10 | 117-04-09 |
| 1747 | 157-00-10 | 164-17-00 |
| 1748 | 209-10-06 | 212-19-00 |
| 1749 | 183-13-08 | 179-04-08 |
| 1750 | 137-07-03 | 137-18-03 |
| 1751 | 150-07-01 | 141-14-06 |
| 1752 | 192-14-08 | 62-02-03 |
| 1753 | 340-05-04 | 276-05-03 |
| 1754 | 175-15-09 | 229-11-10 |
| 1755 | 177-02-06 | 229-01-08 |
| 1756 | 225-16-03 | 151-16-06 |
| 1757 | 212-13-00 | 157-11-05 |
| 1758 | 206-17-00 | 200-08-00 |
| 1759 | 254-00-00 | 158-18-00 |
| 1760 | 198-10-04 | 174-67-03 |
| 1761 | 149-05-02 | 224- 1-07 |
| 1762 | 225-00-00 | 204-11-10 |
| 1763 | 200-14-00 | 276-07-09 |
| 1764 | 227-07-05 | 152 06-04 |
| 1765 | 243-00-06 | 203-03-08 |
| 1766 | 164-01-00 | 135-04-03 |
| 1767 | 114-09-03 | 123-09-00 |
| 1768 | 128-16-01 | 141-09-00 |
| 1769 | 225-14-02 | 205-09-09 |
| 1770 | 266-11-01 | 327-05-01 |
| 1771 | 193-11-00 | 209-04-00 |
| 1772 | 193-17-10 | 189-03-00 |
| 1773 | 291-00-06 | 256-01-05 |
| 1774 | 251-10-09 | 267-14-01 |
| 1775 | 199-10-06 | 195-18-00 |
| 1776 | 251-06-05 | 205-16-10 |
| 1777 | 274-17-05 | 266-14-08 |
| 1778 | 518-04-01 | 441-16-02 |
| 1779 | †1301-08-03 | 686-11-06 |
| 1780 | †1321-16-04 | 819-03-00 |

\* The pound New York currency was $2.50.
† Depreciated Continental currency.

| Years. | Receipts. | Disbursements. |
|---|---|---|
| 1781 | £160-06-00 | £122-15-00 |
| 1782 | 218-17-00 | 197-10-00 |
| 1783 | 171-04-00 | 148-06-09 |
| 1784 | 275-11-10 | 374-18-06 |
| 1785 | 321-03-05 | 323-06-00 |
| 1786 | 364-12-10 | 361-06-08 |
| 1787 | 313-18-00 | 291-05-05 |
| 1788 | 217-02-06 | 241-03-04 |
| 1789 | 408-10-10 | 389-00-00 |
| 1790 | 585-05-01 | 569-07-01 |
| 1791 | 353-10-05 | 353-05-00 |
| 1792 | 488-03-11 | 485-11-06 |
| 1793 | 300-03-07 | 286-08-11 |
| 1794 | 316-16-08 | 304-04-00 |
| 1795 | 684-09-10 | 684-09-10 |
| 1796 | 524-09-03 | 475-16-02 |
| 1797 | 531-06-01 | 378-16-10 |
| 1798 | 393-17-06 | 391-13-00 |
| 1799 | 545-16-10 | 336-09-06 |
| 1800 | 616-19-00 | 654-13-03 |
| 1801 | 537-15-04 | 485-15-04 |
| 1802 | 2,137-15-06 | 2,117-05-00 |
| 1803 | 1,247-10-00 | 1,250-08-03 |
| 1804 | 560-18-00 | 575-15-01 |
| 1805 | $2,057.62 | $1,716.90 |
| 1806 | 3,354.22 | 3,257.27 |
| 1807 | 1,346.46 | 990.62 |
| 1808 to Aug. | 1,100.89 | 744.45 |
| 1808 to Dec. | 2,663.19 | 2,629.00 |
| 1809 | 1,592.27 | 1,353.80 |
| 1810 | 5,414.10 | 5,356.00 |
| 1811 | 1,936.09 | 2,073.10 |
| 1812 | 5,065.19 | 4,826.41 |
| 1813 | 8,470.09 | 9,506.50 |
| 1814 | 8,234.70 | 7,256.92 |

The foregoing table is not strictly an exhibit of the yearly income and expenditures only, but includes receipts and disbursements of all kinds and for all purposes. Thus during the years of 1812 to 1814 large sums were received from subscriptions and expended upon the new Church then building.

A few special reports on the Income and Assets of the Church made from time to time to the Consistory are here subjoined:—

August 27th, 1793. "Yearly income of the Church.

| | |
|---|---:|
| "Ground rents, | £290-13-6¾ |
| Church pasture, | 34- |
| " Mill, | 47- |
| Interest on £662 6-4, | 46-7-2¾ |
| Seat rent, | 100- |
| | £518-0-9½ |

"Expenditures.

| | | |
|---|---:|---:|
| Ministers' salary and wood, | £220 | |
| *Voorzanger*, | 20 | |
| Collecting, | 6. | |
| Bell ringer and wood, | 13. | |
| | | 259. |
| Additional rents out of lands, | | 100. |
| do do do | | 10. |
| | | £369 |
| "Unsettled rents & debts, | £657-12 | |
| do Pew rents, | 40- | |
| Money lent, | 36-69 | |
| | | 733-18-9 |
| Debts due for lot of Potman," * | | £200- |
| | | £533-18-9 |

"State of Income and improvement of fund.
1795. Present income.

| | | | |
|---|---:|---|---:|
| Rent for land in patent | £250. | will be at 1800 about | £300. |
| Old cash rents, | 10. | " " " " " | 10. |
| Wheat rents, 176 skip: @9s | 79-4 | fluctuating, say 52-16 to | 79-4 |
| Mill at present, | 47. | will increase say to | 94. |
| Pasture, | 34. | fluctuating, say | 34. |
| An. int. on obligations near | 42. | " " | 42. |
| Seat money in church, | 100. | " " | 100. |
| In 1795, | £562-4 | " " in 1800 | £659-4 |

---

* This debt was incurred in the purchase of the Lot on the Northerly corner of Union & Ferry Streets for the Academy erected thereon by the Church.

### Present Expenses.

| | |
|---|---:|
| Minister's salary, | £200. |
| Clerk, | 20. |
| Sexton and stove, | 12. |
| Wood, | 30. |
| | £262. |
| Present remains, | 300-4 |
| Add to this subscriptions about, | 30. |
| | £330-4 |

"Improvement of fund may take place, by sale of the [Poor]

| | |
|---|---:|
| Pasture: it yields no more than, | £34. |
| sold for £900 will yeild more free from expense, | 29. |
| ditto Mill, etc., at present £47:—sold for £1.700,—interest free and more, | 72. |
| A. S. Vedder's Lot and house * with East part of old [lot] more say, | 49. |
| Parsonage lot, † say more, | 48. |
| Lands to be leased, rent of which will at least be | 80. |
| In 1800 the fund may be | £937-4 |
| Deduct present expense | 262. |
| and remains | £675-4 |

"This exclusive of subscriptions and what obligations are with the deacons.

"Seat money may be considerably increased by making the repairs, which have been heretofore contemplated and resolved upon but not yet executed.

"In every case the enlarging and increase of funds depend upon our improvement of time. From the present opinion of men and value set on property, it is probable that we might get one fourth more at present than we might be able to obtain five years hence if not 18 months hence." ‡

---

\* The lot owned and occupied by the late G. Q. Carley.
† The lot on which the Church now stands.
‡ This encouraging report seems to have been made in view of the proposed improvement of the old house of Worship.

16th March, 1802. "Report on the annual income of the Church.

| | |
|---|---|
| Quitrents, | £319-10-6 |
| Church [Poor] Pasture, | 58. |
| Church Grist-Mill, | 50. |
| Average amount of annual Seat money. | 35. |
| Annual interest on bonds & notes, principal being £1287, @ 7 % | 90. |
| | £552-10-6 |

Mar. 5th, 1805. "Estimate of Income of the Dutch Church.

| | | |
|---|---|---|
| Annual quitrents, cash. | | £315-5-8 |
| do wheat, 171¼ skiples @ 6s. | | 51-7-6 |
| | | £366-13-2 |
| Arrears of quitrents, cash, | £277-13 10 | |
| do wheat, 500 Skiples, | 150.-0-0 | |
| | £427-13-10 | |
| Income from Poor pasture, seat money and Grist-mill, | | 195. |
| total income, | | £561-13-2 |

Obligations.

| | |
|---|---|
| Principal, | £3.086 00-11 |
| Interest due March 1st, | 409- 1-4½ " |

25th April, 1815. Income.

| | |
|---|---|
| "Cash, | $1,001.77½ |
| Wheat, | 145,53 |
| Obligations, $9966, 50: An: interest | 696,88½ |
| Rent of [Poor] Pasture, | 242. |
| | $2,084.19 |

16th Mar. 1818. "Finances of the Church, Jan. 1st. 1818.

| | |
|---|---|
| Obligations due, Principal, | $8,583.08½ |
| " arrears due, | 1,041.42 |
| Quitrents, arrears due, | 1,484,12½ |
| do wheat arrears, | 738.69 |
| | $11,846.32 |

# HISTORY OF THE CHURCH.

"Yearly Income.

| | |
|---|---:|
| Interest on obligations, | $600.81½ |
| Quitrents in Cash, | 809.20½ |
| do wheat, @ 12s. the skiple | 294.91 |
| Pew rents, | 299.50 |
| Pasture rent, | 257.74 |
| | $2.262.17 |

On the 3d March, 1823. The annual income from all sources is stated to be $2,118.81.—

In 1790 and for some years later there was great scarcity of small change: to meet this inconvenience many individuals, corporations and even Churches issued "shin plasters" for one penny and upwards.

On the 6th of September, 1790 the deacons announced to the Consistory that in consequence of the scarcity of copper money the weekly collections in the Church had fallen off nearly one half, and therefore inquired whether there was no way of remedying this loss.

The reverend Consistory having considered the matter came to the unanimous conclusion,—

1. that the reverend Consistory should immediately have printed £100 in one, two, three and six penny notes;
2. that Domine Romeyn or some other member of the Consistory should sign the same in the name of the Consistory;
3. that these notes shall be issued from time to time by the deacons;
4. that the deacons shall keep an account of all the notes issued and hold the money received in exchange to redeem them on demand;
5. the deacons shall render an account hereof as often as required by the Consistory.

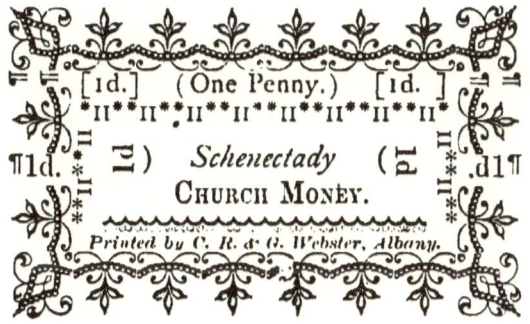

## CHAPTER XVI.

### Church Statistics.

*Baptisms.*—The baptismal Register (*Doep book*) of this Church from 1694 to this time is entire with the exception of ten years during Domine Vrooman's ministry: and as all children were baptised both colored and Indian as well white,—legitimate and illegitimate—it is the only authoritative source, if rightly interpreted, whence the descendants of most of the old Dutch families can derive their pedigrees, In early times baptism was always performed in the Church, unless unavoidably prevented, and within a few days after birth; sometimes on the birthday. And it was the duty of the Domine to register each child so baptised with parents' and sponsors (*getuygen*) names.

The number of registered baptisms from 1694 to 1852 is 19,396.

*Marriages.*—Preliminary to the marriage contract the banns were proclaimed three successive Sabbaths in the Church, or a licence might be granted by the Governor of the Province, after which the rite was solemnised (*bevestight*) by the Domine, or occasionally by a justice of the peace.

The marriage Register or *Trouwboeck* of this church contains the names of 2573 couples married between the years 1694 and 1852.

*Church members.*—The number of members received during the ministry of each pastor was as follows:—

| | | |
|---|---|---|
| ——————————............ | 1694—1700............ | 23 |
| Do. Freeman,............ | 1700—1705............ | 85 |
| ——————,............ | 1705—1715 ............ | 1 |
| Do. Brouwer,............ | 1715—1728............ | 108 |
| Do. Erichzon,............ | 1728—1736............ | 204 |
| ——————,............ | 1736—1740............ | 31 |
| Do. Van Zantvoord,........ | 1740—1752............ | 152 |
| ——————,............ | 1752—1754 ............ | 57 |

| | | |
|---|---|---|
| Do. Vrooman,* | 1754—1784 | 487 |
| Do. Romeyn,† | 1784—1804 | 248 |
| Do. Meier, | 1804—1806 | 10 |
| ———— | 1806—1808 | 18 |
| Do. Bogardus,‡ | 1808—1812 | 157 |
| ———— | 1812—1815 | 12 |
| Do. Van Vechten, | 1815—1849 | 910 |
| Total, | | 2,503 |

A report made to the Classis of Albany, July 14th, 1817 shows the following statistics. ‖

| | |
|---|---|
| Number of families | 426. |
| Total in the Congregation | 2518. |
| In communion by report last year | 342. |
| Received on Confession | 53. |
| do by certificate | 5. |
| Dismissed | 6. |
| Died | 12. |
| Total in communion | 382. |
| Adult baptisms | 7. |
| Infant baptisms | 46. |

For a list of the Deacons & Elders see appendix F.

---

\* From 1772 to 1782 no members are registered.

† There were 414 members living in 1785.

‡ In 1809 Domine Bogardus reported only 270 members of the Church; in 1811 the number was increased to 413.

‖ Consistory minutes.

APPENDIX A.

Plan of Church of 1734.

## REGISTER VAN DE PLAATSEN IN DE KERKE. \*

*Mons Plaatsen.*

### BANK NO. 1 †

Begint achter het gestoelte der Ouderlingen tegen de West Muur en gaat tot aan 't gestoelte der Magistraten, behelsende 12 sit-plaatsen.

1. Johannes Schuyler, 1734; Adam Van Slyck, 1788. 2. Philip Livingston. 1734; Robert Livingston, 1754; Johannes Glen Jr., 1788. 3. Jeremiah Van Rensselaer, 1734; Steven Van Rensselaer, 1754; Stephanus Van Rensselaer, 1788; John Sanders Ten Eyck. 1791. 4. Edward Collins, 1734; Harmanus Bradt, 1754-88. 5. Jan Wemp, 1734; Jan ‚Baptist Van Eps, 1754; Jan Baptist Van Eps, 1806. 6. Arent Bratt, 1734; Arent C. Van Petten, 1754; Nicolaas A. Van Petten, 1788. 7. Isaac Isaacse Truax; Isaac Isaacse Truax, 1754; De kerke, 1798; Abraham Oothout, 1798. 8. Johannes H. Wendell; Evert Wendell, 1754; Harmanus H. Wendell, 1788; Hendrick Glen. 9. Harmen Harm: Vedder; John Cuyler Jr. 10. Petrus Van Driessen; Johannes Van Driessen. 11. Harmanus Adamse Van Slyck, 1754. 12. Jacobus Bratt, 1754.

---

\* This list is made up of those Registers combined, of dates 1734, 1754 & 1788 and include all the names contained therein. The slips or *Bancken* were numbered nearly alike in 1734 and 1754 but the numbers were quite different in 1788. As before stated each sitting in the Church was held by its occupant for life unless forfeited by non-payment of the seat rent, or by removing from the town; and descended to his or her nearest male or female heir. Hence the same sitting was in some cases retained in the family for 3 or 4 generations. It will be noticed also that the males occupied the wall benches (*gestoelte*) chiefly, which were slightly raised above the others; whilst the females sat upon the benches (*bancken*) in the body of the house. The slips for the two sexes were numbered from one upwards,—those of the males from 1 to XIII:—those of the females from 1 to 62. The Deacons and Elders sat in the four benches on each side of the pulpit or *doophuisje*, and the magistrates and other men of note upon the long bench on the West side of the Church extending from the pulpit around to the South door. The date following each name shows the year when this name first appears on the list, and the number *prefixed* to the name indicates the seat on the bench occupied by that person.

† Bench No. 1 (See plan) was occupied by men of note.

BANK II.*

Begint aan de West zyde Van de zuyder Duer tegens de zuydt muur en gaat tot aan Bank No. I: dese is gelaten ten behoeven van de Magistraten, &c.—12 zit-plaatsen.

1. Gerrit Symonse [Veeder], 1733-4; Johannes Helmerse Veeder, 1754-88. 2. Symon Swits, 1734; Isaack Swits, 1754; Nicolaas Hall, 1785. 3. Reyer Schermerhorn, 1734-88; Bartho. R. Schermerhorn, 1794. 4. Jan Barentse Wemp, 1734; Abraham J. B. Wemple, 1788; John A. Wemple, 1803. 5. Nicolaas Schuyler, 1734; Cornelis Van Slyck, 1754-88. 6. Jan Vrooman, 1734; Tobias Ten Eyck, 1754; Tobias Jacobus Ten Eyck. 7. Harmanus Jacobus Van Slyck, 1754-88.

BANK III.

1. John Visger, 1734; John Visger, 1754-88; John Visger, 1794. 2. Joh: Harmense Vedder, 1734-88; Nicolaas Adr: Van Petten, 1791. 3. Nicolaas Van Petten, 1734-54; Michael Tyms. 1788. 4. Jacobus Van Eps. 1734-88; John Post, 1789; Corn: Zeger Van Santvoord, 1794.

BANK IV.

1. Harmen Van Slyck, 1734; Antony Van Slyck, 1754-88. 2. Johannes H. Wendell, 1734; Seth Vrooman, 1754; Adam S. Vrooman, 1788. 3. Johannes Van Slyck, 1734; Carel Hansen Toll, 1754; Johannes S. Toll, 1788. 4. Caleb Beck, 1734-54; Caleb Beck, 1788. 5. Peter Cornu, 1734; Daniel Cornu, 1754; Johannes Van Petten, 1788. 6. Jacobus Vedder, 1754; Jacobus Peek, 1788; Jacobus Jacobuse Peek, 1790. 7. Jacobus Mynderse, 1754; Dirk Van Ingen, 1791. 8. Peter Van Guysling, 1788.

---

* The Magistrates bench, was occupied also by 6 other respectable citizens.

## HISTORY OF THE CHURCH. 201

#### BANK V.

1. Douwe Fonda, 1734; Jacob Fonda, 1754. 2. Arent Stevens, 1734; Willem Stevens, 1754-88. 3 Peter Van Slyck, 1734; Maas Van Vranken, 1754; Nicolaas Van Vranken, 1788. 4. Hendricus Helmerse Veeder, 1754; Hendericus Simonse Van Antwerp, 1803. 5. Isaack Quackenbos, 1754; John Quackenbos, 1780. 6. Abraham Fonda. 1754-88. 7. Adam Vrooman, 1754; Jacob A. Vrooman, 1788. 8. Marten Van Slyck, 1754-88.

#### BANK VI.

1. Symon Vrooman, 1734; Joh: Symonse Vrooman, 1754; Symon Jacobse Vrooman, 1788. 2. Abraham Mebie, 1734; Albert Mebie, 1754; Albert S. Mebie, 1788. 3. Johannes W. Teller, 1734; Johannes Teller, 1754; John Teller, 1785. 4. Cornelis Van Dyck, 1734; Johannes Van Dyck, 1754; Hendrick Van Dyck, Jr., 1788. 5. Abraham Glen, 1734; John S. Glen, 1754-88. 6. Jacob Schermerhorn, 1734; Johannes Schermerhorn, 1754-88. 7. Myndert Wemp, 1734; Myndert Myndertse Wemp, 1754; Jacobus Wemple, 1791. 8. William Teller, 1734; Jacobus Teller, 1754; Wm. Jacobuse Teller, 1785; 9. Andries Bratt, 1734; Johannes Andriese Bratt, 1754; Andries Johannes Bratt; 1788.

#### BANK VII.

1. Jacob Glen, 1734; Jacob Glen Sanders, 1754; John Sanders Jr., 1788. 2. Nicolaas Schuyler, 1734; John Sanders, 1754; Arent Sanders, 1788. 3. Nicolaas Groot, 1754; Nicolaas D. Groot, 1788. 4. Sara Glen, 1754; Elisabeth Sanders, 1788; Elsje Ten Eyck. 5. Maria Sanders, 1754; Margarita Sanders, 1788. 6. Sara Sanders, 1754; Sara J. Glen, 1780. 7. Debora Sanders, 1754; Maria Beeckman, 1788; Maghtelt D. Fonda, 1798.

BANK VIII.

1. Jan Wemp, 1734; John Ryerse Wemple, 1754-88. 2. Hendrick Van Rensselaer, 1734; Seger Van Santvoord, 1754-88. 3. Arent Andriese Bratt, 1734; Abraham Bratt, 1754. 4. Antony Bleecker,1754; Johannes J. Cuyler; Cornelius Cuyler Jr., 1788; Philip Ryley. 5. Barent Sanders, 1734; John Sanders Jr., 1788; Abraham Glen Jr.,; Jacob Sanders Glen. 6. Johannes Bratt, 1734; Reyer Wemple, 1788. 7. Gerrit Lansing, 1734-88; Gerrit G. Lansing, 1792. 8. Bartholomew Vrooman, 1734; Johannes B. Vrooman, 1788. 9. Johannes Symonse [Veeder], 1734; Myndert Veeder, 1754; Johannes M. Veeder, 1788. 10. Symon Volkertse [Veeder], 1734; Barent Veeder, 1754. 11. Joh: Abrahamse Vedder, 1734; Albert Johanese Vedder; Jacob Swits; Isaac J. Swits, 1788; Jacob Abrahamse Swits, 1791. 12. Pieter Veeder, 1734-88, Nicolaas Veeder, 1796. 13. Gerrit Symonse [Veeder], 1734-88. 14. Joseph Yates Jr., 1754; Cristoffel Yates, 1788; Joseph C. Yates, 1790. 15. Hendrick Vrooman, 1734; Cornelis H. Vrooman, 1754; De kerk, 1802; Arent Vrooman, 1806. 16 Albert J. Vedder, 1754-88. 17. Abraham Robertse Yates, 1754-88; Abraham Joseph Yates, 1794. 18. Abraham Van Eps, 1754; Abraham Van Eps, Jr., 1785; De kerk, 1792.

BANK IX.

1. Daniel De Graaf, 1754-88; Daniel Jesse De Graaf, 1791. 2. Jellis Truex, 1734; Abraham Truex, 1754; Arent S. Vedder, 1788. 3. Andries Truex, 1734-88. 4. Claas Van der Volgen, 1734-54; Frans Veeder, 1788. 5. Isaack Jacobse Swits, 1734; Hendrick Swits, 1754-88. 6. Johannes Schoonmaker, 1734-88. 7. Isaack Vrooman, 1734-54; Adam S. Vrooman, 1788.

BANK X.

1. Hendrick Vrooman, 1734; Barent Vrooman, 1754; Samuel Van Slyck, 1788; Adam J. Van Slyck, 1794. 2. Jesse DeGraaf, 1734; Nicolaas DeGraaf, 1754-88. 3. Jan Marselis,

1734 ; Takel Marselis, 1754 ; Ahasuerus Marselis, 1788 ; Hendrick Marselis, 1790. 4. Arent Samuelse Bratt, 1734 ; Samuel Arentse Bratt, 1754 ; Arent Bratt, 1803. 5. Jacob Mebie, 1734; Johannes Mebie, 1754 ; Pieter J. Mebie ; Cornelis Mebie, 1788. 6. Antony Van Slyck, 1734; Cornelis Antony Van Slyck, 1754-88 ; Adriaan C. Van Slyck, 1790. 7. Reynier Mynderse, 1754-88.

BANK XI.

1. Andries Nack, 1734 ; Arent Johannese Bratt ; Nicolaas Arn : DeGraaf, 1754 ; Abraham Arn : DeGraaf, 1788. 2. Abraham DeGraaf, 1734 ; Abraham DeGraaf, 1754 ; Abraham DeGraaf, 1788. 3. Robert Yates, 1734 ; Jos : Robertse Yates, 1754-88 ; Abraham N. Yates, 1804. 4. Pieter Mebie, 1734; Johannes Mebie, 1754-88. 5. Joseph Van Sice, 1734 ; Johannes Van Sice, 1754 ; Cornelis Vander Volgen ; Lourens Corn : Vander Volgen, 1788. 6. Jacob Vrooman, 1734-54 ; Johannes Clute, 1788. 7. Abraham Truex, 1734; Abraham I. Truex, 1754-88.

BANK XII.

1. Marten VanBenthuysen, 1734 ; Pieter Truex, 1754-88. 2. Jillis Fonda, 1734 ; Pieter Fonda, 1754 ; Jillis Pieterse Fonda, 1788. 3. Jan Danielse Van Antwerp, 1734 ; Arent Van Antwerp, 1754 ; Johannes Van Antwerp, 1754 ; Barent Tobias Ten Eyck, 1788. 4. Corset Vedder, 1734 ; Harmanus Vedder Jr., 1754 ; Takerus VandeBogart, 1788; *op de kerke*, 1802. 5. Andries Van Petten, 1734 ; Nicolaas Van Petten, 1754 ; Andries Van Patten, 1788. 6. Hendrick Ten Eyck, 1734; Hendrick Tobias Ten Eyck, 1754 ; Myndert S. Ten Eyck, 1788. 7. Cornelis Veeder, 1734 ; Gerrit Daniel Gerrit Van Antwerp, 1754; Gerrit Connor, 1788. 8. Myndert Myndertse, 1734-54 ; Johannes Myndertse, 1788.

BANK XIII.

1. Jan Dellamont, 1734; Abraham Dellamont, 1754-88. 2. Henricus Wemple, 1734; John Empie, 1754-88. 3. Willem Schermerhorn, 1734-54-88. 4. Henricus Volkertse Veeder, 1734; Hendrick Dellamont, 1754-88. 5. Philip Truex, 1734; Abraham Philipse Truax, 1754-88. 6. Johannes Peek, 1754-88. 7. Carel Hansen Toll, 1754-88.

Register van de Vrouwen sit-plaatsen beginnende voor de justices.

[ Women's seats. ]

BANK NO. 1.

1. Maria Vedder, 1734; Margarita Mebie, 1754; Anna H. Van Dyck, 1788. 2. Elisabeth Van Dyck, 1734; Maria Harmense Bratt, 1754-88. 3. Debora Wemp, 1734; Maria Wempel, 1754-88. 4. Catharina Mebie, 1734; Annatie R. [A?] Mebie, 1754-88. 5. Helena Van Eps, 1734; Helena Pieters, 1754; Annatie Pieters, 1788. 6. Anna Wendell, 1734; Anna Van Antwerp, 1754-88. 7. Anna Mebie, 1734; Engeltie Mebie, 1754-88; Jacomyntie Van Dyck, 1793. 8. Catharina J. Empie, 1754-88.

BANK 2.

1. Engeltie Veeder [Vedder?], 1748; Catrina Van Antwerp. 1754; Engeltie J. Van Antwerp, 1788. 2. Ariaantie Van Antwerp, 1748; Jannetie Peek, 1754; Catharina C. Cuyler, 1788. 3. Helena Bancker, 1748; Elisabeth Bancker, 1754-88. 4. Elisabeth Bancker, 1748; Margarita Van Eps, 1788; Elisabeth H. Peek, 1793. 5. Susanna Vedder, 1754; Catalyntje Van Vleck, 1788. 6. Catalyntje Vedder, 1754; Maria Vedder,

Annatie Vedder, huysvrouw Van J. B. Van Eps Jr., 1788. 7. Jannetie Veeder, 1734; Susanna Veeder; Angenetie Vedder; Jannetie J. B. Van Eps, 1788. 8. Sarah P. Truex, 1754-88. 9. Maria Connor, 1754-88. 10. Maria Empie, 1754; *De kerke*; Elisabeth Baucker Peek, 1793.

BANK 3.

1. Anna H. Vedder, 1734; Susanna Van Petten; Anna J. Cuyler, 1788. 2. Janneke Nack, 1734; Sara Vander Volgen, 1754-88; Margareta Waldron, 1803. 3. Hester Groot, 1734; Hester DeGraff, 1754; Elisabeth Reyly, 1788. 4. Caatie Bratt, 1734; Catalina Clement, 1754-88; Margarita Samlse Clement, 1794. 5. Ingeltie Vrooman, 1734; Elisabet Swits, 1754; Maria Swits, 1788; Susanna Swits, 1793. 6. Dorata Vrooman, 1734; Raghel Wemple, 1754-88; Susanna Jellise Fonda, 1791. 7. Steyntje Vrooman, 1734; Maria Cornelise Veeder, 1754-88; Maria N. Bratt, 1809. 8. Jannetie Mynderse, 1754-88. 9. Catharina Jacobse Bratt, 1754-88. 10. Elisabeth Harmense Bratt, 1754-88.

BANK 4.

1. Christina Truex, 1734; Catalyntje De Graaf, 1754-88. 2. Anna Wendell, 1734; Catarina H. Wendell, 1754; Catrina H. Glen, 1788. 3. Ariaantje Vedder 1734; Neeltje Vander Bogart, 1754-88; Nelly Schermerhorn Clinch, 1804. 4. Anna Veeder, 1734; Maria Van Syse, 1754; Cristina DeGraaf, 1788; Margarita L. Mynderse, 1791. 5. Maria Bratt, 1734; Engeltie Van Petten, 1754-88. 6. Sara Van Slyck, 1734; Kaatje White, 1754-88; Eva Jacobse Bratt, 1790. 7. Elisabet Cornu, 1734; Helena Van Slyck, weduw, 1754-88.

BANK 5.

1. Antje Bleecker, 1734; Maria Pieterse Brouwers 1754; Helena P. Brouwer, 1788; Helena J. Brouwer, 1792. 2. Gerritje Wyngaard, 1734; Maike Tymense, 1754-88. 3.

Cathalyntje Truex, 1734; Helena Jan Baptist Van Eps, 1754-88; Maria Van Petten, 1791. 4. Maritie Truex, 1734-88. 5. Sara Truex, 1754; Margarita Truex, 1788. 6. Catalyntje Van Eps, 1754-88. 7. Hellegonda Damens (?), 1734.

### BANK 6.

1. Eva Vander Volgen, 1734; Alida Reyly, 1754: Geértruy R. Mynderse, 1788. 2. Maria Van [der] Volgen, 1734; Geertruy Reyly, 1754; Margarita R. Mynderse; Elisabeth Volkertse Veeder, 1788. 3. Catharina Vander Volgen, 1734-88; Catharina H. Yates, 1793. 4. Sarah Van Slyck, 1754; Sarah Van Schaick, 1788. 5. Engeltie Fairley, 1754 88. 6. Debora Glen, 1734; Debora Van Eps, 1788.

### BANK 7.

1. Susanna Vedder, 1734; Maria Van Petten, 1754; Catrina J. Cuyler; Emmetje Clerk, 1788. 2. Maria H. Vedder, 1734; Engeltje Campbell, 1754-88; *De kerke*, 1793. 3. Maria Stevens, 1734-88. 4. Susanna Van Eps, 1734; Eva Young, 1754-88. 5. Susanna Mynderse, 1734-88. 6. Ariaantje Van de Bogart, 1754; *De kerk*, 1765-88.

### BANK 8.

1. Elisabeth Bratt, 734; Rebecca Peek, 1754-88. 2. Catalyna Berret 1734; Leena Johannese Van Antwerp, 1754-88. 3. —— Van Vranken, 1734; Margarita Vedder, huysvrouw van Reyer Veeder; Margarita Van Vranken, 1754; Elisabet Truex; Maria R. Van Vranken, 1788. 4. Eva Feelick, 1734; Jannetie Van Guysling, 1754; Suster J. Van Guysling 1788. 5. Engeltie Vrooman, 1734; Maria Sweruse Marselis 1754-88. 6. Anna Bratt, 1734; Maria R. Schermerhorn, 1754-88.

BANK 8.bis

1. Jannetie Symonse Van Petten, 1754-88. 2. Jannetie Johannese Teller, 1754-88. 3. Anna Johannese Teller, 1754-88. 4. Annatie Jillese Van Vorst 1754-88. 5. Elisabeth Van Ingen, 1754-88. 6. Elisabeth P. Clute (McKinney) 1788.

BANK 9.

1. Hester Tymense, 1734-54; Anna Tymense, 1788. 2. Anna Christiaanse, 1734; Immetie Christiaanse, 1754-88; *De kerke*, 1801. 3. Margarita Janse Wemple, 1734; Elisabet Swart, 1754; Sara C. Van de Bogart, 1788. 4. Molly Post, 1734-88; Catalina C. Van Santvoord, 1788. 5. Catarina Van Guysling, 1734-88. 6. Jannetie Andriese Bratt, 1754; Annatie Bancker, 1788.

BANK 9.bis

1. Neeltie Staats, 1754; Deborah Staats; Helena Lansing, 1788. 2. Helena Jac: Van Eps, 1754-88. 3. Margarita Schermerhorn, 1754-88; Engeltie R. Schermerhorn, 1788. . Catriena Banker, 1754; Catriena Banker Van Aernum, 1788; *De kerke*, 1791; Elisabeth Reynex, 1792. 5. Annatie Glen, 1754; Margarita Hosford, 1788. 6. Annatie Adriaanse Van Slyck, 1754-88.

BANK 10.

1. Anna Van Vorst, 1734; Elisabet Schermerhorn, 1754; Annatie Van Vranken, 1788. 2. Maria Arentse Vedder, 1734; Annatie Swart, 1754-88. 3. Helena Swits, 1734; Jannetie Vrooman, 1788. 4. Tanneke Clute, 1734; Tanneke Jac: Clute, 1754-88. 5. Jannetie Swits, 1734; Maria H. Vrooman, 1754-88. 6. Helena Johannese Van Eps, 1734; Catrina Johannese Van Eps. 1754-88.

BANK 11.

*Vacant.*

BANK 12.

1. Annatie Abrahamse Van Antwerp, 1754- . 2. Elisabet Bratt 1754; Rebecca De Graaf ; Debora De Graaf, 1788. 3. Anna Bratt 1754; Elisabet Johannese Van Sice, 1788. 4. Susanna Bratt 1754 ; Annatje Freeman, 1788. 5. Alida Vredenbergh, 1754-88 ; *De kerke*, 9.

BANK 13.

1. Elisabet Cornu, 1734; Elisabet Corna, 1754-88. 2. Maria Corna, 1734-88. 3. Helena Williemse Pieterse, 1734 ; Elisabeth Abrahamse Bratt, 1754-94 ; Eva Abrahamse Bratt, 1794. 4. Sophia Pieterse, 1734-88 ; Cornelia Marselis, 1801. 5. Margareta Van Syse ; 1754 ; Helena Campbell; Mary Van Syce, 1788.

BANK 14.

1. Catrina Adriaanse Van Slyck, 1754-88. 2. Maria Yates, 1754; Maria Cornelise Van Slyck, 1788; Elisabeth Cornelise Van Slyck, 1794. 3. Jacobatie Truex, 1754-94; Catalyntje Truex Conde, 1794. 4. Neeltie Viele, 1754-88. 5. Neeltie Bancker 1754-88. 6. Alida Conde, 1754.

BANK 15.

1. Susanna Toll, 1734; Magdalena Schermerhorn, 1754; Fytje Van Petten, 1788. 2. Elisabeth Toll, 1734; Geertruy Toll, 1754 ; Engeltie Viele, 1788 ; Neeltie Nicholas S. Van Petten, 1791. 3. Claartje Van Slyck, 1734 ; Judick Veeder, 1754; Anna Combs, 1788. 4. Maria Fonda, 1734-54 ; Engeltie Freeman ; Elisabeth Freeman; Maria Vedder: Hannah Warner, 1788 ; Catharine Theresa Romeyn Beck, 1794. 5. Ingeltie Van Petten, 1754-88.

## BANK 16.

1. Eva Swart, 1734; Geertruy M. Mynderse, 1754; Susan Schermerhorn, 1803. 2. Maria Mynderse, 1734-54; Annatie Joseph Mynderse, 1794. 3. Elizabeth Marselis, 1754; Helena Marselis, *weduwe*, 1788. 4. Anna Teller, 1754; Anna W. Teller, 1788. 5. Engeltie Veeder, 1754-88.

## BANK 17.

1. Jannetie Viele, 1734; Catrina Albertse Vedder, 1754-88; Catharina Arent A. Vedder, 1798. 2. Ariaantje Andrz: Bratt, 1734. 3. Margareta Schermerhorn, 1734; Susanna Schermerhorn, 1754-88. 4. Geertruy Groot, 1734; Marrytje Claaz: Van Petten, 1754; Raghel Jacobuse Fonda, 1788. 5. Catalina R. Wemple, 1734; Susanna R. Wemple, 1754; Alida Wemple, 1788. 6. Catriena Swart, 1754-88; Rebecca Groot, 1804.

## BANK 18.

1. Maria Dellamont, 1734; Annatie Dellamont, 1754; Catrina Swits, 1788. 2. Suster Van Guysling, 1734; Suster Swits, 1754-88. 3. Marytje Veeder, 1734; Catharina Van Slyck, 1754-88. 4. Rebecca DeGraaf, 1734; Hester Toll, 1754; Hester C. Toll, 1788. 5. Margarita Dellamont, 1754-88.

## BANK 19.

1. Catharina Livingston 1734. 2. Delia Groenendyck, 1734; Maria Schuyler; Jannetie Van Slyck, 1754; Geertruy Cornelise Van Slyck, 1788; Jannetie Lambert, 1790. 3. Maria Groenendyck, 1734; Sarah J. Mynderse, 1754-88; Alida M. Wemple, 1791. 4. Margarieta Groenendyck, 1734; Geertruy J. Mynderse, 1754-88. 5. Geertruy Mynderse, 1754; Margarita M. Mynderse, 1754-88. 6. Susanna Bratt, 1734; Catharina Akes Van Slyck, 1754; Jannetie Reyley, 1788.

BANK 20,

1.⎱
2.⎰ Predikants Huysgezin, 1754-88. 3. Susanna Toll, 1754-88. 4. Hesje Johannese Toll, 1754-88. 5. Elisabeth Ten Eyck, 1754-88.

BANK 21.

1. Eva Dellamont, 1734-88. 2. Catriena Van Petten, 1734; Catriena S. Veeder 1754-88; Susanna Roseboom, 1803. 3. Cornelia Bratt, 1734; Geertruy Van Slyck, 1790. 4. Grietje Bratt, 1734; Susanna Toll, 1754; Catrina Johannese Glen, 1788. 5. Margarita A. Peeck, 1754-88.

BANK 22.

1. Maria Van Brackell, 1734; Maria Vedder, 1754; Helena Veeder, 1788. 2. Tryntje Bratt 1734; Eva Peek, 1754-88. 3. Maritie Glen, 1734; Maria Van Eps, 1754; Elisabeth P. Van Gysling, 1788. 4. Maria Yates, 1734; Maria Smith, 1754-88. 5. Sara A. Yates, 1754; Eva C. Yates, 1788.

BANK 23.

1. Helena Wemp, 1734; Helena Bratt, 1754; Helena C. Yates, 1788. 2. Elisabeth Yates, 1793. 3. Gerzina De Graaf, 1734-88 Susanna DeGraaf, 1809. 4. Susanna Arentse Bratt, 1734; Susanna P. Mebie, 1754; Maria Mebie, 1788. 5. Margarieta Wemple 1754-88.

BANK 24.

1. Anna Van Dyck, 1734; Aegje Danielse [Van Antwerp], 1754; Ariaantje Yates, 1788. 2. Jacomyntje Van Dyck, 1734; Maria Wendell, 1754-88. 3. Maria Danielse Van Antwerp,

1734; Engeltje Van Antwerp, 1754-88. 4. Anna Pieterse Danielse [Van Antwerp], 1734; Engeltie Groot, 1754; Annatie Groot, 1754; Margarieta A. Van Eps, 1788. 5. Neeltje Van Antwerp, 1754-88.

BANK 25.

1. Catrina Jacobse Mebie, 1734-54; Margarita Brouwer Bancker, 1788. 2. Margarieta Mebie. 1734; Anna Jac: Mebie, 1754; Anna Clute, 1788. 3. Maritie Pieterse Danielse [Van Antwerp], 1734-88. 4. Sara Reyley, Huysvrouw van Daniel Fort, 1734-88; Catrina B. Bancker, 1792. 5. Raghel Vrooman, 1754-88; Catharina Marselis, 1803.

BANK 26.

1. Helena Post, 1734-88; Margarieta Van Santvoord, 1803. 2. Gezina DeGraaf, 1734-54; Gesina Vedder 1788. 3. Debora Van Gysling, 1754; Debora Swits, 1788; Debora N. Hall, 1803. 4. Margarietie Bratt, 1734; Chaartje Vrooman, 1754-88. 5. Margarieta Cornelise Vrooman, 1754; Elisabeth Bratt Vrooman, 1794.

BANK 27.

1. Engeltie Bratt, 1754; Margarieta D. McKinney, 1788. 2. Maria P. Vrooman, 1754; Annatie Johannese Vedder, 1788. 3. Helena Van Deusen, Doghter Van Elisabeth Haff, 1754 to 1788. 4. Jenneke Truax, doghter Van Johannes Truex 1754; *De kerk*, 1793; Elisabeth Johannese Quackenbos, 1794. 5. Jacomyntje Schermerhorn, 1754; Debora Schermerhorn, 1788.

BANK 28.

*Vacant.*

BANK 29.

1. Anna Quackenbos, 1734-54; Anna Isaacse Quackenbos, 1788. 2. Geertruy Van Vranken, 1734; Catharina C. Mebie, 1788. 3. Neeltje Vedder, 1734-54; Sara Schermerhorn, 1788. 4. Catrina Arentse Vedder, 1754-88; Sarah Johannese Toll, 1794. 5. Elisabeth Quackenbos, 1754-88.

BANK 30.

1. Alida Toll, 1734-88. 2. Anneke Toll, 1754-88. 3. Effie Toll, 1754-88. 4. Folkie Vedder, 1754; Ariaantje L. Van Vranken. 1788; *De kerke*, 1803; Angelica Vrooman, 1810. 5. Elisabeth Fairly, 1754-88.

BANK 31.

1. Susanna Bragham, 1734; Catrina Swits, 1754; Catrina S. Bratt, 1794; Catharina Peek, 1803. 2. Eva Groot, 1734; Doortie Vrooman, 1754-88; Maria Van Slyck, 1803. 3. Catarina Veeder, 1734-54; Catharina W. Teller, 1788. 4. Anna Arentse Bratt, 1734-88; Elisabeth Cornelise Bratt, 1801. 5. Catrina Van der Heyden, 1754; Engeltie Jacobuse Van Eps, 1788.

BANK 32.

1. Elisabeth Groot, 1734; Rebecca J. Quackenbos, 1754-88. 2. Catryntje Van Brakel, 1734; Marya Lagrange; Ariaantie Vander Volgen, 1754-88. 3. Elisabeth Van Sice, 1754; Francina Van Ingen, 1788. 4. Sara Marselis, *weduwe*, 1734; Sara Lighthall, 1754-88. 5. Sara Peek, 1754-88.

## HISTORY OF THE CHURCH. 213

BANK 33.

1. Catrina Bartho Vrooman, 1754; Catrina Peek, 1788. 2. Angenitie Danielse [Van Antwerp], 1734; Angenitie Van Slyck, 1754; Susanna Van Antwerp, 1788. 3. Marya Groot, 1734-88. 4 Eva Yates 1734; Jannetie Cornelise Van Slyck; Christina Van Slyck, 1754; Susanna Pieterse, 1788. 5. Catrina Van Slyck, *Weduwe*, 1734; Maria Jacobuse Mynderse, 1754; Margarieta J. Mynderse, 1788.

BANK 34.

1. Maike Van Petten, 1734; Gertie Van Petten, 1754-88. 2. Metie Fairly 1734-88: *De Kerke*, 1792; Engeltie Campbell, 1793. 3. Antje Schermerhorn, 1734; Debora Kettle, 1754-88; Annatie Beek Van Gyseling, 1791. 4. Janne Van Petten, 1734; Jannetie Clement, 1754; Marytje Bratt, 1788. 5. Geesie Vrooman, 1754-88.

BANK 35.

1. Marytje Vrooman, 1734; Jannetie Fonda, vrouw van Jellis Fonda, 1788; Alida A. Vedder, 1801. 2. Folkie Wemp, 1734, Jannetie Stoffelse Yates, 1788. 3. Margarieta Veeder, weduwe, 1734; Folkie Veeder, 1788; Ariaantje L. Van Vranken, 1803. 4. Engeltie Van Driessen, 1754-88. 5. Engeltie Lansing, 1734; Folkie Swits, 1788.

BANK 36.

1. Margarieta Ten Eyck, 1734; Margarita Jac: Ten Eyck, 1754; Anna S. Ten Eyck, 1788. 2. Ragheltie Ten Eyck, 1754; Raghel Ten Eyck, 1787; Marya Ten Eyck, dau: of Henry Ten Eyck, } 1799. 3. Debora Sanders, *Huysvrouw van* John Sanders Jr., } 1754; Sara Sanders, 1799. 4. Elisabeth Sanders, *dogter van* John Sanders, } 1754 tot 1788. 5. Catrina Hendricke Veeder, 1754-88.

## BANK 37.

1. Margarita Van Slyck, 1754-88. Catharina H. Van Slyck, 1797. 2. Helena Van Slyck, 1734 ; Elisabeth Visger, 1754-88. Caatie Van Slyck 1754-88. 4. Sophia Pieterse, 1734; Margarieta Peterse, 1754-88; Engeltie P. Truex, 1800. 5. Jannetie Reyly, 1754 ; Elisabeth Glen, doghter van Henry Glen, } 1788.

## BANK 38.

1. Ariaantje Wemp, 1734; Hesje Toll; Annnatie Glen 1754-88. 2. Marya Wemp, 1734; Susanna Fonda, 1754; Rebecca Yates, 1788. 3. Rebecca Glen, 1734; Cathryna Wendell, 1754-88. 4. Gesina Swits, 1734 ; Susanna DeGraaf, 1754-88. 5. Sara Abrahamse Glen, 1754-88.

## BANK 39.

1. Elisabeth Yates, 1734; Sara Ephraim Smith, 1788. 2. Maritie Vrooman, 1734 ; Engeltie Veeder, 1788 ; Engeltie Ar: Bradt Dens, 1734. 3. Ragheltie Fonda, 1734; Rachel Nieuwkerk, 1788; Tanneke DeGraaf, 1794. 5. Anna Beck, 1734; Christina Isaacse Truex, 1788; Hannah Moyston, 1805. 5. Maria Stevens, 1788 ; Catharina Stuart 1794.

## BANK 40.

1. Jannetie Bradt, 1734; Maria L. Vrooman, 1788. 2. Baata Marinus, 1734; Annatie Vrooman, 1754; Engeltie Vrooman, 1788. 3. Sara Smith, 1734; Sara Van Eps, 1788. 4. Neeltie P. (?) Van Eps, 1734; Elisabeth Van Vorst, 1788. 5. Sarah Marselis, 1754; Eva Yates Jr., 1788; Sarah Peek, 1810.

HISTORY OF THE CHURCH. 215

BANK 41.

1. Engeltie Schermerhorn, 1734; Engeltie Veeder, 1788.
2. Altie DeGraaf, 1734; Eva Schermerhorn, 1788. 3. Jacomyntie Pottman, 1734; Cornelia J. Barhydt, 1788; Nancy J. Barhydt, 1811. 4. Eva Marselis, 1734; Sara Marselis Jr., 1754-88. 5. Caatje Condie, 1788.

BANK 42.

1. Leja Stevens, 1734; Maria Hagadorn, 1754; Annatje Connor, 1788. 2. Dientje Hagadorn, 1734; Rachel Barhydt, 1788. 3. Elisabeth Brouwer, 1734; Margareta Van de Bogart, 1788. 4, Annatje W. Veeder, 1734; Jannetie Jos: Yates Cuyler, 1788. 5. Elisabeth Jos: Yates Van Slyck, 1788.

BANK 43.

1. Sartje Danielse Van Antwerp, 1734; Annatie Wesselse, 1754-88. 2. Marya Danielse Van Antwerp, 1734-88; Geertruy Vander Heyden, 1809. 3. Rebecca Danielse Van Antwerp, 1734-88; Rebecca Putman, 1809. 4. Hillegonda Van Vranken, 1754-88. 5, Margarieta Vrooman, 1788.

BANK 44.

1. Catrina Colon, 1754; Lena Oothout, 1788. 2. Jannetje Bratt, 1788. 3. Magdalena Oothout, 1788; Margarieta Oothout, 1791. 4. Elisabeth A. Joh: Potman, 1788. 5. Margarieta Albertse Vedder, 1788.

BANK 45.

1. Catrina Symon Vrooman, 1734; Lena Vrooman, 1788, 2. Catharina Glen, 1734; Helena Wemple, 1788. 3. Susanna

Glen, 1734; Rachel Wemple, 1788. 4. Anna Truex, 1734; Elisabeth Ab: Truax, 1754-88; Elisabeth Collon. 5. Rachel Clute, 1788; Rachel Gonzalis, 1801. 6. Margarietje Jno: Bapt: Van Vorst, 1788.

### BANK 46.

1. Elisabeth DeGraaf, 1734; Margarieta Jesse Van Slyck, 1788. 2. Anneke DeGraaf, 1734; Alida DeGraaf, 1754; Ariaantje Van de Bogart, 1748. 3. Maria DeGraaf, 1734-88. 4. Ariaantje Schermerhorn, 1734; Alida Clement, 1788. 5. Catrina Hall, 1754-88; Maria Jac: Vedder, 1791. 6. Anneke DeGraaf, 1788.

### BANK 47.

1. Eytie Vrooman, 1734; Maritje Jac: Vrooman, 1788. 2. Maria Isaacse Vrooman, 1734; Maria Marselis, 1788. 3. Johanna Van Vorst, 1734; Sara Marselis, 1788. 4. *Weduwe* Jan Danielse [Van Antwerp], 1734; Catriena Johannese Hall, 1754 88. 5. Willemptje Groot, 1754; Willemptie Mebie, 1788. 6. Hester Van de Bogart, 1754; Maria Albert Vedder, 1788.

### BANK 48.

1. Alida Wemp, 1734; Cornelia Brouwer, 1754; Catharina Van Antwerp, 1788. 2 Lena Fonda, 1734; Brechje Van Slyck, 1754; Clara Van Slyck, 1788. 3. Annatie Van Vleck, 1734; Catharina Van Olinda, 1788. 4. Debora DeGraaf, 1734; Elisabeth Clute, 1788. 5. Maria Van Vleck, 1754; Maria Dellamont, 1788. 6. Maria H. Brouwer, 1754-88.

### BANK 49.

1. Maritie Brouwers, 1734; Elisabeth Brouwers, 1754; Elisabeth Bratt, 1788. 2. Lysbet Toll, 1734; Neeltje Johannese

## HISTORY OF THE CHURCH. 217

Van Eps, 1754; Eva Johannese Van Petten, 1788. 3, Elisabeth Brouwer, 1734; Elisabeth H. Brouwers, 1788. 4. Maritie S. Veeder, 1734; Maria S. Vedder (?), 1788. 5. Catrina Van de Bogart, 1734; Maria McMichael, 1788. 6. Maritie Ar: De Graaf, 1734; Annatie Vedder, 1788.

### BANK 50.

1. Barber Franse [Van de Bogart] 1734; Anna Connor, 1754; Maria Sanderse Vedder; Sara Sanderse Vedder; Margarita A. Truex, 1788. 2. Tryntje Vrooman, 1734; Catriena Yates, 1754-88; Maria Marselis Van Vranken, 1801. 3. Maritie Swits, 1734; Maria Yates, 1754; Maria Yates Teller, 1788. 4. Maria Van Antwerp, 1734; Ariaantje G. Van Antwerp, 1754-88. 5. Margarieta Vedder, 1754; Annatie Albert Vedder, 1788. 6. Elisabeth Johannese Van Eps, 1754-88.

### BANK 51.

1. Gesina Vrooman, 1734; Neeltie Van Antwerp, 1754; Sophia Wessels, 1788. 2. Maritie Van Brakell, 1734; Hester Vrooman, 1754; Marya Ja: Heemstraat, 1788. 3. Jannetie Cornelise Van Slyck, 1734; Geesie Schermerhorn, 1754-88. 4. Elisabeth Peek, 1734; Rebecca Symonse Groot, 1754-88. 5. Alida Wemp, 1734; Eva Yates, 1754-88; Hubertje S. Bratt, 1790. 6. Neeltie H. Van Antwerp, 1734; Catlyntie Yates, 1754-88.

### BANK 52.

1. Margarita Vrooman, 1734; Eva Vrooman, Seth's *Vrouw*, 1754; Alida Adam Vrooman, 1788. 2. Jannetie Van Slyck: 1734; Engeltie Lansing 1754-88. 3. Maria Fonda, 1734; Eva Van Schaick, 1754; Antie DeGarmo, *weduwe*, 1788; Eva H. Van Dyck, 1734. 4. Engeltie Lansing, 1754; Helena Adr , Van Slyck, 1788. Rebecca Fort, 1734; Susanna Cornelise Van

de Volgen, 1754-88. 6. Marya Fort 1734; Maria F. Veeder, 1754-88. 7. Engelina Van Slyck, 1734-54; Catharina Stiers, 1788.

### BANK 53.

1. Margarieta H. Van Slyck, 1754-88. 2. Sara Vedder, 1754|; Sara Van Petten, 1788. 3. Maghtelt Lansing, 1754; Ruth Lansing 1788; Annatje Jac: Beekman, 1799. 4. Breghje Van Guysling, 1754; Suster Peek, 1788; Nancy A. Peek, 1809. 5. Mieke Bratt, 1754; Annatie Berret, 1788. 6. Elisabeth Groot, 1754; Neeltie Groot; Jacomyntje Van Slyck, 1788. 7. Debora Veeling, 1754-88; *De kerke*, 1793.

### BANK 53.

1. Lydia Van Slyck, 1734; Margarieta H. Van Slyck, 1754-88. 2. Sara Vedder, 1734; Sara Van Petten, 1754-88. 3. Rebecca Brouwers, 1734; Magtelt Lansing, 1754; Ruth Lansing, 1788; Annatie Jac; Beekman, 1790. 4. Diewer Viele, 1734; Breghie Van Gysling, 1754; Suster Peek, 1788; Nancy A Peek, 1809. 5. Mieke Bratt, 1734-54; Anna Berret, 1788. 6. Vredtie Van Vorst, 1734; Elisabeth Groot, 1754; Neeltie Groot; Jacomyntie Van Slyck, 1788. 7. Debora Veeling, 1754-88; *De kerk*, 1792.

### BANK 54.

1. Anna Peek, 1734; Annatie DeGraaf, 1754-88. 2. Margarita Van de Bogart, 1734; Marya Morrison, 1754-88. 3. Angenieta Vrooman, 1734; Margarieta Joh$^{se}$ Veeder, 1754-88; The Church, 1801. 4. Antje P. Clements, 1734; Susanna Sixby, 1754-88; The Church, 1801. 5. Margarieta Bisoe, 1734; Maria Wm. Beth, 1754 88. 6. Anna Smith, 1734; Breghie Smith, 1754; Maria Abr$^{mse}$ Fonda; Annatie Van de Bogart, 1788. 7. Sarah Vrooman, 1754; Geertruy Bosie; Sarah S. Schermerhorn, 1788.

BANK 55.

1. Catriena Bratt, 1734; Anna J. Empie, 1754-88. 2. Margarieta Bratt, 1734; Tanneke Van Dyck, 1754 88; Eve Wendell, 1810. 3. Helena Bratt, 1734; Jannetie Joh: Schermerhorn, 1754; Helena Ogden, 1788; De Huysvrouw van Dom: Romeyn, 1792. 4. Ariaantje Bratt, 1734-88; Jannetie Ar. Van Petten, 1794. 5. Debora Wemp, 1734; Folckie Bratt, 1754-88. 6. Catlintje Andr: Bratt, 1734; Annatie Christo. Yates, 1754-88. 7. Rebecca Wemp, 1734; Jannetie Tymis, Maria Van Petten, 1788.

BANK 56.

1. Maria Ab$^{m:e}$ Mebie, 1754; Ragheltje Fonda Jr., 1788. 2. Sara Van Petten, 1754; Catrina A. Bratt, 1788. 3. Elisabeth Groot, 1734; Rebecca DeGraaf, 1754-88. 4. Annatie G. Mebie, 1754; Annatie Erickson, 1788. 5. Eve Van Petten, huysvrouw van Johannes Toll, } 1754; Geertruy Swart, 1788. 6. Catrina Stevens, 1754-88; Eve Mebie.

BANK 57.

1. Neeltie S. Van Eps, 1734-88. 2. Catrina Lansing, 1754; Debora Lansing, 1788. 3. Catrina Dellamont, 1754-88. 4. Lena Sanderse Van Eps, 1754-88; De kerk, 1792. 5. Margarieta Brouwers [Brown?], 1754; Annatie Beck Guysling, 1788; De kerke, 1791; Helena Ogden, 1792. 6. Maria Marselis, 1754-88; De kerk.

BANK 58.

1. Elisabeth Ph. Groot, 1754; Neeltie Ph. Groot; Annatie Petrus Groot, 1788. 2. Alida Nack, 1754; Alida Vedder.

1788; *De kerk*, 1801. 3. Margarieta Van Slyck, 1754-88. 4. Margarieta Peek, 1754; Lena Peek Barhydt, 1788. 5. Elisabeth Isaac Marselis, 1754-88. 6. Maria Arentse J. Vedder, 1754-88.

BANK 59 tot 62.

*De kerkenraadt.*

## APPENDIX B.

### SCHENECTADY ACADEMY AND UNION COLLEGE.

Schenectady Academy, out of which grew Union College, was commenced in 1785. Domine Romeyn, who came to the village the year before, was the soul of this new enterprize. Through his influence the church was induced to erect a commodious building, and the citizens engaged to give it their patronage and furnish it with a library. After a prosperous existence of nearly ten years, a College charter having been obtained, the Academy property was passed over into the hands of its Trustees. The progress of this undertaking can be clearly traced in the minutes of the Consistory. Their first official action was taken on the 21st day of February 1785, when they resolved to construct, as speedily as possible, with the help of the church, a house of two stories, with two rooms in each story, upon the lot of ground belonging to the church upon which the old Guardhouse * now stands ; and that upon the completion of the building three of said rooms shall be assigned for the use of the school and Academy. †

Moreover on account of the cost of the Academy house to the Church it was resolved that said Church shall receive four shillings yearly from every scholar taught in said house ; and if said Academy or *Illustre School* shall become changed into a college, then the President of such College as well as the Rector of said school shall be a member of the Dutch Church and minister of this church—and the said four shillings for each scholar shall be bestowed upon such poor scholars as the Church shall name.

---

* After the erection of the church of 1734, that of 1715, standing at the junction of Church and State streets was used as a fort ; it was not standing in 1754, but a Guard or Watchhouse seems to have been erected in its place.

† Bestolen so spoedig als mogelyk met de hulpe Van hun E. Gemeente, een Huys Van Twee Verdiepingen en twee Verbrekken in yeder Verdiepinge te Bouwen op het Lot grondt tot de Kerk behorende, daar tegenswoordigh het Oude Wacht huys staat ; sullende op volvoeringe van het gebrouw, drie van desselfs Vertrekken worden of gesondert tot school en Academie gebruyk.
—Consistory minutes.

March 5th 1785:—The consistory about this time were still negotiating with the town magistrates for the improvement of the Common schools (*triviale scholen*) of the town and for the establishment of an *Illustre School* or Academy.

March 16th, 1785:—The Consistory order the gathering of materials for the Academy building.

March 25th:—It was considered expedient to build the academy not upon the old Guardhouse Lot but upon the North corner of Union & Ferry streets on land then belonging to Johannes Pootman:—ordered that building materials shall be procured as speedily as possible—also carpenters and Masons.

April 7th 1785:—The Academy building being now well under way the Consistory and 27 respectable citizens of the town met Reuben Simonds [public] House [in Church street] to close the matter of the Academy by signing articles of agreement for the management & support of said academy. *

The names of these 27 respectable citizens were,

Cornelius A$^d$ Van Slyck,
Andries Van Petten,
Joseph Yates,
Cornelius Vrooman,
Samuel A. Brat,
Isaac Quackenboss,
Abraham Swits,
Gerrit A. Lansingh,
Daniel Campbell,
Claes Van der Volgen,
Peter Van Gyseling,
Christ$^r$ Yates,
Henry Glen,
Abraham Oothout.

John Richardson,
Robert Moyston,
William Van Ingen,
Henry Glen, for John Glen,
Abraham Fonda,
Abraham Oothout, for Harmanus Bradt,
Reyn$^r$ Mynderse,
William Mead,
Corn$^s$ Van Dyck,
Isaac Vrooman,
Nicholas Veeder,
D. Romeyn *Prases*.

Signed in presence of
    Ab$^m$ Truex.
    Reuben Simmonds.
    Mynd$^t$ M. Wemple.

---

* This agreement is drawn up with great formality & particularity in eleven sections & is written on fifteen pages of foolscap. It was probably drawn up by Dr. Romeyn who was President of the meeting.

The first board of Trustees elected in accordance with the terms of this contract, were:—

      Do Dirk Romeyn, President.
      Dirk Van Ingen, Secretary.
      Abraham Oothout, Treasurer.
      John Glen.
      Daniel Campbell.
      Henry Glen.
      ——— Frey.
      Claas Van der Volgen.
      John Sanders.
      Peter Vrooman.
      ——— Dietz.

April 22nd 1785:—The Consistory appoint Wm. Schermerhorn to superintend the building of the Academy.

August 1st, 1785:—Committees both of Citizens and Consistory are appointed to urge forward the Academy building. *

An effort was made in 1791 to endow this school by a grant of Indian Lands; and November 16th, Dr Dirk Van Ingen announced to the Consistory that he and others had rented 10,240 acres of land of the Oneida Indians for 21 years on consideration that he paid after five years £100 yearly to said Indians. Dr. V. offered said land to the Consistory to be held for the benefit of the Schenectady church in as much as said Academy unincorporated could not hold real estate. At first the Consistory agreed to receive the land but subsequently gave it up finding doubtless that it could not be legally held by the Church.

On the second day of April, 1793, the Trustees of the Academy ask that the building erected by the Dutch church be made over unto them, to which the Consistory consented. And on September 24th, 1796, the Trustees of Union College ask that the building be made over to them unconditionally, to be sold, and the money put into a more commodious building:—on due consideration this request was granted, and the proceeds of this sale with other moneys were used in building the present Union School edifice.

---

* A stone of an oval shape was built into the front, on which were cut the names of the building committee.
This stone is now in Union College Museum.

APPENDIX C.

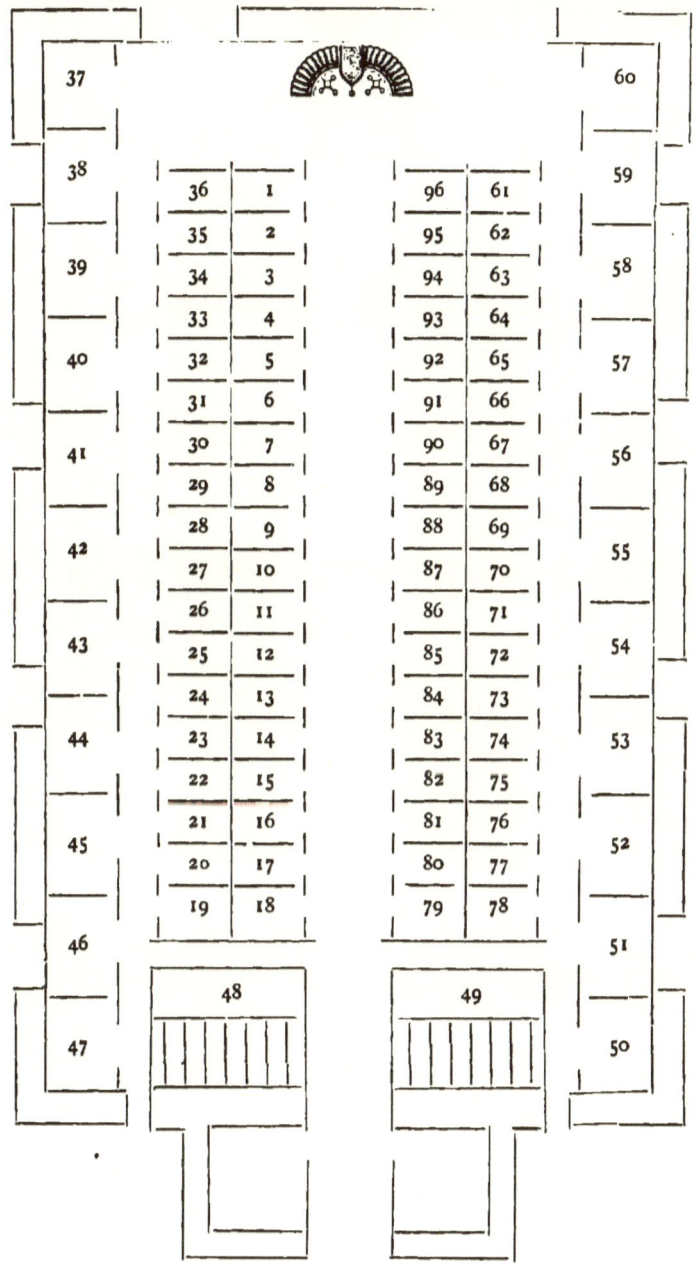

Plan of the Church of 1814.

## NAMES OF THE PEW-HOLDERS IN THE CHURCH OF 1814.*

No. 1. Reserved for the Elders.
" 2. John N. Marselis and Jno: Bapt: Van Epps.
" 3. Widow Volkie Veeder.
" 4. Widow Jane Yates.
" 5. John Sanders; Joseph Horsfall, later.
" 6. Widow Rebecca Van Vranken.
" 7. Abraham Van Ingen; Walter Clute, later.
" 8. Zeger Van Santvoord; Jacob Truax, later.
" 9. Cornelius Van Santvoord.
" 10. Estate of C Roseboom and C Zeger Van Santvoord: Margaret Visger, later.
" 11. Maas Van Vranken and Richard Van Vranken.
" 12. Harmanus Peek.
" 13. Jacob M. DeForest.
" 14. Nicholas A. Marselis.
" 15. Widow Nancy Vrooman.
" 16. Cornelius S. Groot.
" 17. Cornelius Clute and H. Van Huysen.
" 18. John Clark.
" 19. Harmanus Veeder.
" 20. David Kittle, Elizabeth Ouderkirk and Margaret Steers.
" 21. Henry N. Van Petten.
" 22. Abraham S. Groot * * * Richd. McMichael.
" 23. Rudolph Van Huysen and Gerrit Bensen.
" 24. John Yates; 1821, John H. Moyston, Robt. Moyston; 1825, made free by the Consistory.
" 25. Joseph Mynderse.
" 26. Joseph Mynderse for John B. Yates, John Tonnelier.
" 27. Walter Barheit & Nicholas N. Marselis.
" 28. Myndert Van Gysling and Elisabeth Mills.

---

* Prior to this date the Congregation was seated according to sex; afterward in families.

No. 29. Widow Maria Brower.
" 30. Miss Debora Graham
" 31. Simon J. Van Antwerp and Philip Van Vorst.
" 32. ⎱ Jeremiah Fuller.
" 33. ⎰
" 34. Elisabeth Prince and Miss Van Gysling.
" 35. James Rosa.
" 36. Stephen N. Bayard, Rev. Jacob Van Vechten.
" 37. Jacob Swits.
" 38. Gerrit S. Veeder and Jellis Fonda.
" 39. Cornelius A. Groot and John P. Truax, James V. S. Ryley.
" 40. Abraham Oothout.
" 41. Joseph C. Yates, D. D. Campbell, Rev. Jacob Van Vechten.
" 42. Henry Yates Jr.
" 43. Tobias A. Cuyler, Thomas Tripp and Giles F. Yates,
" 44. Peter F. Wendell and Maria Alexander.
" 45. John H. Moyston, Bartho: Schermerhorn.
" 46. Alex: G. Fonda and Jellis A. Fonda.
" 47. John S. Bonny, —— Trip and Tannahill, Free, later.
" 48. Joseph C. Yates.
" 49. Barent S. Mynderse.
" 50. Free.
" 51. Henry Peek.
" 52. John S. Vrooman: M. T. Veeder.
" 53. Isaac De Graaf.
" 54. Abraham Beck: Myndert Vander Volgen.
" 55. John Haverly and Harmanes A. Van Slyck.
" 56. Abraham Van Eps and David Boyd.
" 57. Maas and John S. Schermerhorn.
" 58. Widow Angelica Schermerhorn.
" 59. Jacob Beeckman: Wid: Nancy Beekman.
" 60. Joseph Peek: Jonas Holland.
" 61. James V. S. Ryley: Joseph Consaul.
" 62. Isaac Riggs.
" 63. Philip R. Toll: Frederic Reese.
" 64. John Veeder: Daniel C. Bradt.
" 65. Abraham A. Truax.

No. 66. Maas and John S. Schermerhorn.
" 67. John B. Vedder.
" 68. Maria Morrison and Peter Becker.
" 69. Sybrant Van Schaick; A. Marselis, John S. Ten Eyck.
" 70. Andrew N. Van Petten; Elisabeth Bancker, Margaret Dellamont.
" 71. Gershom Van Voast.
" 72. Oliver Ostrom; John S. Ten Eyck.
" 73. Jacob C. and Joseph Consaul, Alexander Vedder.
" 74. Henry A Fonda; Daniel J. Toll, Abraham Schermerhorn.
" 75. David Vander Heyden, Adrian Van Santvoord.
" 76. Joseph Horsfall.
" 77. John J. Peek.
" 78. Aaron F. Vedder.
" 79. Thomas B. Clinch; Aaron Farnsworth.
" 80. John C. Barheit.
" 81. Widow Helen Linn.
" 82. Douwe Clute.
" 83. Isaac I. DeGraaf.
" 84. Jacob Groesbeck.
" 85. Bartholomew Clute; John B. Clute.
" 86. Jacob I. Clute.
" 87. Daniel L. Van Antwerp.
" 88. Daniel Vedder.
" 89. Takerus Vedder, Elisabeth Vrooman and Catharine J. Schermerhorn.
" 90. Elisabeth Mercer; Abraham Van Ingen.
" 91. Peter Brower.
" 92. John I. and James I Van Eps.
" 93. Daniel S. DeGraaf.
" 94. Widow Mary Teller.
" 95. Jacob Van Antwerp.
" 96. Deacons' Pew.

APPENDIX D.

| 144 | 143 | 142 | 141 | 140 | | | | 35 | 34 | 33 | 32 | 31 |
|---|---|---|---|---|---|---|---|---|---|---|---|---|
| | 136 | 137 | 138 | 139 | | Organ loft. | | | 26 | 27 | 28 | 29 | 30 |
| | | | | | | Pulpit. | | | | | | | |

| | | | | | | |
|---|---|---|---|---|---|---|
| | | | | | | 25 |
| 145 | 135 | 86 | 85 | 36 | | 24 |
| 146 | 134 | 87 | 84 | 37 | | 23 |
| 147 | 133 | 88 | 83 | 38 | | 22 |
| 148 | 132 | 89 | 82 | 39 | | 21 |
| 149 | 131 | 90 | 81 | 40 | | 20 |
| 150 | 130 | 91 | 80 | 41 | | 19 |
| 151 | 129 | 92 | 79 | 42 | | 18 |
| 152 | 128 | 93 | 78 | 43 | | 17 |
| 153 | 127 | 94 | 77 | 44 | | 16 |
| 154 | 126 | 95 | 76 | 45 | | 15 |
| 155 | 125 | 96 | 75 | 46 | | 14 |
| 156 | 124 | 97 | 74 | 47 | | 13 |
| 157 | 123 | 98 | 73 | 48 | | 12 |
| 158 | 122 | 99 | 72 | 49 | | 11 |
| 159 | 121 | 100 | 71 | 50 | | 10 |
| 160 | 120 | 101 | 70 | 51 | | 9 |
| 161 | 119 | 102 | 69 | 52 | | 8 |
| 162 | 118 | 103 | 68 | 53 | | 7 |
| 163 | 117 | 104 | 67 | 54 | | 6 |
| 164 | 116 | 105 | 66 | 55 | | 5 |
| 165 | 115 | 106 | 65 | 56 | | 4 |
| 166 | 114 | 107 | 64 | 57 | | 3 |
| 167 | 113 | 108 | 63 | 58 | | 2 |
| 168 | 112 | 109 | 62 | 59 | | 1 |
| | 111 | 110 | 61 | 60 | | |

Bride's door.     Stairs to gallery.     Forefather's door.

Plan of Church of 1863.

## HISTORY OF THE CHURCH. 233

"The rent price of Pews in the Reformed P. Dutch Church, Schenectady, N. Y., July 24th, 1863, as reported to the Consistory by the Committee appointed by them":—

| Pew. No. | Lessee. | Price. |
|---|---|---|
| 1. | Angelica Van Petten, | $ 8. |
| 2. | B. L. Conde, | 8. |
| 3. | S. O. Hedden, | 10. |
| 4. | C. H. Van Vranken, | 10. |
| 5. | Geo. B. McClyman, | 10. |
| 6. | James G. Caw, | 10. |
| 7. | Duncan Robinson, | 10. |
| 8. | Mrs. T. Combs and Sarah Swits, | 10. |
| 9. | George Harding, | 10. |
| 10. | James B. Clute, | 9. |
| 11. | Mrs. A. E. Harmon, | 14. |
| 12. | Ernestus Putman, | 16. |
| 13. | Jas. H. Barhydt, | 16. |
| 14. | Abraham Veeder, | 16. |
| 15. | Mrs. Abrm. Veeder, | 16. |
| 16. | J. R. Sitterlee, | 16. |
| 17. | N. J. Schermerhorn, | 14. |
| 18. | G. W. Moon, | 11. |
| 19. | A. Vandermore, | 10. |
| 20. | A. C. Van Eps, | 15. |
| 21. | Jno Kilmartin, | 16. |
| 22. | Nic. H. Vedder, | 15. |
| 23. | Sybrant Vandebogart, | 15. |
| 24. | Angus McIntosh, | 14. |
| 25. | Mrs. Geo. Fisher, | 8. |
| 26. | Deacons, | |
| 27. | Miss Arabella Fonda, | 20. |
| 28. | Mrs. A. Lighthall, | 22. |
| 29. | Thos. Pemberton, | 24. |
| 30. | | 24. |
| 31. | | 8. |
| 32. | | 8. |
| 33. | Mrs. R. Perry, | 9. |
| 34. | | 9. |

| Pew. No. | Lessee. | Price. |
|---|---|---|
| 35. |  | 6. |
| " 36. |  | 8. |
| " 37. | A. O. Peterson, | 20. |
| " 38. | Richard Marselis, | 8. |
| " 39. | Richard Marselis, | 12. |
| " 40. | Robt. Stevenson, | 20. |
| " 41. | Daniel Vedder, | 20. |
| " 42. | Nicholas Cain, | 20. |
| " 43. | Geo. Shaible, | 19. |
| " 44. | Mrs. J. N. Barhydt. | 10. |
| " 45. | Charles N. Yates, | 15. |
| " 46. | Gershom Banker, | 14. |
| " 47. | Harriet Barringer, | 20. |
| " 48. | Charles E. Angel, | 20. |
| " 49. | Joseph Horsfall, | 16. |
| " 50. | C. Van Slyck, | 15. |
| " 51. | H. T. Garret, | 16. |
| " 52. | B. Schermerhorn, | 16. |
| " 53. | Mrs. Otis Smith, | 14. |
| " 54. | Wm. Clogston, | 16. |
| " 55. | Miss F. Hook. | 12. |
| " 56. | Wm. H. Schermerhorn, | 15. |
| " 57. | J. L. Landon, | 15. |
| " 58. | Miss Susan Veeder, | 15. |
| " 59. | Mrs. Tannahill and Max: Cox, | 15. |
| " 60. | Joseph Harmon, | 15. |
| " 61. |  | 25. |
| " 62. | James Van Kuren, | 22. |
| " 63. | Spencer Ostrom and Jas: H. Lighthall, | 22. |
| " 64. | Mrs. Nath: Clarke and Mrs. Giles Brower, | 25. |
| " 65. | Jacob N. Vedder, | 28. |
| " 66. | H. H. Swart and Peter Dorsch, | 30. |
| " 67. | T. W. Van Brunt, | 30. |
| " 68. | Jno. N. Vrooman, | 30. |
| " 69. | Jno. Frame and Thos: Cox, | 30. |
| " 70. | Wm. H. Helmer, | 30. |
| " 71. | Aaron Barringer, | 30. |
| " 72. | Corn: S. Thomson, | 30. |

| Pew. No. | Lessee. | Price. |
|---|---|---|
| 73. | Peter B. Yates, | 30. |
| 74. | Peter Holmes, | 30. |
| 75. | Noah? Vibbard, | 30. |
| 76. | The Pastor, | 30. |
| 77. | Jno. Consaul, | 34. |
| 78. | Nicholas Swits, | 30. |
| 79. | Caspar F. Hoag, | 30. |
| 80. | Alex. J. Van Eps, | 30. |
| 81. | S. V. Swits, | 30. |
| 82. | Jno. G Van Voast, | 30. |
| 83. | Albert Van Voast, | 30. |
| 84. | David F. Reese, | 25. |
| 85. | | 10. |
| 86. | | 10. |
| 87. | Mrs. Fonda, Cady and Johnson, | 25. |
| 88. | Albert A. Vedder, | 30. |
| 89. | Miss Deborah Graham, | 30. |
| 90. | Isaac Banker, | 30. |
| 91. | Potter, | 30. |
| 92. | Jno. W. Veeder, | 30. |
| 93. | Edward Rosa, | 30. |
| 94. | N. Van Vranken, | 34. |
| 95. | Martin DeForeest, | 30. |
| 96. | Simon C. Groot, | 30. |
| 97. | Thos. B. Mitchell, | 30. |
| 98. | Alex. M. Vedder, | 30. |
| 99. | Jno. B. Clute, | 30. |
| 100. | Abram Doty, | 30 |
| 101. | Thos. H. Reeves, | 30. |
| 102. | Wm. Van Vranken, | 30. |
| 103. | Jos. Y. Van de Bogart, | 30. |
| 104. | Jno. McNee, | 30. |
| 105. | Richd. V. Benson, | 30. |
| 106. | Jacob F. Clute, | 28. |
| 107. | Isaac Cain, | 25. |
| 108. | C. C. Clute, | 22. |
| 109. | Jno. G. Veeder, | 22. |
| 110. | John Southard, | 25. |
| 111. | Jno. Reaber and P. Frederick. | 15. |

| Pew. | Lessee. | Price. |
|---|---|---|
| No. 112. | Jno P. Becker, | 15. |
| " 113. | Andrew Frame. | 15. |
| " 114. | F. Van de Bogart, | 15. |
| " 115. | Duncan McDonald, | 15. |
| " 116. | D. M. Kittle, | 12. |
| " 117. | Wilson Davis, | 16. |
| " 118. | Jno. Van de Bogart, | 14. |
| " 119. | B. A. Mynderse, | 16. |
| " 120. | Wm. McKerlie, | 16. |
| " 121. | Abraham Vrooman, | 15. |
| " 122. | Catharine Swits. | 20. |
| " 123. | Alex. Holland, | 20. |
| " 124. | Nancy Vedder, | 20. |
| " 125. | Henry Furman, | 14. |
| " 126. | Jno. Van Antwerp, | 15. |
| " 127. | G. L. Oothout, | 10. |
| " 128. | George Ohlen, | 19. |
| " 129. | Henry Rosa, | 20. |
| " 130. | Wm. Chrisler, | 20. |
| " 131. | Nicholas Yates, | 20. |
| " 132. | J. V. Vrooman, | 10. |
| " 133. | Elisabeth Veeder, | 8. |
| " 134. | Mrs. M. Myers, | 20. |
| " 135. | C. C. Clute, | 8. |
| " 136. | D. Ketcham, | 20. |
| " 137. | G. Westinghouse, | 20. |
| " 138. |  | 20. |
| " 139. | Elders, |  |
| " 140. |  | 6. |
| " 141. |  | 9. |
| " 142. | Jacob A. Wick. | 9. |
| " 143. | S. A. Daggett, | 8. |
| " 144. |  | 8. |
| " 145. |  | 8. |
| " 146. | Charles Carr (?), | 15. |
| " 147. | E. Brinton, | 15. |
| " 148. | Edw. Groot, | 16. |
| " 149. | Mrs. J. K. Paige, | 15. |
| " 150. | Mrs. J. K. Paige, | 15. |

## HISTORY OF THE CHURCH. 237

| Pew. | Lessee. | Price. |
|---|---|---|
| No. 151. | Mrs. Stuyvesant, | 12. |
| " 152. | Tayler Lewis, | 14. |
| " 153. | Miss Elisabeth Fuller, | 16. |
| " 154. | Mary Tomlinson, | 18. |
| " 155. | Albert Ward, | 30. |
| " 156. |  | 38. |
| " 157. | Stephen Yates, | 38. |
| " 158. | Robt. Furman, | 34. |
| " 159. | Pettingill and Kelsey, | 30. |
| " 160. | Nich: Van de Bogart, | 30. |
| " 161. | A. Truax, | 28. |
| " 162. | Young & Graham, | 20. |
| " 163. | Mrs. J. C. Van Vranken, | 12. |
| " 164. | O. S. Luffman, | 11. |
| " 165. | Lewis I. Barhydt, | 11. |
| " 166. | Jane Timesen, | 10. |
| " 167. | Maria Van Slyck, | 8. |
| " 168. | Harmen Van Eps, | 8. |

## APPENDIX E.

Twenty-nine leases assigned to the Church December 30th, 1747, by Jan Wemp and Arent Bratt, Patentees of Schenectady:

"One Indenture from Karel Hanse Tol, Gerrit Van Brakelen, Aswerus Marselis, Caleb Beck and Company.

One from Pieter Vrooman.

    do    Laurens Claase [Vander Volgen].
    do    Jan Mabey.

Also the following given by Col. Peter Schuyler, Johannes Sanderse Glen, Adam Vrooman, Geysbert Marselis and Company:

One Indenture given by Benjamin Lanyen,
                Jacobus Peeck,
                Jan Danielse [Van Antwerpen],
                Jellis Fonda,
                Philip Schuyler,
                Abm. & Dirk Groot,
                Abraham Wendell,
                Pieter Vrooman,
                Evert Van Eps,
                Hendrick Vrooman,
                Sander Philipse,
                Claas & Tjerk Franse [Vander Bogart],
                Arent Danielse [Van Antwerpen],
                Arent Vedder,
                Jan Danielse [Van Antwerpen],
                Gerrit Gysbertse [Van Brakelen],
                Dirk Bratt,
                John Lench,
                Jan Baptist & Jellis Fonda,
                Johannes Mynderse,
                Jan Philipse,
                Samuel Bratt,
                Ahasuerus Marselis,
                Jan Vrooman,
                Karel Hansen [Toll].

We, hereunder written, do hereby Certify that we have received the above mentioned Indentures for the behoof of the Church Wardens pr us.

                        Peter Groenendyck,
                        Johannes A. Vedder,
                        John Sanders,
                        Gerrit A. Lansingh."

---

        Church quitrents, 25th May, 1750.
26th May, 1750.
        "Gissinge van de lyst aengaande quit 't gene de Trustees op hunne zyde gestelt hebben, ende kkraad meent de kerke, toe te komen, van Art. Bratt gesond den 26th May, 1750. Also my de menate outbreeckt.

| Tarwe. | Skiples. |
|---|---|
| Cornelis Van Slyck, | 2¾ & 5 g. |
| Hend: Flipse nu Pr. Danielse, | 1. |
| Van Pr. Vrooman erfgenamen, | 4½. |
| Johannes Peeck, | 3 1-5. |
| Jillis Van Vorst nu Gr. Van Vorst, | 9½. |
| N. B.—nu op hun Lyst 7 Schep, | |
| Jan Baptist Van Ebs, | 5. |
| Jonatan Stevens, 1717. | 8. |
| Corn: Groot, | 6. |
| N. B —mischien maet dit maer 3 zyn, | |
| Evert van Ebs, 1712. | 1⅓. |
| Gr. Gysbertse [Van Brakelen], 1717, | 1½. |
| Cornl. Slingerland, 1718. | 1½. |
| Adam Vroom, 1719. | 1¼. |
| John Collins, nu d'erfgenamen V. andries van Sleyck, | ½. |
| Saml. Bratt, 1706, | ⅛. |

[50.]

| Gelt. | £. S. D. |
|---|---|
| Johan: Van Antwerpen, | 0–09–0 |
| Gysbert Marselis Jr., | 09 |
| Philip Livingston voor 't Landt van Dirk Groot | 10 |
| Pieter Brouwer & Broeders, | 04–6 |
| Abrah: nu Gerrit Lansing, | 01 |
| 1717, John Dumbar, | 01 |
| Joh: Cloet & Myndert Wemp, | 04 |
| Douwe Aukes, | 0–00–6 |
| Albert Vedder, | 1 |
| | [£2–00–0.] |
| Bart. Vrooman, | –01– |
| Jan Wempel, | –6 |
| Hendr: Vrooman, | –3 |
| Henrick Hansen, | 1–00–0 |
| | [£2–02–9.] |

Plancken.

Jan Wemp................................... 10
Joh : Teller,................................. 10

[20.]

Wegens de Tarw quit dient onderrechtinge omtrent eenige Schriften van de zo genoemde *Slincksche* Trustees door de andere te confirmeren en ons overgelevert.

| Uytgift tydt. | Betaling tydt. | Schep: |
|---|---|---|
| 1705-6. Thomas Smit. | 1706-7. | ⅔. |
| 1706-7. Dirck Bratt. | 1713. | 3-9. |

N. B.—dit is voor Rosendal niet wel geteykent maer echter van hem besetz Dog 1718 geset ap, - 1.
Claes en Tjerk Fransen [Van de Bogart], - 2.

[4].

N. B.—dit is oock mit geteykent maar 't schynt gezet want het geteykt is van getuyge.—

| | | | | |
|---|---|---|---|---|
| | Jan Philipse, - | - 1708, | - | 0-1 quad. |
| | Henr. Vrooman. - | - 1711. - | - | 1. |
| | Jan Vrooman, - | 1713, | - | 1. |
| | Abrah : Wendel, - | - 1713, - | | ½. |
| 1707, | Arent Danielse. - | - 1714, | - | 1. |
| 1707. | John Lench, - | - 1713, - | | 1⅓. |
| | Arent Vedder. - | - 1713, | - | ¾. |
| 1708. | Benjamyn Lanine, - | 1714, - | | 5. |
| 1709. | Daniel Janse. - | 1714, | - | 5. |
| 1705-6 | Jacobus Peeck, - | - 1706, - | | ½. |
| | 5 jaar en dan, - | ——, | - | 1. |
| 1708. | Sander Pilipse £2 huur to 1720 en dan, | | - | £1. |
| 1705. | 31 x ber Jan Danielse, - | 1705-6, | - | 1 skpiple |
| 1708. | Jan Danielse, | - 1714, - | | 1. |
| 1715-6. | Arent Danielse, | ——, | - | 22. |

Dit is voor 't landt van Reyer Wemp en heeft altyt in 't Boeck 23 gestaen en betalt gewest. Doch 1745 hebben Trusties geordonneert dat sint 3 schep : Voor hun zoude zyn en maer 20 * * * * de kerke en hebben sy die 3 na sich getrocken, en dus tegen 't schrift dan zeker de kk : jaarlyeks 2 schep : te kort gedaen.

Fouten en 't gene Vergeten en onbekent is Uytgesondert.
Ick ondergesz: attesteren dese Copie accorderen met syn orrigenal.   P. FELINCK.

[NOTE. Forty-six leases in the above list yielded a yearly rent of 96 skiples of wheat £3-2-9-in money and 20 boards.]

## APPENDIX F.

#### ELDERS AND DEACONS.

These officers by the charter of this Church must be eight in number—four elders and four deacons, each holding his office two years. The election is held on the first Saturday of December in each year when two of each class are appointed and on New Year's day following ordained [*bevestight*] and inducted into office.

From the founding of the church here to 1701, the number of elders and deacons was generally two each: After Domine Freerman came and to Domine Erichzons' ministry in 1728, the number was increased to three, and from the latter date to the present time the number has been four each.

The following list is as full as the imperfect condition of the consistorial minutes will allow.—

| Deacons. | Elders. |
|---|---|
| | 1680. |
| Hendrick Meese Vrooman, | |
| Jan Pootman. | |
| | 1683. |
| Johannes Pootman, | |
| Sweer Teunise Van Velsen. | |
| | 1687. |
| Johannes Sanders Glen. | Myndert Wemp. |
| | 1688. |
| Claas Lourense Purmerent, | Sweer TeuniseVan Velsen, |
| [Vander Volgen], treasr. | Reinier Schaets, |

| Deacons. | Elders. |
|---|---|
| Adam Vrooman, | Myndert Wemp. |
| Isaac Swits. | |

1689.

| | |
|---|---|
| Adam Vrooman, treasr. | Myndert Wemp, |
| Isaac Swits, | Frans Harmense Van de Bogart. |
| Barent Wemp, | |
| Willem Appel. | |

1690.

Isaac Swits, treasr.

1691.

| | |
|---|---|
| Isaac Swits, treasr., | Johannes Sanderse Glen. |
| Barent Wemp, | |
| Adam Vrooman. | |

1692.

| | |
|---|---|
| Barent Wemp, treasr., | Johannes Sanderse Glen, |
| Adam Vrooman. | Isaac Swits. |

1693.

| | |
|---|---|
| Adam Vrooman, treasr., | Isaac Swits, |
| Jacobus Peek. | Barent Wemp. |

1694.

| | |
|---|---|
| Johannes Hendrickse Vrooman, | Johannes Sanderse Glen, |
| Jacobus Peek, treasr., | Barent Wemp. |
| Adam Vrooman. | |

1695.

| | |
|---|---|
| Arent Vedder, | Claas Lourense Van der Volgen. |
| Johannes Hendrickse Vrooman. | Johannes Sanderse Glen. |

1696.

| | |
|---|---|
| Dirk Arentse Bratt. | Jacobus Peek, |
| Arent Vedder, treasr. | Claas Laurense Van der Volgen. |

1697.

| | |
|---|---|
| Harmen Vedder, | Isaak Swits. |
| Dirk Arentse Bratt, treasr. | Jacobus Peek. |

1698.

| | |
|---|---|
| Abraham Groot, | Adam Vrooman, |
| Harmen Vedder, treasr. | Isaak Swits. |

1699.

| | |
|---|---|
| Johannes Vrooman. | Johannes Sanderse Glen. |
| Abrm. Groot, treasr. | Adam Vrooman. |

| Diaconen. | Ouderlingen. |
|---|---|
| **1700.** | |
| Jacobus Van Dyck, treasr., | Jacobus Peek, |
| Johannes Vrooman. | Johannes Sanderse Glen. |
| **1701 *** | |
| Ryer Schermerhorn, | Adam Vrooman, |
| Gerrit Symonse [Veeder], | Barent Wemp, |
| Jacobus Van Dyck. | Jacobus Peek. |
| **1702.** | |
| Daniel Janse [Van Antwerpen], | Isaac Swits, |
| Ryer Schermerhorn, } treasr | Adam Vrooman, |
| Gerrit Symonse [Veeder] } | Barent Wemp. |
| **1703.** | |
| Nicolaas Van Petten, | Nicolaas Van der Volgen, |
| Johannes Glen, | Johannes Vrooman, |
| Dan'l Janse [Van Antwerpen] treasr | Isaac Swits. |
| **1704.** | |
| Johannes Teller, | Ryer Schermerhorn, |
| Nicolaas Van Petten, } treasrs. | Nicolaas Vander Volgen, |
| Johannes Glen. } | Johannes Vrooman. |
| **1705.** | |
| Gysbert Van Brakelen, | Isaac Swits, |
| Jan Wemp, | Barent Wemp, |
| Johannes Teller | Ryer Schermerhorn. |
| **1706,** | |
| Johannes Teller, † | Ryer Schermerhorn, † |
| **1707.** | |
| Johannes Teller. | Ryer Schermerhorn. |
| **1708.** | |
| Johannes Teller. | Ryer Schermerhorn. |
| **1709.** | |
| Barent Wemp, | Ryer Schermerhorn, |
| Johannes Wemp, | Gysbert Gerritse [Van Brakelen] |
| Johannes Teller. | |
| **1710.** | |
| Johannes Teller. | Ryer Schermerhorn. |

* After this date the number of Deacons and Elders was increased.

† Johannes Teller and Ryer Schermerhorn managed the finances from 1706 to 1713: During this time there was no minister.

| Diaconen. | Ouderlingen. |
|---|---|
| | 1711. |
| Johannes Teller. | Ryer Schermerhorn. |
| | 1712. |
| Johannes Teller. | Ryer Schermerhorn. |
| | 1713. |
| Jan Wemp, | Barent Wemp, |
| Volkert Symonse [Veeder]. | Gerrit Symonse [Veeder]. |
| | 1714. |
| Volkert Symonse [Veeder], | Gerrit Symonse [Veeder], |
| Symon Swits. | Johannes Sanderse Glen. |
| | 1715. |
| Volkert Veeder, treasr. | Gerrit Sanderse [Veeder], |
| Symon Swits. | Johannes Sanderse Glen. |
| | 1716. |
| Jan Dellamont, | Jacobus Van Dyck, |
| Symon Swits, | Gerrit Symonse [Veeder], |
| Volkert Symonse [Veeder]. | Johannes Sanderse Glen. |
| | 1717. |
| Jan Dellamont, | Jan Wemp, |
| Barent Vrooman, | Abraham Groot, |
| Arent Bratt. | Jacobus Van Dyck. |
| | 1718. |
| Barent Vrooman, treasr. | Abraham Groot, |
| Arent Bratt, | Johannes Wemp, |
| Albert Vedder. | Johannes Vrooman. |
| | 1720. |
| Johannes Teller, | Hendrick Vrooman. |
| Volkert Symonse [Veeder], | Arent Bratt, |
| Harmen Vedder. | Jacobus Van Dyck. |
| | 1721. |
| Harmanus Vedder, treasr. | Jacobus Van Dyck, |
| Symon Vrooman, | Adam Vrooman, |
| | 1722. * |
| Nicolaas Schuyler, treasr. | |
| | 1723. |
| Dirk Groot, treasr. | |

* From 1722 to 1728 Domine Brouwer was sick and unable to officiate.

| Diaconen. | Ouderlingen. |
|---|---|
| | 1724. |
| Arent Bratt. | |
| | 1725. |
| Arnout DeGraaf. | |
| | 1728. |
| Cornelis Vander Volgen, | Arent Danielse [Van Antwerpen] |
| Wilhelmus Veeder, | Nicolaas Schuyler. |
| Jacob Glen. | Symon Vrooman. |
| | 1729. |
| Jacob Swits, | Arent Bratt. |
| Robert Yates. | |
| | 1730. * |
| Robert Yates, treasr. | Saml. Arentse Bratt, |
| Jan Barentse Wemp, | Jacobus Van Dyck, |
| Wouter Vrooman. | Dirk Groot, |
| | Cornelis Vander Volgen. |
| | 1731. |
| C. Van der Volgen, | S. Arentse Bratt, |
| Wouter Vrooman, | Dirk Groot, |
| Abraham DeGraaf, | Abraham Mebie, |
| Jan Barentse Wemp, treasr. | Harmanus Vedder. |
| | 1732. |
| Sander Glen, | Abraham Mebie, |
| Myndert Wympel, | Harmanus Vedder, |
| Cornelis Van Dyck, treasr. | Arent Bratt, |
| Abraham DeGraaf. | Jacob Glen. |
| | 1733. |
| Sander Glen, | Arent Bratt, |
| Myndert Wympel, | Harmanus Vedder, |
| Abraham Truax, | Gerrit Symonse [Veeder], |
| Sander Lansing. | Jan Barentse Wemp. |
| | 1734. |
| Sander Lansing, treasr. | Symon Vrooman, |
| Abraham Truax, | Robert Yates, |
| Abraham Glen, | Jan Barentse Wemp, |
| Arent Samuelse Bratt. | Gerrit Symonse Veeder. |

---

\* From this date the number of Deacons and Elders was four each.

| Diaconen. | Ouderlingen. |
|---|---|
| | 1735. |
| Isaac Truax, treasr. | Simon Vrooman, |
| Abraham Glen, | Robert Yates. |
| Arent Samuelse Bratt. | |
| | 1736. |
| Hendrick Vrooman, Jr., | Arent Danielse[VanAntwerpen] |
| Andries Van Petten, | Nicolaas Schuyler, |
| Isaac Truex, | Abraham DeGroff, |
| Hendrick Brouwer. | Hehner Veeder. |
| | 1737. |
| Hendrick Vrooman, | Abraham DeGraaf, |
| Willem Teller, | Abraham Mebie, |
| Hendrick Brouwer, | Wilhelmus Veeder, |
| Barent Wemp. | Arent Bratt. |
| | 1738. |
| | Abraham Mebie, |
| | Sander Lansing. |
| | Jacob Glen. |
| | 1739. |
| | Isaac Truax. |
| | 1740, |
| Abraham Glen. | Arent Danielse[VanAntwerpen] |
| Harmanus Van Antwerpen. | C. Van Dyck. |
| Alexander Van Eps. | |
| | 1741. |
| Johannes Bratt, | Daniel DeGraaf, |
| Hendrick Van Rensselaer, * | C. Van Dyck, |
| Pieter Groenendyck, | ———— Vrooman, |
| Alexander Van Eps, treasr. | Arent Danielse[VanAntwerpen. |
| | 1742. |
| Pieter Groenendyck, | Jan Barentse Wemp, |
| Alexander Vedder, | Abraham Mebie, |
| Johannes Bratt, treasr. | Arent Danielse Van Antwerpen. |
| | Abraham Glen. |

\* H. V. Rensselaer moved to Claverack and P. Groenendyck was chosen in his place in March, 1741.

| Diaconen. | Ouder |
|---|---|
| **1743** | |
| Nicolaas Groot, | Simon Swits. |
| Nicolaas Arentse Van Petten, | Jacob Glen, |
| Pieter Groenendyck, | Jan Barentse Wemp |
| Alexander Vedder. | Abraham Mebie. |
| **1744.** | |
| Meindert Meindertse, | Isaack Truex, |
| Johannes Veder, | Jacob Vrooman. |
| Nicolaas Groot, | Simon Swits, |
| Nicolaas Arentse Van Petten. | Jacob Glen. |
| **1745.** | |
| Andries Arentse Bratt. | Alexander Lansing. |
| Albert Arentse Vedder, | Jacob Swits, |
| Myndert Myndertse, | Isaac Truex, |
| Johannes Veder. | Jacob Vrooman. |
| **1746.** * | |
| Cornelis Van Slyck, | Jacob Schermerhorn, |
| John Sanders. | Johannes Albertse V |
| **1747.** | |
| Gerrit Lansing, | Abraham Glen, |
| Gerrit Van Antwerpen. | Pieter Groenendyck. |
| **1748.** | |
| Jacobus Van Slyck, | Jan Barentse Wemp |
| Joseph Robertse Yates. | Nicolaas Groot. |
| **1749.** | |
| Seth Vrooman, | Jacob Glen, |
| Jacobus Meinderts. | Daniel DeGraaf. |
| **1750.** | |
| Claas DeGraaf, | Jacob Vrooman, |
| Johannes Vischer. | Alexander Vedder. |
| **1751.** | |
| Isak Quakkenbos. | Abraham Truex, |
| Jan Baptist Van Eps. | Willem Teller. |
| **1752.** | |
| Simon Tol, | Hendrick Brouwer, |
| Johannes Hall. | John Sanders. |

* The names following this date to 1826 are the *newly* electe Deacons for each year; the full board consisted of these and tho preceding year.

| Diaconen. | Ouderlingen. |
|---|---|
| | 1753. |
| Elias Post, | Gerrit Lansing, |
| Johannes A. Van Antwerpen. | Cornelis Van Slyck. |
| | 1754. |
| Tobyas Ten Eyck, | Abraham Mebie, |
| Jellis Truax. | Joseph Robt. Yates. |
| | 1755. |
| Jacobus Van Eps, | Jacob Glen, |
| Willem Schermerhorn. | Jacobus Meynderts. |
| | 1756. |
| Abraham Yates, | Simon Toll, |
| Pieter Truex. | Nicolaas Groot. |
| | 1757. |
| Reynier Meyndertse, | Willem Teller, |
| Harmen Peek. | Abraham Glen. |
| | 1758. |
| Abraham Fonda, | Alexander Vedder, |
| Takerius Van de Bogart. | Isaak Quakkenbosch, |
| | Seth Vrooman. |
| | 1759. |
| Isaac Vrooman, | Gerrit A. Lansing, |
| Isaac Marselis. | Claas Van Petten. |
| | 1760. |
| Claes Van der Volgen, | Albert Vedder, |
| Jacob Fonda. | Johannes Sanders, |
| | 1761. |
| Isaac I. Swits, | Reynier Mynderse, |
| Harmanus Bratt. | Tobias Ten Eyck. |
| | 1762. |
| Hendrick Van Dyck, | Jacob Van Slyck, |
| Cornelis Van der Volgen. | Joseph R. Yates. |
| | 1763. |
| Abraham Wempel, | Jacobus Mynderse, |
| Thomas Brouwer Baucker. | Nicolaas Groot. |
| | 1764. |
| Hendericus T. Veeder, | Gerrit A. Lansing, |
| Reuben Horsford. | Jan Bapt. Van Eps. |
| | 1765. |
| Caleb Beck, | Henderick Brouwer, |
| Maas Van Vranken. | Johannes Vischer. |

## HISTORY OF THE CHURCH.

| Diaconen. | Ouderlingen. |
|---|---|
| | 1766. |
| Abraham Van Eps, | Johannes Sanders, |
| Johannes J. Vrooman. | Alexander Vedder. |
| | 1767. |
| Isaac I. Truax, | Daniel DeGraaf, |
| Petrus Vander Volgen. | Takerius Vander Bogart. |
| | 1768. |
| Claas Veeder, | Isaac Quakkenbosch, |
| Albert Mebie. | Tobias Ten Eyck. |
| | 1769. |
| Zeger Van Santvoord, | John Baptist Van Eps, |
| Arent Vedder. | Joseph Yates. |
| | 1770. |
| Jacob S. Vrooman, | Gerrit A. Lansing, |
| Jacob Cloet. | Abraham Fonda. |
| | 1771. |
| Johannes Cuyler, | Jacobus Van Slyck, |
| Jan Baptist Wendell. | Reynier Mynderse. |
| | 1772. |
| Cornelis Vrooman, | Harmanus Bratt, |
| Andreas Truex. | Willem Schermerhorn. |
| | 1773. |
| Adam Van Slyck, | Isaac Vrooman, |
| Jacobus Bratt. | Nicolaas Vander Volgen. |
| | 1774. |
| Simon Van Petten, | Nicolaas Van Petten, |
| Abraham Swits. | Caleb Beck. |
| | 1775. |
| Asuerus Marselis, | Isaak Swits, |
| Johannes Visger. | Abraham Wemple, |
| | 1776. |
| Johannes Van Petten, | Harmanns Peek, |
| Arent S. Vedder. | Jacob S. Vrooman. |
| | 1777. |
| Frederick Clute, | Gerrit A. Lansing, |
| Abraham Oothout. | Johannes Cuyler. |
| | 1778. |
| Jacobus Teller, | Arent Albertse Vedder, |
| Johannes Roseboom. | Johannes B. Van Eps. |

32

| Diaconen. | Ouderlingen. |
|---|---|
| | 1779. |
| Asuerus Marselis, | Daniel DeGraaf, |
| Johannes Clement. | Corn: Vander Volgen. |
| | 1780. |
| Lancaster Connor. | Tobias Ten Eyck, |
| Myndert M. Wemple. | Claas Vedder. |
| | 1781. |
| John Wemple, | Johannes Sanders, |
| Jesse DeGraaf. | Willem Schermerhorn. |
| | 1782. |
| Daniel Cornu, | Claas Van der Volgen, |
| Arent A. Vedder. | Zeger Van Santvoord. |
| | 1783. |
| Abraham Dellamont, | Johannes Cuyler, |
| Corn: Van Slyck. | Jacobus Teller. |
| | 1784. |
| Abraham Dellamont, | Johannes Cuyler, |
| Cornelis Van Slyck. | Jacobus Teller. * |
| | 1785. |
| Johannes Clute, | Willem Schermerhorn. |
| Nicolaas Yates. | Johannes Roseboom. |
| | 1786. |
| Cornelis Van Dyck, | Abrm. Oothout, |
| John Sanders. | Claas Veeder. |
| | 1787. |
| Johannes Peek, | Joseph Yates, |
| Frans Veeder. | Jacob Fonda. |
| | 1788. |
| Johannes Myndertse, | Nicolaas Van der Volgen, |
| Johannes Erickson. | Jacobus Bratt. |
| | 1789 |
| Adam Vrooman, | Claas Veeder, |
| Johannes Post. | Cornelis Van Dyck. |

\* Nov. 1 *Anno* 1784.—"Jacobus Teller een onser Medebroeders, wegens noodtsakelyke besighede sig op wegh naar D' Troit begeven hebbende is in het begin van dit najaar aan de Grand Rivier op het Lake Erie tot onse en des Gemeentens groote droefheit ongelukkiglyke door de Indianen Vermoort.'
—Consistory Minutes.

| Diaconen. | Ouderlingen. |
|---|---|
| | 1790. |
| John B. Vrooman, | Andries Truax, |
| Johannes Toll. | Cornelis Vrooman. |
| | 1791. |
| Claas Hall, | Abraham Oothout, |
| Gerrit S. Veeder. | Thomas B. Bancker. |
| | 1792. |
| Simon J. Van Antwerpen, | Abraham Swits. |
| Nicolaas Vedder. | Frederick Clute. |
| | 1793. |
| Bernardus F. Schermerhorn, | Arent S. Veeder, |
| Carel Hansen Toll. | Johannes Van Petten. |
| | 1794. |
| Maas Van Vranken, | Corn: Adn. Van Slyck, |
| Gerrit Van Antwerpen. | Jacobus Clute. |
| | 1795. |
| Corn: Van Santvoord, | Claas Veeder, |
| Johannes A. Vedder. | Lancaster Connor. |
| | 1796. |
| Peter Van Guyseling, | Nic: Van der Volgen, |
| Harmen Wessels. | Johannes Peek. |
| | 1797. |
| Jellis Jac: Fonda, | Abraham Oothout, |
| Corn: Christiaanse. | Arent A. Vedder. |
| | 1798. |
| John P. Truex, | John S. Glen, |
| Jesse Peek. | Carel H. Toll. |
| | 1799. |
| Hendrikus Yates, Jr., | Thomas B. Bancker, |
| Volkert D. Oothout. | Gerrit S. Veeder. |
| | 1800. |
| John Jas: Yates, | Nicolaas Hall, |
| John Jac: Schermerhorn. | Johannes Myndertse. |
| | 1801. |
| Jacob Swits, | Claas Veeder, |
| Jellis A. Fonda. | Jesse D. DeGraaf. |
| | 1802. |
| John N. Marselis, | Abraham Oothout, |
| Jacob S Schermerhorn. | Nicolaas Vedder. |

| Diaconen. | Ouderlingen. |
|---|---|
| | 1803. |
| John N. Veeder, | Arent S. Veeder, |
| Josias Swart. | Maas Van Vranken. |
| | 1804. |
| Johannes F. Clute, | Francis Veeder, |
| Jeremiah Fuller. | John Sanders. |
| | 1805. |
| Abraham DeGraaf, | Corn: Van Santvoort, |
| Isaac J. DeGraaf. | John Yates. |
| | 1806. |
| James V. S. Ryley, | Jellis J. Fonda, |
| Joseph C. Yates. | Simon J. Van Antwerp. |
| | 1807. |
| John Is. Peek, | Adam S. Vrooman, |
| Peter F. Veeder. | Jacob Swits. |
| | 1808. |
| Joseph Peek, | Gerrit Van Antwerp, |
| Peter C. Van Slyck. | Maas Van Vranken. |
| | 1809. |
| David Vander Heyden, | John A. Vedder, |
| Douwe Clute. | John N. Marselis, |
| | John Veeder. * |
| | 1810. |
| Aaron Vrooman, | John James Schermerhorn, |
| David Pruyme. | James V. S. Ryley. |
| | 1811. |
| Gerrit Bensen, | John I. Peek, |
| Jacob I. Clute. | Corn: C. Christiaanse. |
| | 1812. |
| Aaron Van Antwerp, | Abraham Oothout, |
| Jno. Baptist J. Van Eps. | Gerrit S. Veeder. |
| | 1813. |
| Isaac DeGraaf, | Maas Van Vranken, |
| Rudolph Van Husen. | Jacob Swits. |

\* chosen in place of John A. Vedder deceased.

| Deacons. | Elders. |
|---|---|
| | 1814. |
| Cornelius Clute, | Corn: Z. Van Santvoord, |
| Abraham Oothout, Jr. | Jacob S. Schermerhorn, * |
| | Arent Vrooman, |
| | John J. Peek. |
| | 1815. |
| Maas Schermerhorn, | John N. Marselis. |
| John Quackenbos. | Jeremiah Fuller. |
| | 1816. |
| Peter Brouwer, | Abraham Oothout, |
| Zeger Van Santvoord. | Gerrit Bensen. |
| | 1817. |
| Alexander G. Fonda, | Rudolph Van Husen, |
| Peter I. Clute. | Jacob I. Clute. |
| | 1818. |
| Cornelis S. Groot, | Maas Schermerhorn, |
| John S. Vrooman. | James V. S. Ryley. |
| | 1819. |
| Philip Van Vorst, | Maas Schermerhorn, |
| John H. Moyston. | Cornelis Clute. |
| | 1820. |
| Adrian Van Santvoord, | David Vander Heyden, |
| Daniel S. DeGraaf. | Abraham Oothout. |
| | 1821. |
| Myndert Van der Volgen, | Maas Schermerhorn, |
| John B. Clute. | Philip Van Vorst. |
| | 1822. |
| Oliver Ostrom, | Corn: Z. Van Santvoord, |
| Jacob C. Consaul. | Maas Van Vranken. |
| | 1823. |
| Bartholomew Schermerhorn, | Myndert Van der Volgen, |
| Harmanus Van Housen. | Cornelius S. Groot. |
| | 1824. |
| Albert Vedder, | John N. Marselis, |
| John H. Brooks. | Gerrit S. Veeder. |

\* Jacob S. Schermerhorn died and on January 29th, 1814, Arent Vrooman was chosen in his place ; the latter died and March 12th, 1815, John J. Peek was appointed elder.

| Deacons. | Elders. |
|---|---|
|  | 1825. * |
| John J. Vedder, | Bartholomew Schermerhorn, |
| Robert Moyston, | Jacob I. Clute, |
| Albert Vedder, | John N. Marselis, |
| John H. Brooks. | Gerrit S. Veeder. |
|  | 1826. |
| Joseph Horsfall, | Jacob Swits, |
| Daniel S. DeGraaf, | James V. S. Ryley, |
| Jacob J. Vedder, | Bartholomew Schermerhorn, |
| Robert Moyston. | Jacob J. Clute. |
|  | 1827. |
| Oliver Ostrom, | Myndert Vander Volgen, |
| Jacob DeForeest, Jr., | Gerrit Bensen, |
| Joseph Horsfall, | Jacob Swits, |
| Daniel S. DeGraaf. | James V. S. Ryley. |
|  | 1828. |
| Giles F. Yates, | Maas Schermerhorn, |
| Wm. B. Schermerhorn, | Jeremiah Fuller, |
| Jacob DeForest, Jr., | Myndert Vander Volgen, |
| Oliver Ostrom. | Gerrit Bensen. |
|  | 1829 |
| John G. Van Voast, | Peter I. Clute, |
| John G. Veeder, | Adrian Van Santvoord, |
| Giles F. Yates, | Maas Schermerhorn, |
| Wm. B. Schermerhorn. | Jeremiah Fuller. |
|  | 1830. |
| Daniel S. DeGraaf, | Rudolph Van Housen, |
| Sebastian Vrooman, | Oliver Ostrom, |
| John G. Van Voast, | Peter I Clute, |
| John G. Veeder. | Adrian Van Santvoord. |
|  | 1821. |
| Wm. Schermerhorn, | Jacob I. Clute, |
| John I. Vedder, | Alexander G. Fonda, |
| Daniel S. DeGraaf, | Rudolph Van Housen, |
| Sebastian Vrooman. | Oliver Ostrom. |

* After this date all the members of the Consistory are named.

| Deacons. | Elders. |
|---|---|
| | **1832.** |
| Nicholas Van Vranken, | Gerrit Bensen, |
| John P. Swits, | Joseph Horsfall, |
| Wm. Schermerhorn, | Jacob S. Clute, |
| John J. Vedder. | Alexander G. Fonda |
| | **1833.** |
| Barent J. Mynderse, | John B. Clute, |
| Frederic T. Tupper, | Peter I. Clute. |
| Nicholas Van Vranken, | Gerrit Benson. |
| John P. Swits. | Joseph Horsfall. |
| | **1834.** |
| Nicholas Swits, | Wm. B. Schermerhorn, |
| Abraham G. Veeder, | John G. Van Vorst, |
| Barent J. Mynderse, | John B. Clute, |
| Freder.c T. Tupper. | Peter I. Clute. |
| | **1835.** |
| Jacob M. Vedder, | Joseph Horsfall, |
| John Davis, | Peter Brouwer, |
| Nicholas Swits, | Wm. B. Schermerhorn, |
| Abraham G. Veeder. | John G. Van Voast. |
| | **1836.** |
| James A. Van Vorst, | James V. S. Ryley, |
| John Holliday, | Daniel S. DeGraaf, |
| Jacob M. Vedder, | Joseph Horsfall, |
| John Davis. | Peter Brouwer. |
| | **1837.** |
| Duncan McDonald, | Nicholas Van Vranken, |
| Daniel Nellis, | Barent J. Mynderse, |
| James A. Van Vorst, | James V. S. Ryley, |
| John Holliday. | Daniel S. DeGraaf. |
| | **1838.** |
| John B. Schermerhorn, | Jacob I. Clute, |
| Jonas Holland, | John G. Van Voast, |
| Duncan McDonald, | Nicholas Van Vranken, |
| Daniel Nellis. | Barent J. Mynderse. |
| | **1839.** |
| Nicholas Yates, | John B. Clute, |
| Simon C. Groot, | John G. Veeder, |
| John B. Schermerhorn, | Jacob I Clute, |
| Jonas Holland. | John G. Van Voast. |

| Deacons. | Elders. |
|---|---|
|  | 1840. |
| Peter J. Wemple, | Adrian Van Santvoord, |
| Caspar F. Hoag. | Oliver Ostrom, |
| Nicholas Yates, | John B. Chute, |
| Simon C. Groot. | John G. Veeder. |
|  | 1841. |
| Thomas Houston, | Cornelius S. Groot, |
| John McNee, | Abraham Veeder, |
| Peter J. Wemple, | Adrian Van Santvoord, |
| Caspar F. Hoag. | Oliver Ostrom. |
|  | 1842. |
| Francis Van de Bogart, | Caspar C. Ham, |
| Henry Ramsay, | John P. Swits, |
| Thomas Houston, | Cornelius S. Groot, |
| John McNee. | Abraham Veeder. |
|  | 1843. |
| Christopher Reagles, | Wm. B. Schermerhorn, |
| William Van Vranken, | Peter J. Wemple, |
| Francis Van de Bogart, | Caspar C. Ham, |
| Henry Ramsay. | John P. Swits. |
|  | 1844. |
| Bartholomew Tymesen, | Gerrit Bensen, |
| George Wagner, Jr., | Nicholas Yates, |
| Christopher Reagles, | Wm. B. Schermerhorn, |
| Wm. Van Vranken. | Peter J. Wemple. |
|  | 1845. |
| John McNee, | John G. Van Voast, |
| John Van Santvoord, | Caspar F. Hoag, |
| Bartholomew Tymesen, | Gerrit Bensen, |
| George Wagner, Jr. | Nicholas Yates. |
|  | 1846. |
| B. Teller Schermerhorn, | Duncan McDonald, |
| George Anderson, | Nicholas Swits, |
| John McNee, | John G. Van Voast, |
| John Van Santvoord. | Caspar F. Hoag. |
|  | 1847. |
| G. W. Winne, | Peter I. Clute, |
| Otis Smith, | Barent J. Mynderse, |
| B. T. Schermerhorn, | Duncan McDonald, |
| George Anderson. | Nicholas Swits. |

## HISTORY OF THE CHURCH. 257

| Deacons. | Elders. |
|---|---|
| | 1848. |
| Charles A. Lee, | Adrian Van Santvoord, |
| James Van Kuren, | Simon C. Groot, |
| G. W. Winnee, | Peter I. Clute, |
| Otis Smith. | Barent J. Mynderse. |
| | 1849. |
| Ernestus Putman, | William Van Vranken |
| Alexander J. Van Eps, | Stephen H. Johnson, |
| Charles A. Lee, | Adrian Van Santvoord, |
| James Van Kuren. | Simon C. Groot. |
| | 1850. |
| John Erkson, | Peter J. Wemple, |
| Francis J. Van de Bogart. | Nicholas Yates, |
| Ernestus Putman, | William Van Vranken, |
| Alexander J. Van Eps. | Stephen H. Johnson. |
| | 1851. |
| Daniel Vedder, | Caspar C. Ham, |
| F. N. Wetmore, | Casper F. Hoag, |
| John Erkson, | Peter J. Wemple. |
| Francis J. Van de Bogart. | Nicholas Yates. |
| | 1852. |
| Frederic N. Clute, | Otis H. Smith, |
| Jacob F. Clute, | Abraham Veeder, |
| Daniel Vedder, | Caspar C. Ham, (resigned). |
| F. N. Wetmore. | Casper F. Hoag. |
| | John G. Van Voast (vice Ham). |
| | 1853. |
| Abraham Vrooman, | Christopher Reagles, |
| Ernestus Putman, | Simon C. Groot, |
| Frederic N. Clute, | Otis Smith, |
| Jacob F. Clute. | Abraham Veeder. |
| | 1854. |
| Charles S. Vedder, | Alexander G. Fonda, |
| George S. Hardin, | Gideon Moore, |
| Abraham Vrooman, | Christopher Reagles, |
| Ernestus Putman. | Simon C. Groot. |
| | 1855. |
| Daniel Vedder, | Wm. B. Schermerhorn, |
| George Wagoner, | Oliver Ostrom, |
| Charles S. Vedder, | Alexander G. Fonda, |
| George S. Hardin. | Gideon Moore. |

| Deacons. | Elders. |
|---|---|
| | 1856. |
| Ira Van Pelt, | Duncan McDonald, |
| Charles Yates, | Bartho. Teller Schermerhorn, |
| Daniel Vedder, | Wm. B. Schermerhorn, |
| George Wagoner. | Oliver Ostrom. |
| | 1857. |
| Chas. N. Yates, | B. T. Schermerhorn, |
| Ira Van Pelt, | Duncan McDonald, |
| John McNee, | Nicholas Swits, |
| Chas. S. Vedder. | Jacob T. Clute. |
| | 1858. |
| John McNee, | Nicholas Swits, |
| C. S. Vedder, | Jacob T. Clute, |
| T. B. Mitchell, | Nicholas Van Vranken, |
| Daniel Vedder. | John G. Van Voast. |
| | 1859. |
| Daniel Vedder, | Nicholas Van Vranken, |
| T. B. Mitchell, | John G. Van Voast, |
| Aaron Barringer, | Casper F. Hoag, |
| Daniel M. Kittle, | Ernest Putman. |
| | 1860. |
| Aaron Barringer, | Casper F. Hoag, |
| Daniel M. Kittle, | Ernest Putman, |
| T. H. Reeves, | Thos. B. Mitchell, |
| H. Van Vechten Clute. | Jacob T. Clute. |
| | 1871. |
| T. H. Reeves, | T. B. Mitchell, |
| H. Van Vechten Clute, | Jacob T. Clute, |
| Abraham Vrooman, | Simon C. Groot, |
| Chas. Yates. | Daniel Vedder. |
| | 1862. |
| Abraham Vrooman, | Simon C. Groot, |
| Chas. Yates, | Daniel Vedder, |
| Joseph G. Van Debogert, | Nicholas Swits, |
| Chas. E. Angle. | Casper F. Hoag. |
| | 1863. |
| Joseph G. Van Debogert, | Nicholas Swits, |
| Chas. E. Angle, | Casper F. Hoag, |
| Abram Doty, | Ernestus Putman, |
| Jacob V. Vrooman. | Thos. B. Mitchell. |

| Deacons. | Elders. |
|---|---|
| | 1864. |
| Abram Doty, | Ernestus Putman, |
| Jacob V. Vrooman, | Thos. B. Mitchell, |
| T. H. Reeves, | John G. Van Voast, |
| Nicholas Cain. | Daniel Vedder. |
| | 1865. |
| T. H. Reeves, | John G. Van Voast, |
| Nicholas Cain, | Daniel Vedder, |
| Martin DeForest, | Wm. Van Vranken, |
| James H. Barhyte. | Casper F. Hoag. |
| | 1866. |
| Martin DeForest, | Wm. Van Vranken, |
| James H. Barhyte, | Casper F. Hoag, |
| Benj. L. Conde, | Thomas B. Mitchell, |
| Daniel M. Kittle. | Abram. Vrooman. |
| | 1867. |
| Benj. L. Conde, | Thos. B. Mitchell, |
| Daniel M. Kittle, | Abram. Vrooman, |
| A. T. Veeder, | Duncan McDonald, |
| John W. Veeder. | Abram. Doty. |
| | 1868. |
| A. T. Veeder, | Duncan McDonald, |
| John W. Veeder, | Abram Doty, |
| Wm. Schermerhorn, | Jacob F. Clute, |
| Jacob V. Vrooman. | T. H. Reeves. |
| | 1869. |
| Wm. K. Schermerhorn, | Jacob F. Clute, |
| Jacob V. Vrooman, | T. H. Reeves, |
| Duncan Robinson, | Nicholas Cain, |
| James H. Barhyte. | Casper F. Hoag. |
| | 1870. |
| Duncan Robinson, | Nicholas Cain, |
| James H. Barhyte, | Casper F. Hoag, |
| John Westinghouse, | Thos. B. Mitchell, |
| Wm. Van Dermore. | John Van Derveer. |
| | 1871. |
| John Westinghouse, | Thos. B. Mitchell, |
| Wm. Van Dermore, | John Van Derveer, |
| Abram. H. Van Vranken, | John DeNee, |
| Andrew T. Veeder. | Daniel Vedder. |

| Deacons. | Elders. |
|---|---|
| | 1872. |
| Abram. H. Van Vranken, | John McNee, |
| Andrew T. Veeder, | Daniel Vedder, |
| E. Nott Schermerhorn, | B. L. Conde, |
| James Milmine. | Daniel Kittle. |
| | 1873. |
| E. Nott Schermerhorn. | B. L. Conde, |
| James Milmine, | Daniel Kittle, |
| Jonas H. Clute, | Duncan Robinson, |
| Richard Marcellus. | Abram Vrooman. |
| | 1874. |
| Jonas H. Clute, | Duncan Robinson, |
| Richard Marcellus, | Abram. Vrooman |
| Geo. H. Doty, | Duncan McDonald, |
| Harmon Consaul. | Casper F. Hoag. |
| | 1875. |
| Geo. H. Doty, | Duncan McDonald, |
| Harmon Consaul, | Casper F. Hoag, |
| James H. Barhyte, | T. H. Reeves, |
| John Westinghouse. | J. V. Vrooman. |
| | 1876. |
| James H. Barhyte, | T. H. Reeves, |
| John Westinghouse, | J. V. Vrooman, |
| Albert Van Voast, | Jonas H. Clute, |
| Alex. Thompson. | Daniel Vedder. |
| | 1877. |
| Albert Van Voast, | Jonas H. Clute, |
| Alex. Thompson, | Daniel Vedder, |
| Harmon Consaul, | Duncan Robinson, |
| C. E. Kingsberry. | J. Westinghouse. |
| | 1878. |
| Harman Consaul, | Duncan Robinson, |
| C. E. Kingsberry, | J. Westinghouse, |
| Albert Van Voast, Jr., | John Van Derveer, |
| Andrew T. Veeder. | T. H. Reeves. |
| | 1879. |
| Albert Van Voast, Jr., | John Van Derveer, |
| Andrew T. Veeder, | T. H. Reeves, |
| Wm. Van Dermore, | Cornelius Lansing, |
| J. W. Clute. | J. V. Vrooman. |
| | 1880. |
| Wm. Van Dermore, | Cornelius Lansing, |
| J. W. Clute, | J. V. Vrooman, |
| Welton Stanford, | Wm. Van Vranken, |
| Jonas Hallenbeck. | John Westinghouse. |

# INDEX.

Albany, 59, 67.
Andros, Governor, 63, 64, 65.
Antwerp, 37, 51.
Archives, *See Records.*
Banker screen, 19.
Baptism, 8, 38, 41, 52, 80, 94, 194, 195.
Barclay, Rev. Thomas, 39, 74, 85.
Bell, 8, 41, 42, 52, 97.
Beukendal. *See Massacre of* 1748.
Bibliography, 75, 80, 107, 137, 138, 139, 154.
Bi-centennial celebration, 7.
Bogardus, Rev. Cornelius, 48, 134, 135, 137.
Bride's door, 7, 20, 155.
Brouwer, Rev. Thomas, 39, 40, 86.
Burying-grounds. *See Cemeteries.*
Calls, text of, 111-113, 129-132.
Charter, 98-105.
Church money, 193.
Cemeteries, 14, 15, 59, 40, 84, 167-171, 177.
Classis, the First in America, 36.
" of Amsterdam, 65, 66.
" of Schenectady, 44, 45, 52, 55.
Cock of St. Nicholas. *See Vane.*
Coetus, 40, 79, 117.
College. *See Union College.*
Committees, 6, 28, 39.
Communion, 52.
Consistorial minutes, 55.
Corwin, Rev. E. T., 7, 35.
Deacons, 102, 241-258.
Dellius, Rev. Godfrey, 37, 68.
Dimensions of 5th church edifice, 155.
Dixon, Rev. Alexander, 143.
Documents. *See Records.*
Doolittle, Rev. T. S., 7.
Dortrecht, 37, 43, 56.
Dutch Language, 46.
" Settlers, 31-34.
Edifices—First, 7, 17, 35, 36, 62, 63, 171.
" Second, 17, 39, 80-84, 146.
" Third, 18, 20, 40, 41, 42, 48, 94, 96, 147, 197.
" Fourth, 18, 48, 146-148.
" Fifth, 7, 50, 51, 152-157.
Eenkluys, Hans Janse. *See Poor Pasture.*

Elders, 102, 241-258.
Endowments, 170-179.
English Language, preaching, 125-128, 46.
Erichzon, Rev. Reinhart, 18, 40, 86-105.
Finances, 179-193.
Fire of 1861, 25, 42, 49, 50, 150.
Flags; 8, 10. 46.
Foot-stoves, 41, 95.
Forefather's door, 7, 19.
Freeman, Rev. Bernardus, 17, 37, 69-80, 85.
Funerals, 163.
Great Consistory, 5, 10, 13.
Griffis, Rev. Wm. Elliot, 10. 14, 52, 145.
Holland. *See Dutch*, 32, 33.
Hour-glass, 8, 13, 41, 52.
Indians, (See also Mohawks,) 36; 37, 38, 39, 43, 48, 58, 74.
Inscriptions, 7, 19, 20, 155, 156.
Labadists, 35, 36.
Lawrence, Rev. E. C., 10, 26.
Leases, 176, 237-241.
Lewis, Taylor, 18.
Leyden, 32, 36.
Lists. *See Elders, Deacons, Pews, etc.*
Lovelace, Governor, 59, 174.
Lydius, Rev. Johannes, 73, 74, 85.
Marriages, (See Statistics,) 8, 38, 52, 194.
Massacre of 1690, 14, 17, 36, 37, 59, 67.
Massacre of 1748, 21, 43.
Meier, Rev. I. H., 37, 121. 123, 129-134, 137.
Memberships, 194, 195.
Memorial Tablet, 12, 36.
Memorial Exhibition, 16, 17, 18,
Mill, and mill pasture, 175.
Missionary work, 37, 38, 39, 73.
Mission Schools, 52, 145.
Mohawks, 17, 33. 37, 73, 80.
Mohawk River, 34, 67.
Mohawk valley. Game, 34. Flowers, 19. Products, 20,
Monument on State Street, 14, 15, 40, 84, 146, 177.
Monuments, 169, 170.
New Castle, 63, 64.
New Netherlands, 55, 59.
New Year's greeting, 22.
Niskayuna, 44, 57.
Niskayuna patent, 178
Nott, Rev. Eliphalet, 49, 148.
Palisades, 34, 34, 43, 57, 67.
Papers. *See Records.*

# INDEX.

Paper Currency, 193.
Parsonages, 44, 35, 48, 62, 63, 150.
Pastors. *See names of*, 9.
Pearson, Prof. J., 35, 45.
Pelican feeding her young, 8, 32.
Pews, 41, 48, 94, 95, 199-237
Pine trees, 34.
Poor Pasture, 56, 59, 60, 172-174, 179, 183.
Potter, Edward Tuckerman, 18, 50, 152-156, 159.
Potter, Rev. Eliphalet Nott, 10.
Princeton patent, 177.
Pulpit, 8, 19, 41, 93.
Records, 22, 42, 44, 45, 55.
Romevn, Rev. Dirck, 9, 15, 36, 39, 40, 45, 46, 47, 51, 117-128, 137.
Sabbath School, 27, 52.
Salaries, 76, 77, 87, 115, 119, 132, 134, 160, 162.
Schaets, Rev. Gideon, 35, 37, 59, 60.
Schenectady, 33, 34, 37, 57; 58, 67, 85.
Schenectady Academy, 15, 47, 119.
Scotch element in the church, 12.
Seal, 42, 100.
Seelye, Rev. Edward E., 50, 140, 141, 159.
Seelye, Rev. Julius, 23, 50, 139, 140.
Sexton, Klokluyer, 161-167.
Sickles, Rev. Jacob, 46, 120, 129.
Stanton, Rev. H. C., 22, 25.
Statistics, 39, 43, 44, 46, 48, 49, 52, 69, 80, 85, 86, 87, 95, 117, 135, 137.
Stoves 41, 95, 96. [194, 195.
Stuyvesant, Governor, 56.
Symbolism, 8, 19.
Subscription Lists—Third Edifice, 89-93.
" " Fourth " 146
Tablet, 12, 158, 159.
Tassemaker, Rev. Petrus, 35, 36, 60, 63-69.
Taylor, Rev. W. J. R., 10, 15, 15, 22, 49, 50, 138, 139.
Thesschenmaecker. *See Tassemaker.*
Tortoise, the Mohawk totem, 8, 17, 33, 38.
Union College, 15, 27, 45, 46, 47, 48, 49, 52, 119.
Vander Volgen, Nicholas, 48, 148-151.
Vane, 41, 44, 51.
Van Curler, Arent, 27, 33, 34, 57.
Van Derwart, Rev. Herman, 14.
Van Santvoord, Rev. Cornelis, 12, 42, 43, 106, 107.
Van Santvoord, Rev. Staats, 10, 12, 15, 16.
Van Vechten, Rev. Jacob, 49, 155, 139.
Vedder, Rev. Charles E., 10, 11.
Vermilye, Rev. Ashbel G., 24, 51, 52, 144.
Voetius, Prof., 35, 36.

Voor-lezer, 12, 14, 35, 160, 161.
Voor-zanger, 12, 14.
Vrooman, Adam, 44, 109.
Vrooman, Rev. Barent, 44, 51, 108, 109-117.
Wortman. Rev. Denis, 22, 51, 142-144.
Yates, Rev. Andrew, 18, 49, 148.
Yates, Governor, 47.

*COPIES OF THIS BOOK* may be obtained at the book store of Mr. James H. Barhyte, No. 111 State street, Schenectady, N. Y.

Also, "MANUAL OF THE REFORMED CHURCH IN AMERICA," by the Rev. E. T. Corwin, D. D. "HYMNS OF THE CHURCH." "CONSTITUTION OF THE REFORMED CHURCH," embracing Catechism, Confession of Faith, Liturgy, Formulas, Rules of Order, &c., &c. Price 10 cents.

"MANUAL AND DIRECTORY of the First Reformed Church of Schenectady," with list of members and families, and a Historical Sketch, 1878. Price 10 cents.

"STATEMENT OF CONSIDERATIONS," which influenced the Architect in the building of the First Reformed Church in Schenectady. By Edward Tuckerman Potter. Price 25 cents.

---

STEREOSCOPIC PICTURES of the interior of the church edifice, showing the decorations of the Anniversary exercises of June 20th and 21st, may be had of Burgess and Buskerk, No. 105 State street, Schenectady, N. Y.

# An Encyclopedia of the Reformed Church.

## MANUAL OF THE REFORMED CHURCH IN AMERICA

(Third Edition, 1879. pp. 676.)

By Rev. Edward T. Corwin, D. D., Millstone, N. J.

This volume is unique in denominational literature. It covers completely the history of the Reformed (Dutch) Church during the first 250 years of its existence in America.

Part first contains a General History of the rise and progress of the American-Dutch in Colonial times; its struggles with the English Governors in their attempts to establish Episcopacy by law; its own internal commotions in its efforts after ecclesiastical independence, with its subsequent general progress and development in its Constitution and ecclesiastical organizations, its educational institutions, and its missionary operations at home and abroad.

Part second treats of the ministry in particular. It is a biographical dictionary; and more, for it contains the names of *all* who have ever officiated in the Reformed (Dutch) Church in America, with the chief data of their lives, and about 300 characterizations of the worthy dead. Lists of publications of authors are also given, and references to authorities.

Part third treats of the churches in particular. It gives their names in alphabetical order, dates of organization, pastorates, with references to local histories. Complete chronological list of ministers and churches are also added in an Appendix. Eighteen beautiful steel portraits adorn the work. Twenty-two views of the church buildings and institutions illustrate an admirable article on Church Architecture, by Professor Doolittle, of New Brunswick.

---

### PRICE, THREE DOLLARS.

*Board of Publication, Reformed Church in America, 34 Versey St., N. Y.*

For sale by James H. Barhyte, 111 State street, Schenectady N. Y.

www.ingramcontent.com/pod-product-compliance
Lightning Source LLC
Chambersburg PA
CBHW032004230426
43672CB00010B/2248